ASPECTS OF LIBERA

Aspects of Liberal Judaism

Essays in Honour of John D. Rayner

Editors
DAVID J. GOLDBERG AND
EDWARD KESSLER

VALLENTINE MITCHELL
LONDON • PORTLAND, OR

First published in 2004 in Great Britain by
VALLENTINE MITCHELL
Suite 314, Premier House, 112–114 Station Road
Edgware, Middlesex HA8 7BJ

and in the United States of America by
VALLENTINE MITCHELL
c/o ISBS, 920 NE 58th Avenue, Suite 300
Portland, Oregon 97213-3786

Website hhtp://www.vmbooks.com

British Library Cataloguing in Publication Data

A catalogue record for this book is available
from the British Library

ISBN 0-85303-601-2 (cloth)
ISBN 0-85303-593-8 (paper)

Library of Congress Cataloging-in-Publication Data

A catalog record for this book is available
from the Library of Congress

Typeset in 11/13pt Palatino by Vitaset, Paddock Wood, Kent
Printed in Great Britain by
MPG Books Ltd, Bodmin, Cornwall

Contents

Preface

It is a great pleasure to pen these introductory words to the *Festschrift* in honour of the eightieth birthday of my dear friend and close colleague John Rayner, although I must confess that many times over the recent months, as he lay in hospital fighting for his life, I feared that this might turn out to be his eulogy. Fortunately, thanks to medical skill, a benign Providence, the staunch support of his wife Jane and family, and not least his own great strength of will, he has pulled through the valley of the shadow; and if he will never again be as physically mobile as once he was, we give thanks that mentally he is as alert, curious and involved as ever.

Over a year ago, I suggested to fellow rabbis of Liberal Judaism's Rabbinic Conference that producing a *Festschrift* would be an appropriate way of marking John's fourscore years. The initial response was enthusiastic, but then my own illness and the pressure of other demands on colleagues, meant that the project stagnated and seemed unlikely to see the light of day.

That was when, by happy coincidence, Dr Edward Kessler got in touch with me to inquire if anything was being done for John's forthcoming birthday. I told him of our stillborn idea, and it was due to his energy, enthusiasm and unique ability to chivvy contributors with a steely charm that the promised essays started to arrive. Several eminent scholars reluctantly had to decline our invitation to contribute, due to other commitments, and because they have too much respect for John to fob him off with a reheated previous effort. Nevertheless, we are more than pleased with the scope and variety on display; it represents a broad spectrum of current Liberal Jewish thought, as well as including contributions from distinguished 'outsiders' like Rabbi Dr Louis Jacobs and Rabbi Professor Jonathan Magonet.

What of the man who is being honoured? When, in future

centuries, historians come to write about the development and growth of Progressive Judaism in Europe and the United States, I have no doubt that John Rayner will be linked with giants from the past like Abraham Geiger, Kaufmann Kohler, Isaac Mayer Wise, Claude Montefiore and Israel Mattuck. Indeed, his powerful intellect, widely-ranging scholarship, reasoned arguments and impeccably logical, gracefully constructed sermons, lectures, essays and books, most naturally put me in mind of Geiger himself, although John would instantly and blushingly reject the comparison.

John is of the generation irredeemably marked by the experience of the Shoah. He was lucky enough to escape himself, although his parents were not. He saw it as his responsibility, in the words of Isaiah, 'to preserve the tribes of Jacob and to restore the survivors of Israel'. And it was in Liberal Judaism, particularly in the Liberal Jewish Synagogue, under the influence of Israel Mattuck, that he found the expression of Judaism that most happily accorded with his religious beliefs, ethical principles and system of universal values. For almost half a century his has been *the* voice of Liberal Judaism, both in the United Kingdom and further afield. As teacher, pastor, liturgist, tireless expounder of Judaism – and on occasion its polemicist – his inspiration will endure for future generations.

What has won him grudging acknowledgement, even from those most vehemently opposed to his religious and political stances, is the patent sincerity, personal honesty and moral integrity with which he upholds a cause. As one of the many younger rabbis who regard him as their mentor and exemplar wrote about him recently:

> In him I found someone who embodied in a high degree all the traditional virtues of the *Talmid Chacham* ... including a love of study for its own sake, a meticulous attention to detail in the name of truth, an unswerving devotion to rationality tempered by a playful joy in words, scrupulousness in personal behaviour, modesty, patience, a passion for justice, love of his fellow human beings and a determination to strive for their well-being.

I would not, however, want readers to gain the impression that my virtuous friend is not without his few, minor faults.

Like many with a reputation for cleverness and an Oxbridge education, on occasion he can be bemused by the inability of less formidably endowed minds to grasp a point that, to him, is blindingly obvious. As a perfectionist, he is made impatient by slovenly thought, careless mistakes and casual ill-preparedness. Sometimes, too, he relishes pursuing an argument to its logical conclusion, but beyond its intrinsic worth.

Along with many colleagues, I have on occasion winced in fearful anticipation when an envelope with John's distinctive handwriting on it has dropped through the letter box. The letter's format is invariable. Two paragraphs of effusive praise and commendation will be followed by the inevitable *but*, then a lengthy, pained rehearsal of instances of faulty theological reasoning, mispronounced Hebrew words, wrongly attributed Talmudic sources or homiletic deficiencies.

Some time ago I came across a book review by George Steiner of the collected writings of Henri Bergson, the French humanist philosopher. In it, Steiner commented on Bergson's voluminous correspondence with his peers, which always began with two paragraphs of exquisitely polite praise, followed by withering criticism. I cut the review out and gave it to John, asking if Bergson was the man from whom he had learnt his epistolary technique. He chuckled and replied that he would have been proud to have been taught by such a great master!

May he be spared for many years to come, not only to keep us lesser mortals on our toes, but also to continue adding his own valuable contributions to the moral and spiritual well-being of the Jewish people.

David J. Goldberg

Acknowledgements

We wish to record our grateful thanks to Carolyn Simon for the speed, competence, meticulous proof-reading and editorial skill with which she prepared the essays in this *Festschrift* for publication; to Bryan Diamond and Gene Price for help in locating, scanning and identifying the photographs; also to Abigail Bloom, for typing up and making disk-ready a number of the contributions.

The Honorary Officers of the Liberal Jewish Synagogue provided the financial guarantee which enabled publication to proceed; without their support, the project would not have come to fruition. We acknowledge their role with gratitude.

Frank Cass and the editorial team at Vallentine Mitchell have been positive and supportive throughout. It has been a pleasure to work with such skilled and sensitive publishers.

Lastly, but most importantly, the contributors themselves; they responded enthusiastically and – for the most part! – promptly when we told them of our idea to mark John Rayner's special birthday with a *Festschrift* and asked them, at short notice, for an original piece to include. It was Dr Johnson who famously remarked that no man (or woman) ever wrote except for money, but it is a mark of the high esteem in which our dedicatee is held that in his case busily engaged scholars and rabbis willingly made an exception to that general rule. We hope they will feel suitably rewarded when they see what a handsome volume this is, in tribute to an outstanding rabbi and teacher in Israel.

1

Travelling Through the Night: On the Road with John D. Rayner

ALBERT H. FRIEDLANDER

Often, when John and I have met, I think of shared journeys. We were not aware of each other on the initial trip. The Theodor Herzl School was too compartmentalized: John's class, even though we shared Zvi Silberstein as a teacher, was above mine; who speaks with students from a lower class? These days, I think of it as a closed night train rushing through the darkness. At the end, when it – the school – had been burned, we were deposited at different stations: John went via a *Kindertransport* to London, and my ship landed in Cuba just before the borders closed. We met much later, in Amsterdam, at a World Union of Progressive Judaism (WUPJ) conference. After that, our lives intertwined. John's urgings helped to bring me to Great Britain, and we shared much within Liberal and Progressive Judaism as well as in our personal lives. Two journeys, in particular, come to mind.

It is late at night, and John is driving us through France, on our way to a WUPJ conference in Switzerland. We are driving through Troyes, and the window is open. John breathes in the air with pleasure. 'This is real Rashi country,' he tells me. 'Can't you feel it?' Sadly, John lives in the commentaries far more than I do; I had been reciting Schiller's *Wilhelm Tell* in my mind. But, as always, John brings me back into our shared heritage.

Another time, another place. Our families had shared a holiday near Perpignan, in Canet Plage. The Friedlander car was in the critical ward of a garage in Montpelier, and so John was driving us to Andorra 'for a new experience'. He kept his word. As we roared down the mountain passes, he turned to us with a pained expression on his face. 'That's funny,' he said, 'the brakes have gone.' And so they had. I think I learned much about fervent prayer that night.

These days, our journeys are more in books than on the road, but there is also much to share and to learn from one another. I am working on a Bonhoeffer text these days, and there is much for me to learn from my friends who have worked in this field. I talk with John, and we recall inter-faith conferences we have attended. After all, John has founded inter-faith groups! Once, in Sigtuna in Sweden, I spent much time with Eberhard Bethge, the great friend of Dietrich Bonhoeffer (the Protestant pastor and theologian hanged for his role in the attempted assassination of Hitler in 1944). Another journey comes to mind which fits this theme ...

I once visited Eberhard Bethge in Villiprot, and he had to rush me to Bonn for my lecture. As we drove along, Bethge noted: 'Albert, I am almost blind now. I really cannot see to drive. However, Renate, next to me, has excellent eyesight, and she directs me.'

I was almost frozen in horror, quite catatonic. But what could I do?

It was quite true. Every minute, there would come instructions: 'You are getting too close to the car in front, Eberhard. Slow down ... You are veering a bit to the left. Move over.'

'Renate,' I said. 'Why don't *you* drive?'

'Normally, I would,' she replied, 'but I have injured my left leg, and it is very stiff. Every ten minutes or so, we will have to stop, so that I can get out and walk up and down for a short time. Then, it is almost OK.'

Great.

As it happened, we were caught in a traffic jam; nothing moved.

'A great chance for me to exercise,' said Renate. She got out and walked up and down on the side of the highway. And, of course, the cars immediately started moving once more, except for those behind us, their cursing drivers blowing their horns at Bethge's car, which remained stationary until Renate, very slowly, joined us again.

My lecture in Bonn was a bit hesitant that night.

On that occasion, I compared Bonhoeffer with Leo Baeck. I placed him in the 'open prison' which the two shared. In 1933, Germany had become such a prison, well concealed from the outside world, for all who resisted the Nazi doctrine and tried to express this in some way. Sermons are also part of the literature of a society; the right Goethe quotation can be an act of resistance. Religious institutions and their insistence upon ethical actions at times defy evil even though, often, they make an uneasy concordat with the state in order to ensure a tainted survival.

Bonheffer and Baeck are examples of men imbued with religious decency fighting against the darkness. Here, in this *Festschrift* for John, I want to share some of the thoughts I have written concerning Bonhoeffer.

In 1939, Dietrich Bonhoeffer was engaged in an important task of teaching in Manhattan. In a way reminiscent of Baeck in London at the same time, he was urged to continue his work in a community that needed him desperately. Then, like Baeck, he heard a call from Germany. As Eberhard Bethge saw it:

> Berlin called New York, the Marienburger *Alee* called the Prophet's chamber on Broadway. 'Come over and help us!' And Bonhoeffer, after hearing the voice, 'immediately endeavoured to go … assuredly gathering that the Lord had called [him]'. Yet he did not return as a normal missionary to the slums or to the posh quarters of Europe in its version of the city of Berlin. He returned as someone who was prepared to pay the costly price for a terrible misused Christian message.
>
> The content of that call was apparently saying something like this: Now, be who are. Win your inescapable identity by crossing your special ecclesiastical theological Bosphorus, in identifying yourself with the victims of your homeland. Here in the USA, theology alone waits for you, but not the living Christ. He waits for you in the midst of the disgraced and disfigured Jews of your homeland and in the company of your own guilt-stricken folk and friends.[1]

No one can do justice to Bonhoeffer's profound exploration of Christianity in a few pages. We are concentrating upon one aspect of his life and work: his prison texts. This is not an ancillary exploration. Whitehead's warning concerning the 'fallacy of misplaced concretion' underscores that one aspect of the totality cannot be viewed as the totality. The concentration camp experience must not obscure all of his work. Bonhoeffer, however, brought the fullness of his teachings into Tegel prison. There, it was sharpened and clarified; we see it through the perspective of his martyrdom. As Bethge saw it, this was the time when Bonhoeffer became most aware of himself: when he was linked with Jewish suffering and the failure of Christianity.

This is Bethge's analysis: Bonhoeffer, just before the failed 20 July 1944 attempt to assassinate Hitler, in his letter of 18 July, wrote statements that bring the Messianic suffering event of Christ and of Israel as well as the happenings of the present into full inclusivity. *Metanoia*, in this context, is 'letting oneself be pulled along into the way of Jesus Christ, into the Messianic event, so that Isaiah 53 will now be fulfilled'. Isaiah 53, in terms of the vicarious suffering of Christ and of Israel for the nations, is not fulfilled within those days (*damals*) but in a now, the present, as 'life participating in the *"Ohnmacht Gottes"*, God's weakness in this world'.[2] It is thus the Jews who keep the Christ question open.

Two days earlier, Bonhoeffer had fashioned the formula of 'Before and with God we live without God',[3] interpreting it:

- Before and with the biblical God we live without the Greek God.
- Before and with the crucified God we live without the enthroned God.
- Before and with the suffering God we live without the omnipotent God.

A prophet needs listeners, and a teacher needs disciples. (Indeed, viewing Jeremiah and Baruch, or Elijah and Elisha, a prophet also needs a disciple.) 'Discipleship', in Bonhoeffer's terms, is an ultimate, total commitment to the task assigned by God. Viewing this as a rabbi, I would call it a sacred *mitzvah*, which is both commandment and task. I recognize that in Bonhoeffer the parallel path differs from Judaism: it is an absolute commitment to serve Christ in this world. It is the task of the individual which must not be abandoned. The task changes the individual, and here Bonhoeffer turns to Luther, whom he quotes: 'It is by living and even by dying and being damned that one becomes a theologian, not by understanding, reading, and speculating.' Radical faith must be transmitted, even and particularly when it moves outside the dimension of the official Church and Synagogue. In Judaism, the transmission had its parallel lines within the Tradition. The *Sayings of the Fathers* traced the *Shalshelet ha-Kabbalah*, the Chain of Transmission, from Moses to the Men of the Great Assembly and to the Rabbis. Nevertheless, as Israel became a wandering people with its *theologia viatorum*, it allowed the Revelation for each generation to find its expression outside the establishment, even though the *cherem*, the ban, was often pronounced against the 'heretics' who could be the prophets/teachers of their time. Certainly, Bonnhoeffer suffered a similar fate when the Church was aligned with the unjust state. He recognized that a Church cannot be divorced from its environment and is permeated by external evils. As early as 1933, a few days after the 'German Christians' had appointed Ludwig Müller as their National Socialist bishop, Bonhoeffer tried to come to terms with this aching wound in the heart of the Church.

Bonhoeffer's sermon in Berlin's Kaiser Wilhelm Gedächtnis Kirche on 28 May 1938 also reveals his closeness to the Hebrew Bible and judges Christianity in terms of its Jewish roots. One must go back to this earlier moment in his life to understand his testimony of the last years. Bonhoeffer preached about: Moses, the first prophet, Aaron, the first priest. Moses, called by God, chosen without respect of person, the man with the heavy tongue, the servant of God who lives totally in listening to the word of his Lord. Aaron, the man with the purple vestment and the holy crown, the sanctified and sacred priest, who has to preserve the divine service for the priest.[1] Set against the austerity and moral demands of Moses, Aaron's 'church' was a rich outpouring of ritual that could satisfy the populace, even if it was a church without God. It was the 'National Church' of Bishop Müller which would diminish the sense of guilt in a people who felt no compassion for the suffering Jewish people.

What else was happening in the Germany of 1933? Arnold Schoenberg had ceased working on the third act of his *Moses and Aaron* opera. Adorno later remarked that the work was 'a preventive action against the looming of Nazism' in a time when Hitler was marching towards his triumphs. In his essay on this opera, George Steiner noted that Schoenberg here influenced the history of the modern theatre, of modern theology, of the relationship between Judaism and the European crisis.

> Schoenberg made of this archaic, obscure antagonism a conflict of ultimate moral and personal values, of irreconcilable formulations or metaphors of man's confrontations with God. Working on the principle – discernible at the roots of Greek tragic drama – that fundamental human conflict is internal, that dramatic dialogue is in the final analysis between self and self, Schoenberg gathered the entire force of collision into a single consciousness.
>
> This is the drama of Moses. Aaron is one of the possibilities (the most seductive, the most humane) of Moses' self-betrayals. He is Moses' voice when that voice yields to imperfect truth and to the music of compromise. Schoenberg remarked in 1933: 'My Moses more resembles – of course only in outward respect – Michelangelo's.'[5]

In the opera, Aaron is the victor. Moses cries out, 'O word, thou word that I lack!' and falls to the ground, broken. As George Steiner saw this:

> This is one of the most moving, dramatic moments in the history of opera and of the modern theatre. With its implicit allusion to the *Logos*, to the Word that is yet to come but which lies beyond speech, it gathers into one action both the claims of music to be the most complete idiom, the carrier of transcendent energies, and all that is felt in twentieth-century art and philosophy about the gap between meaning and communication.[6]

Schoenberg saw the Bible text within his Jewish faith and brought it into German culture. In a similar way, Bonhoeffer sees the Church turning away from the Word of Sinai, into the intoxicating incense of Aaron's beguiling worship. It wants to experience all of the emotions of the moment of Revelation in its worship, without listening to the commanding voice of Sinai. And so Bonhoeffer demands a return to the Church of Moses against the Church of Aaron, and preaches in his 1933 sermon, at the time of Schoenberg's struggling:

> Out of the impatient church there comes to be the time of the silent waiting, out of the church of stormy striving for the fulfilled desire, for seeing, there comes the church of sober faith, out of the church of self-dedication there a rises the church which prays prayer to the one God. Will that church receive the same dedication, the same sacrifices [made for the church of Aaron]?[7]

It was not that much later that Bonhoeffer entered the Holocaust Kingdom and came closer to Moses and his people.

At Christmas in 1942, in a text hidden in the rafters of his parents' house, he wrote about the conspiracy against Hitler in which he was involved, and about the 'civil courage' which can grow only out of the free responsibility of the free man. Then, it was his hope that Germans were truly beginning to discover what free responsibility meant. He had also begun to realize the meaning of Luther's 'by living and even by dying'.

In those last days, Bonhoeffer wrote his poem *'Christen und Heiden'* ('Christians and Pagans') which is the heart of his *Prison Writings*:

> Humanity goes to God in its need,
> for help, for luck and for bread does it plead,
> to be saved from illness, debt and from death indeed.
> So do they all, all, Christians and pagan.

> To God in His weakness humanity goes.
> Find Him maligned, poor, without shelter and bread,
> Sin, weakness and death hold Him in their throes.
> Christians stand with God, in His pain, in His dread.

> God goes to all humans who live in their need,
> their souls and their bodies with his bread He does feed,
> dying on the cross for them all is His deed
> and forgives them as only He can.

I gave these lines as part of a lecture at a Bonhoeffer conference in Amsterdam. Eberhard Bethge agreed that I had followed Bonhoeffer's rhythm and rhyme, but would not accept my second verse as a correct translation. He was right, but I felt that the structure, here, was essential for the translation of Bonhoeffer's answer to Feuerbach. Anyway, 'all translators are traitors'.

Beyond the obvious differences between a prison and a concentration camp, we recognize that they represent different worlds. A prison is normally part of a penal system based upon agreed standards of justice, and many inmates grudgingly accept that they have broken the law even when they claim that in their case the judgment was unfair. It is still a grey area, and the state must also be judged. Is it following the prejudices of its time rather than striving for eternal verities? How would Oscar Wilde, a giant of *de profundis* literature, be judged today? And even the military courts of the First World War which executed the 'cowards and traitors' who were simply soldiers suffering under battle fatigue have had their sentences reversed in recent times. Courts are fallible and sometimes criminally flawed, but even the worst prisons are not inherently evil places.

Leo Baeck's loyalty was given to the People of Israel, whom he also viewed as part of the Revelation. It is, in fact, a similar path to Bonhoeffer's reaching out to the Divine suffering on the Cross; Israel's suffering is also an anguishing, searing pain existing in God. God existed in the camp, 'hanging on the gallows of Auschwitz', as Elie Wiesel writes in his novel *Night*. That is what makes the texts rising out of the concentration camps more significant than the *de profundis* writings of those who were incarcerated. Those other texts are also an inward search for meaning, letters addressed to an outside world with whom the authors still corresponded. Bonhoeffer and Baeck were beyond that world, in the Holocaust kingdom where one spoke to God through the psalms of the twentieth century and in which an anguished faith can become a beacon of light for the next generation of humans walking through the Vale of Weeping, searching for the dawn.

John Rayner and I are still journeying towards the dawn. Sometimes, a traveller needs a companion carrying a lamp in the night. For me, that is John; his oil lamp has been ignited by the *ner tamid* in our synagogues.

NOTES

1. E. Bethge, 'Acts 16:9, for 19th June' (Amsterdam, 1988), in G. Carter et al. (eds), *Bonhoeffer's Ethics: Old Europe, New Frontiers* (Kampen: Kok Pharos, 1991), p. 231.
2. C. Gremmels, E. Bethge and R. Bethge (eds), *Widerstand und Ergebung : Briefe und Aufzeichnungen aus der Haft Dietrich Bonhoeffer* (Gütersloh: Chr. Kaiser, 1998) p. 396.
3. Ibid., p. 394.
4. D. Bonhoeffer, *Predigten (1925–1935)*, ed. O. Dodzus (Munich: Kaiser Verlag, 1984), pp. 364–5.
5. G. Steiner, 'Moses and Aron', *Language and Silence* (New York: Atheneum, 1967), pp. 155–6.
6. Ibid., p. 161.
7. D. Bonhoeffer, *Predigten*, p. 314.

Soon after writing this chapter, Rabbi Dr Albert Friedlander passed away. One of his last public acts was to participate in the Sabbath service celebrating John Rayner's eightieth birthday.

2

Leo Baeck and Reconciliation

HARRY M. JACOBI

'We must have met, but I cannot remember us speaking to each other,' John said to me when we discovered we had both been pupils at the same school in Berlin. The Theodor Herzl School had a lasting and beneficial influence on both our lives. Modern Hebrew was taught for one hour every day, Zionist songs were sung, and saplings were planted on *Tu b'Shvat*. Our young teachers were tolerant, respected and excellent motivators; we were even on first-name terms with some of them. Sadly, the school was damaged during *Kristallnacht* and had to close soon afterwards.

This first conversation with John took place at the World Union for Progressive Judaism conference in 1949. At similar events in the early 1950s, John and I listened to Leo Baeck's presidential addresses. Then, more regularly, we sat at his feet at the Monday seminars held in London.

Rabbi Dr Leo Baeck was born in 1873 in Lissa, a small town on the German–Polish border. He received *semicha* from the Hochschule für die Wissenschaft des Judentums in the winter semester 1896/97 at the age of twenty-three and gained a doctorate from Berlin University. For ten years he served as rabbi to the Jewish community in Oppeln. He showed great courage as a chaplain in the First World War, and then by attending the Zionist Congress in Basle at a time when most rabbis, the so-called *Protestrabbiner* (protest rabbis), were vehemently opposed to Zionism. In 1900 Adolf Harnack published a book called *The Essence of Christianity*. It contained many false accusations and insinuations against Judaism. Leo Baeck responded by writing *The Essence of Judaism*,[1] a clear and classic refutation and exposition, published in 1905.

During the Nazi period, Leo Baeck was the undisputed and greatly revered leader of German Jewry. He protested frequently and bravely against the Nazi regime and was arrested a number of times. Although he received many offers of escape, he insisted, 'A shepherd does not leave his flock.' He stayed until he was sent to Theresienstadt in January 1943. There his lectures gave spiritual sustenance to his fellow prisoners. In his spare time, on scraps of paper, he wrote a book, *This People*, published in 1955. Through a mix-up of names he was miraculously saved. After liberation he came to London, where his only daughter lived, and resumed the presidency of the World Union for Progressive Judaism.

Although officially identified with Progressive Judaism, Leo Baeck avoided and disliked adjectival Judaism. In his presidential address at the 1951 conference he said: 'It was finally called "World Union for Progressive Judaism". But it had been possible, and perhaps auspicious also, plainly to call it "World Union for Judaism".'

The *Avot d'Rabbi Nathan* (Chapter 23) says: 'He who makes his enemy into a friend, he is the true hero.' In this respect Leo Baeck proved a true hero. After his suffering in the concentration camp, and the loss of most of his family (he was one of eleven children), it would have been perfectly understandable if he had said, as did so many others: 'I want nothing to do with the Germans. I never want to set foot in Germany again.' But he saw the need for reconciliation, and understood that only through reconciliation could one hope to build a saner and safer world. So, after the war he returned frequently to Germany to visit his old community, to lecture and to preach. By so doing he won great respect, and soon became a close friend of the first post-war President of Germany, Theodor Heuss, receiving from him the *Grosse Verdienstkreuz* – the highest German honour.

Leo Baeck shouldered the responsibility of reconciliation bravely, proudly and steadfastly. In *The Essence of Judaism* he draws our attention to the fact that: 'The commandment to love one's neighbour (Lev. 19) is preceded by the interdiction: "Thou shall not avenge, nor bear any grudge against the children of thy people." Before this interdiction comes still another: "Thou shalt not hate thy brother in thy heart." For according to ancient interpretation, a hostile feeling already amounts to hatred.'[2] He also makes the point that: 'With good reason do these conceptions all begin with the negative, "Thou shall not". "Thou shalt not take revenge, thou shalt not retaliate." For only through the negative is the way opened to the positive ... To love means first and foremost not to hate.'[3]

In English we call *Yom Kippur* the 'Day of Atonement', from the Hebrew *kapar*, to expiate, atone for or pardon. In German, however, and to Leo Baeck, it was called *Versoehnungstag*, which means 'Day of Reconciliation': 'Judaism is the religion of reconciliation. That, in the final analysis, is the purpose of life. "It was evening and it was morning – one day", that is the day of reconciliation. Yom Kippur has become the holiest day of the year, because it is the day of reconciliation.'[4] Later in the same work, he comments: '[Our old prayers] contain no esoteric doctrine or fanciful speculation; everything rests on the firm ground of religious certainty; the messianic expectation takes the form of the simple yet great idea of the responsibility, and ultimate reconciliation of all nations.'[5]

Leo Baeck died in 1956. His teaching, and personal example of reconciliation, profoundly influenced both John and myself. We were inspired and motivated to follow in his footsteps by taking *semicha*. (John studied at the Hebrew Union College in Cincinnati and graduated in 1965 and I received *semicha* from the Leo Baeck College in 1971.) It is most fitting that Leo Baeck College Centre for Jewish Education – which has trained so many rabbis since its inception in 1956 – bears his name.

NOTES

1. L. Baeck, *The Essence of Judaism* (New York: Schocken, 1948).
2. Ibid., p. 214.
3. Ibid.
4. Ibid., p. 167.
5. Ibid., p. 245.

2

Ernst Leitz of Wetzlar and Altruism During the Holocaust

FRANK DABBA SMITH

Photography was greatly exploited as a communications and propaganda device during the Holocaust.[1] At an early stage in my research, it was clearly evident that the still camera was a tool of choice whether the objective was to inculcate anti-semitism and report and/or publicize officially approved versions of anti-Jewish activities engaged in by the Nazi state. In addition, individual Germans also turned to photography to record their own enthusiasm or even disapproval of such anti-Jewish measures. Furthermore, against all the odds, individual Jews relied on cameras to leave their historical testimonies of this period, and those involved in the resistance conveyed photographic warnings of Nazi activities. Finally, at the end of the war, the Allies used still photography to portray themselves as the liberators, bringing freedom to the suffering innocents and defeat to the bestially evil enemy.[2]

A vital factor in the achievement of the spontaneous and revealing photography that so characterizes the work of this period was the development of the miniature camera in Germany. The most successful camera was the Leica, first produced commercially in 1925. It was extremely compact and could be fitted with high-quality lenses that enabled photographers to work in ordinary indoor settings without special lighting. It was always instantly ready to capture life and action effortlessly from any angle and often enabled the photographer to remain unnoticed. Without cumbersome equipment, photographs of people no longer had to be confined to stiff or conventionally artistic poses.

The dominance of the miniature camera in German photo-journalism was made official by the Minister of Propaganda, Joseph Goebbels, on 1 August 1937: 'Photojournalists who do not understand that the use and promotion of small modern cameras constitute a duty inherent to their mission should remove their official photojournalist armbands.'[3] Press photographers who insisted on clinging to what were considered old-fashioned and heavy cameras were banned from their profession. Since the camera was viewed as an effective tool for the Nazi mission of proving the racial and athletic superiority of Aryans and conveying the touristic and architectural glories of Germany, Goebbels saw fit to mandate modern methods so that professional photographers would produce dynamic propaganda images efficiently. When it came to the urgent task of publishing the heroic achievements of the Nazi revolution, even the cameras used were required to be radical German designs.

Undoubtedly, there were also economic motives for Goebbels's directive concerning the adoption of the latest German equipment. Surely, Goebbels would have been aware that it would be desirable to enhance the sales figures and public respect of world-famous companies such as Ernst Leitz of Wetzlar, the manufacturer of the Leica. Here was an opportunity to promote simultaneously the Nazi ideal of German economic self-sufficiency and the public perception of the German optical industry as offering the world's most technologically advanced professional equipment.

The miniature camera was not just destined to capture professionally the political, industrial and military successes of the Reich, it also figured in Nazi plans to control the leisure activities of the nation. Famous photographers such as Paul Wolff extolled the virtues of the Leica as he instructed the amateurs who devoured his best-selling books. Here, lightweight and easy to use cameras were seen as playing the decisive role in forging a new German collective visual memory.

One textbook, produced as part of a course organized by the German Labour Front, defined the purpose of a new kind of conformist photography:

> Amateur photography is the patrimony of the whole people and it should perform a useful task the nature of which is more manifest in the Germany of today than it

has even been before. The education of the people includes photography and should provide each and every citizen with the technical knowledge to enable them to persevere responsibly in this domain and to control their own cameras. But they should not stop there. The skill required for handling a camera is not enough to create a true photographer but it does set up all the conditions necessary for his creation so that amateur photography may aspire to be one of the major factors in the history of civilization. Furthermore, it makes possible to leave to one's children and grandchildren a collection of images whose influence is far greater than that of any number of speeches.[4]

The consumer advertising produced by Leitz, for example, during the Nazi period reflects this authorized version of the historical significance of the German family's snapshots.[5] Vacationing Aryan females balance themselves on the ends of diving boards and pose with pets on the beach. Aryan infants frolic waterside, school-aged sisters wearing plaited hair and dressed in folk costumes smile agreeably. Young men with straight noses and sporting Alpine hats gaze upon snow-covered mountains. A very masculine uniformed teenager holds a model aeroplane aloft; to the right of this erect youth, an eagle perches on a stone column. The thrust of these advertisements is that the Leica will enable its owner to produce lasting evidence of his family's rightful adherence to Nazi ideals of beauty, strength and co-operation.

In addition to supplying both professional and amateur photographers with cameras and accessories, Leitz also produced much for the German military. Exact quantities are not known, but it appears that most of the equipment was first sent to a governmental purchasing agency in Berlin. Often the cameras were specially engraved when placed into service. The Luftwaffe was a major customer and their cameras were engraved *Luftwaffe-Eigentum* (air force property) and also with the military contract numbers. The Leica was prized by the military for its properties and was routinely used for intelligence and publicity work. In one prominent instance, Propaganda Kompanie 689, attached to the army forces in Warsaw, used Leicas to photograph extensively the Jews in that city's infamous ghetto.[6]

Behind this 'whiter than white' Leica corporate image,

however, there lay another reality: the top management at Leitz was systematically saving Jews. Activities enabling Jews to emigrate began shortly after Adolf Hitler became Chancellor in 1933 and intensified after the nationwide *Kristallnacht* pogrom of 9–10 November 1938. With Germany's invasion of Poland and the sealing of its borders in August 1939, however, these activities largely came to an end.

During the early years of the Nazi regime, the German policy of forced emigration and the Jewish interest in escaping persecution coincided. Before the peaceful conquest of Austria in 1938, approximately 150,000 Jews – around one-quarter of the population of Jews in Germany – had left the Reich. But, by July of 1938, when representatives of international relief agencies sought help from the emissaries from over thirty governments at the Evian Conference, there were very few places left for asylum seekers to go. At this gathering, which was a symbolic gesture urged by President Roosevelt, profound sympathies were routinely expressed by all but were not manifested in the way of positive action.

Within days of the Nazis' assumption of power in Germany, however, the Leitz organization responded to the pleas of Jewish people. One early example is that of Nathan Rosenthal (born in 1881 in Wetzlar) who had served with Dr Ernst Leitz II on the local board of the Deutsche Demokratische Partei (DDP), later known as the Deutsche Staatspartei (DSP). Dr Leitz had also served on the town council 1916–33 and publicly opposed the Nazi Party. In a letter to Dr Leitz dated 10 February 1947, Rosenthal recalls with gratitude how:

> When I pleaded my plight to you fourteen days after Hitler's rise to power, when my son Paul, who was in the upper fifth of the high school and who could no longer shield himself from the anti-semitism of his teacher, and you immediately accepted him into your firm without taking into account the political [consequences]. His training with you and later employment in your firm here [in New York] made a way for us to emigrate which would otherwise have been completely impossible.

Rosenthal's seventeen-year-old son Paul was first interviewed by Dr Henri Dumur (*Direktor*) and Alfred Turk (*Verkaufsleiter*) and then offered a contract as an apprentice. Paul Rosenthal was placed into a three-year sales training programme, supervised by Dr Hugo Freund (*Leiter der Verkaufsabteilung*) that included a lengthy course in mechanics so as to give him a strong practical background.

Upon completing this training in 1936, Paul Rosenthal asked if he could be recommended for employment at the Leitz agency in New York. Rosenthal was supplied with a letter of introduction and gained a position in the scientific instrument division at the firm's New York office. In addition to providing an immediate career prospect to a vulnerable young man, Leitz also rented warehouse space from the elder Rosenthal, after he was forced to close his own business of fifty years' standing, thus providing a Jewish family with an indispensable source of income.

Another example of a young Jewish person helped by the Leitz organization is Kurt Rosenberg (1918–44). According to apprenticeship documents, he completed four years of training at Leitz in Wetzlar to become a *feinmechanik*, between 4 April 1933 and 4 April 1937. Rosenberg received compliments and pay increases as he progressed with his training. At the end of January 1938, Rosenberg emigrated to the United States and Leitz paid all his expenses. Once arrived in America, he worked repairing cameras for Leitz and was even awarded a patent for inventing a close-up attachment. Sadly, after joining the United States Army, Rosenberg was among those killed on 20 April 1944 when the troopship *Paul Hamilton* was sunk in the Mediterranean.

According to Norman Lipton, a Leitz employee in New York and an eyewitness to the arrival of 'Leitz refugees', these individuals also included:

> The New York photographer, Julius Huisgen [who] was a Catholic with a [partly] Jewish wife [whom the Nazis regarded as racially Jewish], who had been employed at the Wetzlar factory and had volunteered for transfer [overseas] to keep his wife out of danger. He had a long career after the war as a Leica salesman in Pennsylvania.
>
> Dagwood [originally 'Dagelbert'] Horn, a Leica dealer in Wetzlar [or, possibly, Wiesbaden?] was 'adopted' as a Leitz employee and sent on to New York, where the Leitz firm

set him up as a Leica dealer on Fifth Avenue, one block
south of the Empire State Building. Any customer who
came to the Leitz showroom, [part of the company's offices
located on 730 Fifth Avenue] and decided to purchase
equipment, was referred to Horn's shop.[7]

It is not clear to what extent Horn was 'adopted' as a Leitz
dealer in the United States. Within the highly competitive
marketplace in Manhattan, the practice of a manufacturer referring customers to only one retail outlet would seem doubtful.
In fact, Norman Lipton, who was periodically assigned to the
agency showroom, recognized this to be a potential issue when
he was specifically directed to make such referrals by the showroom manager, George Moran. When Lipton mentioned his
concerns to his boss, Augustus Wolfman, he was told that 'Horn
had been a Wetzlar dealer and that Leitz had been responsible
for his *setting up shop* [italics mine] in New York.'[8] It would be
fascinating, indeed, to learn if Horn was assisted financially by
Leitz in any exceptional way, e.g. special credit terms for the
merchandise that he held in stock or credits received for equipment repurchased by Leitz in Germany.

Even if Leitz supported Jewish refugees merely by supplying
letters of reference, this alone constituted a potentially danger-
ous activity. On one occasion, such a letter supplied by Leitz to
a Frankfurt camera dealer relocating to the United States had
serious consequences for Alfred Turk, *Verkaufsleiter* at Leitz.

In August 1938, a photographic dealer based in Frankfurt was
advised by Ernst Leitz II, Henri Dumur and Alfred Turk on how
he could liquidate his business and re-establish himself profit-
ably in the United States. Unfortunately, on 9 November 1938,
during the events of *Kristallnacht*, the man's shop was looted
and destroyed. Both he and his brother were incarcerated at
Buchenwald, but then the Nazis released him on 21 November
as he had an appointment with the United States Consul in
Stuttgart to have his visa application processed.[9]

On 30 December 1938, just prior to his leaving Germany, the
photo dealer received a letter of recommendation from Leitz
addressed to the New York office asking that assistance be
offered to him after his arrival. The man learned just after he
had left Germany, however, that a copy of this letter, signed by
Ernst Leitz II, had fallen into the hands of the Gestapo. As a

result, Alfred Turk had been jailed on 27 January 1939 and then released after three weeks only because of an arrangement whereby he was to be retired immediately from his duties at Leitz.

In his post-war letter of 10 February 1948 to Ernst Leitz II, Nathan Rosenthal hints that the aid provided to Jews by Leitz reached well beyond the ranks of employees and dealers. 'How many innumerable young Jewish people from Glessen, Frankfurt, Darmstadt, etc., did you train in your photo business during the Hitler period in order that they were able to earn a living on emigration without taking into account whether your assistance pleased the Nazis or not?'

Norman Lipton's eyewitness testimony also points to an image of Leitz responding actively to help Jews leave Germany:

> I observed [the absorption of refugees] in action soon after I was hired by the New York office of Leitz on 18 May 1938. On alternate weeks, I witnessed the arrival and processing of thirty or more Leitz-sponsored refugees who were lined up along the wall of our office waiting to be interviewed by Alfred Boch, Executive Vice President ... Boch put them up at the nearby Great Northern Hotel and spent the succeeding days on the telephone finding jobs for them throughout New York and the nation.[10]

The efforts that Leitz made to resettle refugees at its 'absorption centre' in New York did not go unnoticed by American Jewish self-help organizations. Unequivocal gratitude is expressed in a letter written to Alfred Boch by Nell Mann, Employment Supervisor, Greater New York Co-ordinating Committee for German [Jewish] Refugees:

> We wish to convey this expression of appreciation on the part of our Committee for your generous contribution to our work of rehabilitating German refugees. We know that you will be glad to hear that the two young men you retrained in American methods of photo finishing were placed most constructively ... These individuals could not have qualified for the positions which came into our office without this preliminary period of instruction.[11]

In the late 1930s, New York was the centre of what can only be described as a miniature camera 'boom' in America. Picture-led magazines such as *Life*, *Collier's* and the *Saturday Evening Post* were dominated by the work of photographers using the Leica. Kodachrome colour transparency film – available only in the 35mm miniature camera format – was a sensation after its introduction in 1936–37. The biggest single market for sales of Leitz cameras and scientific instruments was now the United States.

It is not difficult to imagine that Leitz-sponsored refugees were well placed to succeed within this rapidly expanding economic sector. Whether it was in retail sales, marketing, distribution, teaching, repairing, photo finishing or manufacturing, skilled personnel were needed all over the United States. Those trained in various aspects of the Leica and its already vast system of interchangeable lenses and accessories arrived at America's shores at a time of great opportunity.

Alfred Boch, who spearheaded the absorption operation in New York, had himself once been a refugee.[12] Boch, a Protestant, was born in Wilno in 1904. During the First World War, he and his family were imprisoned in Siberia. After the war, they returned home to Wilno but decided to flee when war broke out between Russia and Poland in 1919. Together with his brother, Karl, Boch reached relatives in Wetzlar after escaping through Lithuania to the German border. After his arrival in Wetzlar he gained employment at Leitz as an apprentice mechanic. In addition to his commercial astuteness, Boch's own personal history gave him a sense of urgency when it came to the plight of the refugees from Germany.

But what about the senior management at Leitz in Wetzlar? Other than sensing a good opportunity for exporting useful personnel overseas, what other factors might have motivated them to enable Jews to flee persecution on a systematic basis? Might Ernst Leitz II (1871–1956), for example, have been guided by principles other than purely 'pragmatic self-interest'?

The Leitz family had long been known for its positive paternal outlook towards employees. Since 1869, under the direction of Ernst Leitz I (1843–1920), the company had become one of the world's major makers of microscopes and scientific instruments.

As early as 1885, a company health insurance scheme was made available to workers and their families. In 1899, there was a pension scheme and company funds were made available for workers to build homes. In the prosperous town of Wetzlar an unemployment insurance scheme for industrial workers there had been instituted in 1888. These workers' benefits were, however, broadly in accordance with the state social provisions introduced by Bismarck. To be sure, the aim was for a healthier and more stable workforce. In this age of rapid industrial growth, illness represented a threat to production.

During the period of strong industrial growth in Germany in the late nineteenth century, skilled engineers were in great demand. According to sixty-year Leitz employee Emil Keller, retaining this talent was important for an industrial enterprise of this period:

> Beginning with the end of the last century, Leitz attracted engineering talent from all over Germany. We would call them mechanical engineers today, but they themselves preferred to be simply called 'mechanics'. They were widely travelled, rugged individualists with a bent for practical solutions to new mechanical problems. They were high-salaried employees to whom the relationship with management was most important. Ernst Leitz I hired most of these men personally. [His son] Ernst Leitz II was particularly adept at maintaining a cordial relationship with them. In fact, he knew almost all of his employees by their first names and this cordiality was freely reciprocated, resulting in a strong interdependence between them and the administration. *'Du kannst mich gar nicht reize, mein Vater ist bei Leitze,'* school kids would respond to one who might make a deprecating remark about the other's father. ('You can't get *me* into fights, *my* dad works for Mr Leitz.')[13]

The post-First World War period leading up to the introduction of the Leica camera was particularly difficult. Most traumatic was the runaway inflation during the period 1923–24. In order to ameliorate the effects of this inflation in Wetzlar, on 9 November 1923 Ernst Leitz II announced to his employees a programme in which:

> A part of their wages would be paid in paper credit printed and signed by the firm in order to allow its workers to purchase groceries in the appropriate shops at pre-

determined prices, but these prices would be subject to change, and these changes would be listed in future announcements. What Leitz had done was to import food-stuffs from Denmark with foreign exchange, earned through export sales, and then truck the food to Wetzlar for distribution through designated merchants.[14]

It was during this unstable period that Ernst Leitz II decided to launch the Leica camera at the spring 1925 Leipzig Fair. Here was a new product clearly designed for an international market. Fortunately, this miniature camera, the brainchild of Oskar Barnack, one of Leitz's most brilliant engineers, rapidly took the world by storm with sales rising from 857 units in 1925 to 19,895 units in 1930. As sales of microscopes and scientific equipment had fallen, the continued employment of 1,500 workers and the future of the company had been at stake.

So, it is quite plausible that not only did the Leitz refugee programme make sound economic sense at the end of the 1930s, but, also, these actions reflected long-held company traditions of behaving humanely towards a highly valued workforce. The refugee activities were conducted with the involvement of the very highest management personnel including Dr Ernst Leitz II and Dr Henri Dumur (1885–1977). Dumur was a cousin of Ernst Leitz II and a company director for many years. He was also a Swiss citizen and, apparently, a man of formidable intellectual and linguistic abilities, not to mention the possession of consid-erable panache when it came to negotiating with Nazi bureau-crats during the war:

> In his office, behind his desk, there was a large picture of the Prussian King Frederick the Great, for all to see when they came in. When representatives of the NSDAP (National Sozialistische Deutsche Arbeiterpartei) called on him to make demands on Leitz which in Dumur's opinion couldn't be fulfilled or were contrary to company policy, he would refer his visitors to the picture and say: 'I am quoting from what Frederick the Great said 200 years ago: "We were not born in chains and we cannot live in chains either."' That almost always ended the conversation and the subject matter was decided in Leitz's favour. Dumur would later turn to his assistant, after the visitors were

gone, and say: *'Das hat der alte Fritz nie gesag!'* ('Old Fritz never said that.')[15]

Dr Henri Dumur was to play a key role in negotiating with the American Occupation Authorities and guiding the way for the company to get back on its feet rapidly. During the period of 19–26 November 1946, Dumur assisted investigators from the British Intelligence Objectives Sub-Committee in their inquiries concerning 'the methods of manufacture and constructional details of the Leica Camera with particular reference to finish, assembling and testing'.[16]

With regard to the Leitz labour force, the British investigators concluded that sound labour practices made for the Leica camera still being 'worthy of its pre-eminent position':

> The Leitz factory is a well-run, happy organisation, this being due in no small measure to the family nature of the business and to its importance in the neighbourhood. Discipline is strict without being severe and one gets the impression of great interest by employees of every grade in the work being performed.
>
> This pride in workmanship and the just pride all have in their world-wide reputation for quality work is the permeating spirit of the place and helps greatly to offset apathy caused by the present dismal state of the country.[17]

This 'well-run, happy organisation' rapidly gained its post-war footing through excellent productivity and the introduction of extraordinarily successful innovations such as the Leica M-3 camera and the Summicron lenses.

The wartime activities of Ernst Leitz II's daughter, Dr Elsie Kühn-Leitz (1903–85), however, point towards another facet of the concern for the welfare of Jews and other victims of Nazism. In a written testimony completed in 1946, she details the emotional and physical suffering that she witnessed among female forced labourers (*Zwangsarbeiter*) and how she sought to improve their living conditions.[18]

As Leitz was supplying equipment to the military and had lost a great number of workers to the war, approximately 700–800 Ukrainian women were attached to the factory as forced labourers, beginning in 1942.[19] Elsie Kühn-Leitz's efforts to better the living conditions of these Ukrainian women included improving their food, obtaining clothing and radios [!], setting up a sewing room and organizing a schedule so the workers could bathe regularly. Elsie Kühn-Leitz's frequent visits to the camp housing these women aroused the suspicions of the Gestapo.

According to Kühn-Leitz, in May 1943, there was renewed persecution against Jews – at this point those in mixed marriages especially – in the Hessen-Nassau district. She was approached by Julie Gerke, who sought help for another woman, Hedwig Palm, a member of a Wetzlar family that was well known locally for making spectacles. Kühn-Leitz helped them to flee to her aunt in Munich and, after some time, the two women attempted to escape to Switzerland. Unfortunately they were caught as they were searching for the place where they intended to cross the border.

Elsie Kühn-Leitz was implicated and arrested by the Gestapo. From 10 September to 28 November 1943 she was imprisoned by the Gestapo in Frankfurt. The cost to her physical and emotional health was considerable and it was only through the payment of a massive 'ransom' by her father (negotiated by Dr Willi Hof, a prominent advocate of the *autobahn* and family friend) that she was released. Months of medical care were required to heal her head injuries. After her release Kühn-Leitz was subjected to regular harassment by the Gestapo until the end of the war.

It is with the testimony of Elsie Kühn-Leitz that an image emerges of a humane and altruistic personality.[20] She was very concerned with improving the day-to-day conditions of forced labourers. She voluntarily assisted the attempted escape of a Jewish woman without seeking any reward for herself. Even while imprisoned by the Gestapo, she took an active interest in the welfare of Jewish and non-Jewish inmates and shared the care packages that she received from her family. Elsie Kühn-Leitz had much to lose: a privileged existence consisting of wealth, high social position, a university education and motherhood.

When Norman C. Lipton approached Ernst Leitz II's youngest son, Gunther (1915–69), with whom he was well-acquainted, about his desire to write the story of the 'underground railway out of Germany' for *Reader's Digest*, he was told 'absolutely not':

Gunther, who was usually very soft spoken, almost lost his temper. 'Not while I'm alive,' he practically shouted. 'My father did what he did because he felt responsible for his employees and their families and also for our neighbours. He was able to act because the government needed our factory's military output. No one can ever know what other Germans had done for the persecuted within the limits of their ability.'[21]

Gunther Leitz's refusal in 1967 to have the story published during his lifetime could well have been the result of an innate modesty about his family's actions. For him, there was no heroism involved. Helping Jews in the way that they had was what any decent human being would have done, given the opportunity.

Given the overall history of how photography was employed by the Nazis during the Holocaust, it is certainly remarkable to learn of the rescue activities engaged in by one of the most celebrated camera manufacturing firms in Germany.[22] Not only did the saving of Jews by Leitz make good long-term pragmatic sense, but the apparently selfless actions and words of the Leitz family strongly suggest altruistic motivation. This story of humanity and compassion merits considerably more research.[23]

NOTES

1. F. D. Smith, 'Photography and the Holocaust', *Journal of Progressive Judaism* 1 (1993), pp. 5–56.
2. Ibid., p. 5.
3. J. C. Legmany and A. Roille, *A History of Photography, Social and Cultural Perspectives* (Cambridge: Cambridge University Press, 1996), pp. 150–7.
4. Legmany and Roille, *A History of Photography*, p. 154.
5. A sampling of such advertising may be found in F. W. Ruttinger, *Leica in der Werbung 1925–1950* (Huckelhoven, Germany: Wittig-Fachbuchverlag, 1986).
6. The definitive published collection of this work is U. Keller (ed.), *The Warsaw Ghetto in Photographs* (New York: Dover, 1984).
7. I have learned much through my correspondence with Norman C. Lipton, a Leitz employee in New York who witnessed these activities.
8. Ibid.
9. A letter of testimony dated 17 February 1961 and written by Henry Enfield, a Florida photographic retailer. In addition, his son, Kurt, was assisted by Leitz to find a position at Wallace-Heaton in London until able to rejoin his father and other family members in the United States in 1939.

10. Norman C. Lipton correspondence.
11. Letter dated 18 April 1939.
12. E. G. Keller, *E Leitz Inc., New York: The Odyssey of an Enterprise Importing Leitz Scientific Instruments and Leica Cameras from Germany Between 1893 and 1930* (New York: Keller, 1996), p. 28.
13. E. G. Keller, *The Source of Today's Thirty Five Millimeter Photography, Part I* (New York: Butts Hollow Services, 1989), unpaginated.
14. Ibid.
15. Ibid.
16. H. J. Bigg and L. G. H. Cantle, *The 'Leica' Camera* (London: British Intelligence Objectives Sub-Committee, 1946), p. 1.
17. Ibid., p. 11.
18. E. Kühn-Leitz, 'The Time of My Imprisonment by the Gestapo in Frankfurt/ Main from 10th September to 28th November 1943' (England: Leica Historical Society, 1984). Elsie Kühn-Leitz's account of her imprisonment is included with other letters and experiences in C. Otto Nass (ed.), *Elsie Kühn-Leitz Mut Zut Menschlichkeit, Vom Wirken einer Frau in ihrer Zeit* (Europa Union Verlag, 1994).
19. The camp housing the *Zwangsarbeiter* where Elsie Kühn-Leitz engaged in her humanitarian efforts was located virtually across the road from the Leitz-Werke. Today, there is a sports stadium on the site of the labour camp. The barracks that housed the labourers were 'recycled' after the war and some are still in use in Wetzlar. On a site near the former labour camp, they house some ethnic/cultural organization and they are still referred to as 'Leitz-Barracks' on the signs posted outside.
20. For a systematic study that explores the personal characteristics of rescuers of Jews during the Nazi era, see S. P. Oliner and P. M. Oliner, *The Altruistic Personality, Rescuers of Jews in Nazi Europe* (New York: Macmillan, 1988).
21. Norman C. Lipton correspondence.
22. Leitz's chief competition came from Carl Zeiss Optics, located in Jena. There, too, efforts were made to safeguard a few prominent Jewish managers and scientists. See G. Gilbert, *The Illustrated World Wide Who's Who of Jews in Photography* (New York: George Gilbert, 1996), p. 151. At the firm of Franke and Heidecke, producers of the Rolleiflex, there may have been efforts to help a few Jewish employees escape. The picture at the Rollei factory is coloured, however, by a staunch association with the Nazi Party. This tie led to the abandoning of the production of a 9x9cm format studio camera whose prototype had been utilized by a well-known Jewish portrait photographer in Berlin, Soloman Kahn. See I. Parker (ed.), *Rollei TLR: The History* (Jersey: Club Rollei, 1992), pp. 89–104.
23. Further research would be well served by interviewing additional Leitz personnel and others who were actually helped. In addition, any further evidence such as boat tickets, letters, personnel files, diaries and Gestapo reports would be immensely useful. I am also trying to gain an understanding of the complex subject of the *Zwangsarbeiter* who were assigned to Leitz. I would be very interested in hearing from anyone who may be able to help me, particularly eyewitnesses or survivors.

There is also, of course, the basic question: how many people were actually saved by Leitz? One history of the Jewish communities in Hessen discusses the wartime fates of Jews in Wetzlar and also mentions the rescue activities at Leitz, but numbers are not mentioned nor is it possible to infer anything from the meagre population statistics offered. See

P. Arnsberg, *Die judischen Gemeinden in Hessen* (Germany: Societats-Verlag, 1967). George Gilbert and Norman Lipton have claimed on various occasions that the Leitz family helped union leaders, gays, radicals and other anti-Nazis. For example, see Gilbert's article 'About Leica Cameras and the Freedom Train', *Viewfinder – Quarterly Journal of the Leica Historical Society of America* 35 (2) (2002), p. 26. Norman Lipton never shared any details of such claims with me, nor have I seen any other relevant evidence. I do not want to risk embellishing what is already a remarkable piece of history by repeating such unsubstantiated assertions. Clearly, extensive archival work is necessary.

4

Jewishly Responsible Investment

MARK GOLDSMITH

Rabbi Ilai said that people show their quality in three ways: *b'choso*, *b'chiso*, *b'chaso*. *B'choso* is 'by their cup', presumably meaning the way that they deal with alcoholic drink; *b'chiso* is 'by their purse', meaning the way they use and value money; *b'chaso* is 'by their anger', meaning their disposition and temperament. This is of course a play on words but, as Richard Hirsch points out, our most significant religious actions might seem from the outside to be just part of day-to-day behaviour. He writes, 'This can be done best not in the comparatively rare moments of prayer or communion with God on important holidays ... but in the daily relations with his fellow men,' such as through our behaviour in business.[1]

In the twenty-first century the contents of our purses are becoming ever more complex. Within a Western economy people of comfortable means will often hold cash and bank deposits, equity in the houses in which they live, various insurances, investments which are being built up to finance pensions, and stocks and shares held either directly or indirectly through fund managers. It is the aim of this article to investigate how Jews might make decisions about the stocks and shares element of this multi-pocketed purse so as to be consistent with Jewish values and principles.

Judaism sees the acquisition of wealth as morally neutral in itself. Israel Mattuck interpreted the eight and tenth commandments – prohibitions against stealing and coveting – to imply the right of a person to own property.[2] The source of someone's wealth, however, is of concern within Judaism. Daniel Sperber cites two passages which show judgments being made on how we earn our money.[3] The first concerns money used in the religious setting: 'You shall not bring the hire of a harlot, or the price of a dog [essentially the proceeds of gambling], into the house of your Eternal God for [the payment of] any vow; for these are both abominations to your Eternal God.'[4] The second concerns the reputation for trustworthiness of those who make their money by frowned-upon means: 'These are ineligible [to be witnesses or judges]: a gambler with dice, a usurer, a pigeon-trainer, and traders [in the produce] of the sabbatical year.'[5] Our purses should not be filled with money from sources contrary to Jewish values.

In Judaism, the way in which we conduct ourselves in business in order to gain wealth falls into a moral framework. For example, sellers are expected to disclose whatever a buyer needs to know in order to make a decision about the true value of a purchase; they must not seek to gain from withholding information.[6] As a further example, the requirement 'not to put a stumbling block in the path of the blind'[7] can be interpreted to mean that Jews in business must not give advice or sell goods that they know might be to the detriment of the recipient or purchaser.[8]

When wealth is acquired it carries with it obligations. Jewish values place humankind in a custodial relationship with the wealth of the world. Thus those who own the means of generating wealth have a responsibility to dedicate some of their output to the needs of society at large. Classically this responsibility has been derived from the requirement in the biblical 'Holiness Code' to leave a corner of your field for the poor and the stranger to glean.[9]

The biblical and Talmudic regulations which are the foundation of Jewish values in the conduct of business and economic activity were, of course, framed and developed in response to an agrarian society which, on the face of it, shares few of the characteristics of the Western economy of the twenty-first century. The pace of technological change in previous millennia was far slower than that in current times. Even the largest enterprises such as shipyards and tanneries were tiny by the standards of today's multinational corporations. Owners were normally the operators of any economic enterprise – the farmer, the wine-maker, the baker. As Meir Tamari writes, however: 'Unlike the changes in physics or chemistry, economic activities have remained the same – production, distribution, transfer of wealth and so on ... while the techniques change over time, both the motivations and the spiritual challenges remain similar ... the promptings and drives of economic behaviour – uncertainty, greed, wants and jealousy – so deeply imbedded in human nature, do not basically change.'[10]

A central plank of today's Western economy – the holding of stocks and shares in corporations – was, not long ago, restricted to a small section of the economically active population. In recent years, however, a far greater proportion of UK residents now hold shares. These may be held by direct ownership, either as part of an income-producing portfolio of investments or as shares that they have bought or been granted as a result of one of the mass privatizations of utilities or de-mutualizations of building societies and insurance companies. Alternatively, shares may be held indirectly through one of the government-sponsored savings schemes. These have encouraged many people to take part in various kinds of mutual trusts, where a fund manager stewards a series of equity investments on behalf of clients. Typically, investors select from the manager's funds the one in which they want to invest their money. Most pension schemes have been based largely on a spread of stocks and shares and thus most of us can expect to live out our days on the proceeds of these investments. Pension funds alone have over £180 billion invested in the UK stock market, more than matching the £165 billion invested directly by individuals.[11]

This trend makes most UK residents the partial owners of a number of business operations. The nature of most popular investments in stocks and shares, however, is that they are in large businesses with many thousands, if not millions, of shareholders. Can we be said to have any responsibility for their activities?

Many of these businesses operate across national borders and their size in terms of turnover matches that of the economy of some nation-states. Businesses are among the most powerful institutions in today's world. A parallel can be drawn with the prophets' duty, as described in the Bible, to hold to account the powerful people of their day. As John Rayner writes, 'Judaism has always taught that God cares about, and therefore religion must concern itself with, the way a society is governed.'[12]

The term 'Socially Responsible Investment' (SRI) has come into use to describe the efforts of investors to square their moral and ethical responsibilities with the investments they have made. Perhaps the earliest modern exponents of SRI were the Society of Friends (Quakers) whose Friends Provident institution was founded in 1832 to provide life assurance. Friends Provident was set up with the intention that it would never invest money in companies with business activities involving slavery. Since the 1900s, the Methodist Church has invested substantially in the stock market[13] but not in companies with alcohol, tobacco and gambling as part of their businesses.[14] In 1971 a mutual fund called the Pax World Fund was set up in the USA by two Methodist ministers for investors who did not want to invest in businesses involved in supplying the Vietnam War. The international campaign against apartheid in South Africa provided a further boost to SRI when, in 1974, the Interfaith Center on Corporate Responsibility (ICCR) was set up by American churches to encourage businesses in which they had investments to adopt anti-apartheid policies through shareholder resolutions and screened investing. The ICCR in 2002 represented 275 faith organizations with a combined portfolio of $110 billion.[15]

In Britain recently, the £30 billion Hermes pension fund (primarily for post office and telecommunications employees) published ten principles by which its future management would be governed. These included requirements for the ethical, environmental and social performance of those companies in which pensioners' funds were invested. The Pension Disclosure Regulations became legislation in 2000. They require UK pension funds to disclose the degree to which they take into account ethical, social and environmental considerations. As a result of the disclosures which have been made, in 2001 it was possible to assert that over £100 billion of UK assets were held by funds which invest using some principles of Socially Responsible Investment.[16]

While a lead in Socially Responsible Investment has been taken by churches worldwide, the Jewish community has been slow to follow suit. This may be partly because the principles which a Christian community might wish to follow in screening investments are not necessarily those uppermost in the ethical and moral priorities of Jews. For example, a Jew may see no need to disinvest from companies in the alcoholic drinks industry, as Judaism uses moderate amounts of alcohol in many of its ceremonies. The Jewish historical experience and the situation of the State of Israel has meant that pacifism is not considered a practical option and thus disinvestment from arms-related industries might not be priority for some Jews.

One can, however, propose a straightforward set of principles which could form a basis for a Jewish vision of Socially Responsible Investment, based on biblical texts which have been extensively interpreted in later Rabbinical works. The following examples give a flavour of the ethical values founded on biblical teachings.

- Businesses should carry out their activities with a view to minimizing their negative impact upon the environment.[17]
- The employment practices of a business should be just and fair to its workers.[18]
- A business worthy of a Jew's investment funds should be one known to make transactions in good faith.[19]
- Such a business should avoid being involved in abuses of human rights or the taking or giving of bribes.[20]
- If a business is involved in the military sector it should not be party to the promotion of conflict.[21]
- If a business is involved in the health sector it should not engage in practices which unduly restrict access to health-care.[22]
- If a business is in the financial sector its policies and practices should not discriminate against groups in society who find it difficult to access capital for businesses.[23]
- If the activities of the business require it to work with animals it should take care not to treat them with cruelty.[24]

A Jew or a Jewish institution which wishes to act as a socially responsible investor can do so in a number of ways. Companies known to engage in activities contrary to the principles above can be screened out of the investment process and not be recipients of funds. Conversely businesses which are the best performers in their sector in terms of their contribution to social, economic or environmental sustainability or which display exemplary employee practices can be targeted for investment.

Owners of businesses, either directly through stocks and shares or indirectly through unit trusts, investment funds and pension funds, can use their shareholder influence to help bring about positive social and environmental change within these organizations. This can include corporate engagement (communicating with management on particular issues), gaining support for shareholder resolutions and using the threat of disinvestment to bring about positive change. A further tool is the investment of a proportion of a person or institution's portfolio in small enterprises or micro-finance funds which enable people in disadvantaged communities to become active in business.

It is not easy for an individual or a small institution to make the tool of corporate engagement effective. This would be greatly facilitated were there to be Jewish 'Ethical Funds' which grouped the shareholdings of many people. The fund managers could then be charged to use their leverage and engage with the companies in which the investments were held. Alternatively Jews and Jewish institutions interested in effective corporate engagement could join organizations such as the ICCR and International Interfaith Investment Group (3iG) in order to pool the rights associated with share ownership and strengthen their voice in engagement. Screening investments is undoubtedly an effective way to build a Socially Responsible Investment portfolio, where investment returns can be measured not only by financial gain but also by the putting into action of Jewish values. Corporate engagement also puts into practice the responsibility to reason with those with whom we disagree and whom we are able to influence.[25]

While businesses exist first and foremost to make money, it is quite reasonable for their owners, the shareholders large and small, to expect them to do so within the context of their ethical standards. Even one of the strongest advocates of free enterprise, Milton Friedman, wrote that business managers are responsible for conducting the business in accordance with the desires of shareholders, 'which generally will be to make as much money as possible while conforming to the basic rules of the society, both those embodied in law and those embodied in ethical custom'.[26] Current research into the financial performance of SRI funds suggests that there is little difference in financial return between a well-managed and well-spread SRI portfolio of investments and a well-managed and well-spread portfolio with no selection criteria.[27] Jewish shareholders might say that legislation will prohibit any undesirable actions by the businesses in which they have invested. To leave it to legislation, however, abdicates one's responsibility to act ethically *lifnin mishurat hadin* (beyond the letter of the law) where one can.[28]

Current *halachic* opinion treats a corporation of any size as simply an extension of a partnership – all of the shareholders are seen as partners. Therefore if our purse is filling with the proceeds of the companies in which we hold shares we should act as if we were partners in a small enterprise. As Meir Tamari writes, 'shareholders would seem to be required to dismiss their corporate officers if these would perform, on their behalf, policies that would be considered *halachically* to be immoral or non-permissible; otherwise the responsibility, moral and legal, devolves on them as it would in the case of partnership or single owner firms.'[29]

The tools of corporate engagement exist to enable us to take up this responsibility. Other tools, such as a Jewish Ethical Fund, could be created. We need not live out our days in ignorance of whether we are doing so on the proceeds of environmental carelessness, exploitation and sharp business practices.

NOTES

1. R. G Hirsch, *The Way of the Upright*. (New York: UAHC, 1973), p. 64.
2. I. I. Mattuck., *Jewish Ethics* (London: Hutchinson's University Library, 1953), p. 100.
3. D. Sperber, untitled paper presented to the International Interfaith Investment Group, London, 2002.
4. Deuteronomy 23:19.
5. Mishnah Sanhedrin 3:3.
6. Mishneh Torah, *Hilchot Mechirah* 15:6.
7. Leviticus 19:14.
8. For a concise summary of the basic principles of Jewish business ethics see T. Meir, *The Challenge of Wealth*. (New Jersey: Jason Aronson, 1995), pp. xxi–xiv.
9. Leviticus 19:9–10.
10. M. Tamari, *Al Chet: Sins in the Marketplace* (Northvale, NJ: Jason Aronson, 1996), p. xv.
11. *Share Ownership* (London: Department of National Statistics, 2002), p. 26.
12. J. D. Rayner,, *Principles of Jewish Ethics* (London: New Jewish Initiative for Social Justice, 1998), p. 11.
13. The Methodist Church's General Board of Health and Pensions (USA) held equity investments of well over $10 billion in value in October 2003.
14. A. Reese, *A Short History of Sustainable and Responsible Investment*, presented at Limmud Conference, 2003.

15. L. Bush, J. Dekro and M. Leibling, *Jews and the Corporate Responsibility Movement*, <www.socialaction.com> October 2002. The authors note that only two out of the 275 members of ICCR are Jewish organizations, representing a tiny percentage of the probable Jewish philanthropies' investable assets of over $25 billion.

16. The figure of £100 billion includes assets held by unit trusts and similar 'mutual funds', churches, charities and pension funds. See R. Sparkes, *SRI: A Global Revolution* (London: John Wiley & Sons, 2002).

17. This first principle would have as its biblical source text Deuteronomy 20:19, the *Bal Taschit* text requiring an besieging army to preserve fruit trees for the future.

18. The text in Leviticus 19:13, commanding that the wages of a worker are paid promptly is an example of this requirement.

19. 'When you buy or sell anything to your neighbour's hand you shall not wrong one another' in Leviticus 25:14 was primarily interpreted in Rabbinic texts to apply to fair pricing, but could be interpreted more widely, to give rise to the general Jewish responsibility for fair dealing codified in *Shulchan Aruch Choshen Mishpat* 228:6 and *Mishneh Torah, Hilchot De'ot* 5:13.

20. Exodus 23:7–9.

21. Isaiah 2:4.

22. *Shmor naph'shcha m'od*, e.g. Deuteronomy 4:9.

23. The anti-usury regulations have at their root the needs of the poorest members of society to have access to funds, e.g. Exodus 22:24.

24. *Tza'ar ba'alei chayyim*, e.g. Deuteronomy 22:4, 6.

25. Leviticus 19:17.

26. M. Friedman (1970) quoted in M. L. Pava, *Business Ethics – A Jewish Perspective* (New York: Yeshiva University Press, 1997), p. 148.

27. The United Methodist Church of the USA has been managing its funds according to SRI principles since before 1979. Their ethically screened fund has on average gained 12.7 per cent per annum from 1979–mid-2003. The Standard and Poor 500 Index has on average gained 12.8 per cent over the same period.

28. Pava, *Business Ethics*, Chapter 6, presents an extensive analysis of this proposition.

29. Tamari, p. 96.

5

Is There a Specific Jewish Ethic?

LOUIS JACOBS

For all the discussions, ancient and modern, on Jewish ethics[1] the fact remains that there is no equivalent term for ethics in the classical Jewish sources of the Bible and the Talmudic literature.[2] Like religion, ethics is too abstract a term to be used in the very concrete Hebrew and Aramaic of these sources. As Israel Zangwill remarked: 'The Rabbis were deeply religious men, yet they had no word for Religion.' Although the actual word 'ethics' never occurs in the sources, however, there are a number of terms denoting moral conduct over and above the requirements of the Law, the *Halachah*. The *Halachah* is heteronomous and categorical, whereas these terms refer to situations in which there is much scope for choices governed by individual character and temperament.

TERMS

1. Derekh eretz, 'the way of the earth'

This term refers to the way in which well-mannered, decent people generally conduct themselves. The term is universal in application. It is nowhere suggested that *derekh eretz* has been invented by Jews or that its practice is confined to Jews. On the contrary, Jews, as human beings, are expected to live up to the standards accepted as the norm by all human beings. The minor tractate of the Talmud, *Derekh Eretz*,[3] does deal with the good manner demanded specifically of the Jew but this means only that guidance is offered on how the Jew can best realize his humanity, not his Jewishness. It is true, however, that the ethical demands of the tractate are presented in a Jewish religious context.[4] The concept *derekh eretz* is applied anthropomorphically even to animal behaviour in a remarkable Talmudic passage (*Eruvin* 100b): 'Rabbi Johanan said, "If the Torah had not been given we could have learnt modesty from the cat, robbery [i.e. to be industrious and co-operate with others rather than steal from them] from the ant, chastity from the dove, and good manners (*derekh eretz*) from the cock who first coaxes and then mates."' The implication is that in ethical matters the Torah simply confirms what is known in any event from the way various creatures have been made.[5] Another Talmudic passage (*Sotah* 44a) is in similar vein. It explains that the Torah (Deuteronomy 20:7) lists those exempt from military service – the man who has built a house, the man who has planted a vineyard and the man who has taken a wife – in that particular order so as to teach *derekh eretz* that a man should first build a house and plant a vineyard and then take a wife he can afford to keep. The meaning here is that the sequence is of no relevance to the Deuteronomic law itself, which simply states three exemptions, but is given because ideally that is how things should be. The Midrash (*Leviticus Rabbah* 9:3) states that *derekh eretz* preceded the giving of the Torah by twenty-six generations, which can mean only that *derekh eretz* was the universal property of all mankind independent of Revelation.[6]

2. Maasim tovim, *'good deeds'*

This expression, denoting general acts of benevolence, is usually found in association with 'repentance'. In the so-called 'Ethics of the Fathers' (a common misnomer for tractate *Avot* in the Mishnah)[7] we find: 'repentance and good deeds are as a shield in the face of punishment' (4:11) and 'better is one hour of repentance and good deeds in this world than all the life of the world to come; and better is one hour of calmness of spirit in the world to come than all the life of this world.' The latter is a paradoxical saying that presumably seeks to achieve the correct balance between this-worldly and other-worldly religious attitudes. The actual term 'good deeds' is not found in precisely this form in the Babylonian Talmud.[8] This expression is not to be confused with 'Torah and *mitzvot*' (e.g. in *Shabbat* 30a; *Pesahim* 50b). The essential difference between the two expressions is that the latter is legalistic, calling attention to obedience to the study and practice of the precepts, whereas the former refers to the response of the individual character.[9]

3. Lifnim mi-shurat ha-din, *'beyond the line of the law'*

This term refers to what we call 'equity'. It has a quasi-legal connotation. Even where the strict law does not demand compensation for an offence it is said to be good to go beyond the line of the law in order to compensate the one who has been offended. The Talmud (*Bava Kama* 99b) tells, for instance, of the second-century teacher, Rabbi Hiyya, who advised a woman that a *denar* she had shown was good currency whereas in fact she was unable to spend it because it turned out to be a bad coin. Strictly speaking, Rabbi Hiyya had no obligation to compensate the woman for her loss since he was not an expert in coin evaluation and as such was exonerated when he erred. For all that, Rabbi Hiyya did provide the woman with a good *denar* out of his own pocket since he wished to act 'beyond the line of the law'.

Nahmanides (1195–1270), in a famous comment on the verse: 'Do what is right and good in the sight of the Lord' (Deuteronomy 6:18) extends the concept[10] to embrace general ethical conduct, although by so doing he can be said to be going beyond the line of the law, so to speak, since the whole concept in the Talmud is applied only to individual, legal cases. Nahmanides writes:

> At first, the Torah tells us to keep the laws which God has commanded but now it goes on to say: Do that which is right and good also in matters where He has issued no command, for He loves the right and the good. This is an important idea. For it is impossible for the Torah to mention all matters regarding a man's behaviour towards his fellows and neighbours, all his business dealings and matters concerning the improvement of society and political matters. Hence, after mentioning many of them such as 'Thou shalt not go about as a tale-bearer' [Leviticus 19:16]; 'Thou shalt not take revenge or foster hatred' [Leviticus 19:18]; 'Thou shalt not stand idly by the blood of thy neighbour' [Leviticus 19:16]; 'Thou shalt not curse a deaf man' [Leviticus 19:14]; 'Thou shalt rise before the

hoary head' [Leviticus 19:32] and so forth, the injunction is further given to do that which is right and good in all matters so as to include the need for compromise and to go beyond the line of the law, as, for example, the law regarding the sale of a neighbouring field [that precedence should be given to the one who has an adjacent field] and even that of which the Rabbis say that a man's conduct should be beyond reproach and that he should speak gently to others so that he can be called right and upright in everything.

4) Musar, *'reproof'*

This all-embracing term is based on the verse: 'Hear, my son, the instruction (*musar*) of thy father' (Proverbs 1:8). The term denotes urging people to improve their character and conduct but the appeal embraces religious as well as ethical obligations. The *Musar* literature produced during the Middle Ages covers the whole range of Jewish obligations, whether ethical or religious. Bahya Ibn Pakudah's *Duties of the Heart*, for instance, is, as its title denotes, a call to inwardness in the fulfilment of the Torah in all its ramifications. The same applies to the *Musar* movement, founded by Rabbi Israel Salanter in the nineteen century.[11] It is, consequently, quite incorrect to translate the term *Musar* as 'ethics', though this happens frequently. *Musar* falls under the heading of 'ethics' only in so far as every call to follow the path of duty and obligation is 'ethical'. Rabbi Moshe Hayyim Luzzato (1707–1746) writes in the introduction to his *Path of the Upright*, a foremost work of Musar,[12] that he has not compiled the book to teach his readers things of which they have no knowledge but only to remind them of the obligations they know they have without being informed what these are. This calls to mind Abraham Lincoln's statement that it was not the scriptural passages he did not understand which bothered him but the passages he understood only too well.

5. Middot tovot, *'good qualities' of character*

This term is not found in the Talmud[13] but originated in the mediaeval, moralistic literature. The word *middah* in itself means 'measures' and, so far as character dispositions are concerned, refers also to bad qualities, *middot raot*. A *baal middot*, literally, 'master of qualities', is, however, applied to a person with not-able good character traits. The emphasis is on these rather than the actions that inevitably result from them.[14]

JEWISH VALUES

As with the term 'ethics' itself, the abstract term 'values' is not found in the classical sources of Judaism. This is not to say, of course, that there are no teachings about justice, compassion, benevolence, modesty and generosity. These and similar desir-able traits, again like ethics as a whole, are not advocated as specifically Jewish. When, for example, the Talmud (*Yevamot* 79a) states that there are three distinguishing marks of the Jewish people – compassion, bashfulness and benevolence – the bizarre notion is certainly not postulated that these are virtues *because* Jews possess them. On the contrary, the implication is that these are admirable traits in all human beings but are especially prominent among Jews, who are thereby singled out as examples of true humanity. The statement is naturally hyperbolic, par-taking far more of apologetics and preaching than of any assess-ment of human virtue. The meaning is surely: if you want to be a true Jew you must strive to realize those virtues implanted by nature into the human character. Even when it is said (*Betzah* 32b) of one who has no compassion, that his ancestors did not stand at the foot of Sinai, the meaning is not that the Revelation created Jewish compassion but that Revelation reinforced it.[15]

Is there a Jewish ethic?

It follows from the above that there is no such thing as a specific Jewish ethic. Since ethics are universal it makes as little sense to speak of kosher goodness as to speak of kosher mathematics. To be sure, the *Halachah* contains rules about how a Jew should conduct himself ethically but that is because *Halachah*, in the course of its development, has appropriated certain ethical practices to treat them as law rather than ethics. Questions such as whether artificial insemination, abortion and contraception are forbidden belong not to ethics but to religious law. Until recent times no attempt was ever made by the *Halachists* to treat such questions as whether and when a man may lose his temper or whether and when a man should be modest as falling under the scope of *Halachah*.[16]

Relevant here is Maimonides' statement (*Yad, Berakhot* 11:2) on why the special benediction over the precepts is not recited over ethical precepts such as the practice of benevolence. Solomon Ibn Adret of Barcelona (d. *c.* 1310), the *Rashba*, in a famous Responsum (Number 18) explains it differently from Maimonides. According to *Rashba*, there can be no benediction over 'ethical' precepts because the recipient may be unwilling to accept the act of benevolence performed on his behalf and a benediction is recited only where the act depends solely on the one who performs it. Maimonides' analysis is quite different. Maimonides writes: 'It is necessary to recite a benediction ["who has sanctified us with His commandments"] before carrying out a precept *between man and the Omnipresent*, whether the precept is obligatory or whether it is not obligatory' (italics mine). The very popular Orthodox Bible commentator, Baruch Epstein (1860–1942),[17] understands Maimonides' statement to mean that a Jew cannot say 'who has sanctified *us*' before carrying out the ethical precepts because with regard to these there is no specifically Jewish form of 'sanctification' since, with regard to ethical norms, Jews are no different from Gentiles. Such an interpretation is not implausible, but it is better to understand Maimonides as saying that 'who has *commanded* us' is inappropriate since the Jew ought to carry out these ethical precepts not because God has so commanded but because it is right and proper for him to be the sort of person who would carry them out even if he were not commanded. The Jew who is benevolent solely in obedience to a divine command is not really benevolent. There is a divine command in these matters but the command is for him to strive to be the sort of person who is naturally benevolent.[18]

This, I suggest, is the significance of the distinction Maimonides makes between precepts 'between man and the Omnipresent' (religious precepts) and those 'between man and his fellow' (ethical precepts). Take, as an example of the first category, hearing the sound of the *shofar* on *Rosh Hashanah*, and, as an example of the second category, giving alms to the poor. Even the authority who holds that a man has fulfilled his religious obligation notwithstanding the absence of any express intention – 'precepts do not require intention'[19] – this only means that if a man had heard the blowing of the *shofar* without any intention so to do, for instance simply because he happened to pass by the synagogue, where the blowing takes place, he has fulfilled his obligation. But it is obviously meritorious to hear the sounds of the *shofar* with the intention of carrying out the divine command and this is the purpose of the benediction, as if to say: 'I do this because God has commanded me to do so.' If there were no command there would be no meaning to the act; the act gains all significance from the fact that it is a divine command. With regard to almsgiving, on the other hand, the ideal is for a man to be naturally of so benevolent a disposition that even were he not commanded so to do he would still wish to help the poor. Almsgiving is an act significant in itself. With regard to a religious obligation, the ideal is for the act to be carried out with the clear intention of performing God's will. With regard to an ethical obligation, the ideal is rather for a man to be 'caught in the act' that stems naturally from his benevolent and caring nature. Religious precepts should ideally be carried out with intention. Ethical precepts should ideally be carried out without intention or, rather, the intention should follow on the disposition, not the disposition on the intention. The Jew who says: 'I eat *matzah* on Passover because God has so commanded' is a good Jew because of this very intention. Why else would he eat the *matzah*? But the Jew who says: 'I give charity because the God has so commanded' is inferior in his ethical stance to the Jew who simply gets on with it.

ETHICS – JEWISH AND HUMANISTIC

It is interesting to find two *halachists* of the old school discussing the relationship between Jewish ethical standards and the standards of a humanistic ethic, significantly enough, in the introductions to their Responsa collections, which deal with the demands of the *Halachah*. Rabbi Yitzhak Schmelkes (1828–1906), in the introduction to his *Bet Yitzhak*,[20] argues that Kant's categorical imperative is virtually identical to the basis of *Jewish* ethics. He finds this notion stated in 'Ethics of the Fathers' (*Avot* 2:1): 'Which is the right course that a man should choose for himself? That which he feels to be honourable to himself, and which also brings him honour from mankind.' It is doubtful, however, whether this saying can be interpreted in the way Schmelkes does.[21] He also relies on the saying attributed to Hillel (*Shabbat* 31a): 'That which is hateful unto thee do not do unto thy neighbour.' For all that, Schmelkes remarks, Hillel added, 'The rest is commentary, go and study.'[22] Schmelkes understands this to mean that a humanistic ethic in itself is ineffectual in drawing up a detailed ethical scheme. The 'commentary' to be studied is the aspect of revelation, i.e. the Torah ethic which provides the detailed rules. Thus, according to Schmelkes, the basis of ethics is not revelation. Man knows the distinction between good and evil and for this no revelation is required. Revelation is necessary so that man may know how to apply his innate understanding of what is good in the details of his ethical life. Furthermore, says Schmelkes, a humanistic ethic cannot result in individual perfection, which can be attained only through ethical behaviour in obedience to a divine command.

Schmelkes contends that the Torah says little about the cultivation of good character traits because if such descriptions were found in the Torah this would make them very attractive in themselves, whereas they should not be attractive but should be cultivated because God wills it so. This is an extremely odd notion. If Schmelkes is correct it would mean that good character traits should ideally be unattractive in themselves – the very opposite of the idea, mentioned above, that with regard to ethical conduct spontaneity alone is wholesome and it is this spontaneity that the Torah wants human beings to have with regard to the ethical life.

The second *halachist* to discuss our question is Abraham Zevi Perlmutter (d. 1926), in the introduction to his Responsa collection, *Damasek Eliezer*.[23] Perlmutter admits that ethical obligations are innate but maintains that the ethical laws of the Torah go far beyond a purely humanistic ethic in the following respects:

1. A humanistic ethic urges a man not to harm his neighbours but the Torah ethic enjoins positive love of the neighbour.
2. A humanistic ethic does not frown on usury, as does the Torah.
3. A humanistic ethic does not demand that the life of the neighbour be saved from danger, whereas the Torah enjoins:

'Thou shalt not stand idly by the blood of thy neighbour' (Leviticus 19:16).

4. The Torah enjoins love and care not only for the native but also for the alien.

5. The Torah ethic enjoins a man to be a loving husband and a woman to be a loving wife, i.e. the marriage ideal is based on revelation and is not necessarily demanded by a humanistic ethic.

In point of fact, most of these ethical principles are found in all Western ethical systems, though Perlmutter could argue that this is due largely to the fact that the humanistic ethics of the West owe much to the Hebrew Bible and are, in a way, the Torah ethic.

Imitatio Dei

The religious dimension is added to the ethical in the Rabbinic idea of imitating God. The *Sifre* comments on the verse 'to love the Lord your God, to walk in all His ways' (Deuteronomy 11:21): 'Just as He is called[24] "merciful" be thou merciful; just as He is called "compassionate", be thou compassionate.' A third-century teacher spells it out in greater detail (*Sotah* 14a):

> What is the meaning of the verse 'Ye shall walk after the Lord your God' [Deuteronomy 13:5]? Is it possible for human beings to walk after the *Shechinah*? Has it not been said: 'For the Lord your God is a devouring fire' (Deuteronomy 4:24)? But the verse means to walk after the attributes of the Holy One, blessed is He. As He clothes the naked – for it is written: 'And the Lord God made for Adam and his wife coats of skin and clothed them' [Genesis 3:21] – so do thou clothe the naked. The Holy One, blessed be He, visited the sick, for it is written: 'And the Lord appeared to him by the oaks of Mamre' [Genesis 18:1]. So do thou visit the sick. The Holy One, blessed be He, comforted mourners, for it is written: 'And it came to pass after the death of Abraham, that God blessed Isaac his son' [Genesis 25:11]. So do thou comfort mourners. The Holy One, blessed be He, buried the dead, for it is written: 'And He buried him in the valley' [Deuteronomy 34:6]. So do thou bury the dead.[25]

The suggestion is not that clothing the naked, visiting the sick, comforting mourners and burying the dead are good only *because* of the doctrine of *Imitatio Dei*. The implication is rather, as suggested above, that by doing these things in the imitation of God, another dimension, the religious, is added to acts decent human beings would do of their own accord.

ETHICS AND RELIGION

It seems to follow that, in Jewish teaching, ethics do not depend on religious beliefs and attitudes. An atheist can also be virtuous. From this point of view, the basic ethical stance is the same whether adopted by a Jew, a Christian or an atheist. Benevolence is benevolence whether practised by a Jew or a Gentile. Yet the Jewish religion does have something to say about ethics by introducing the dogmatic and the legal into some of the details of the ethical life. To make this more clear, examples should be given of some of the ways in which Judaism stresses ethical conduct differently from, say, Christianity. These emphases do not stem from different views of the ethical as such, but are based on the difference in dogma between the two religions.[26]

- Both Judaism and Christianity frown on divorce. Generally speaking Christianity has refused to allow the dissolution of a marriage so that there can be a second marriage while the spouse is still living. The difference between the two religions in this matter is essentially because Christianity believes marriage to be a 'sacrament', which husband and wife vow to keep and which cannot be abolished by the marriage vow being annulled. This difference owes everything to differing, dogmatic attitudes towards the rite of marriage and can hardly be said to express different ethical standards.[27]
- Generally speaking, Judaism, unlike Christian monasticism, does not consider celibacy to be in any way meritorious.[28] This is due not to any basic difference in ethical stance, however, but to the fact that Judaism regards procreation to be a religious duty.
- Both religions frown on contraception[29] but the Christian opposition is based on the practice being unnatural while in Judaism the opposition is on the grounds of 'wasting seed'.

These considerations are religious, not ethical, in nature. Both religions are concerned with the promotion of a just society; there are few if any differences regarding the means of achieving that just society and these differences cut across the religious divide in any event.[30] Risking a generalization, it can be said that Judaism places greater stress on the ethical deed while in some versions of Christianity faith is greater than works.[31] But this, too, owes much not to different ethical norms but to the Jewish, religious concept of the *mitzvah* ('divine command'). As it had been said more than once, Judaism is the religion of *doing* the will of God.

NOTES

1. The basic theme of this study is discussed in the following works: M. Lazarus, *Die Ethic Des Judenthums* (Frankfurt, 1899); A. Lichtenstein, 'Does Jewish Tradition Recognise an Ethic Independent of Halakha?', in M. Kellner (ed.), *Contemporary Jewish Ethics* (New York, 1978), pp. 102–23; D. W. Halivni, 'Can a Religious Law be Immoral?', in A. A. Chiel (ed.), *Perspectives on Jews and Judaism: Essays in honor of Wolfe Kelman* (New York, 1978), pp. 165–70; L. Jacobs: 'The Problem of the *Akedah* in Jewish Thought', in R. L. Perkins (ed.), *Kierkegaard: Fear and Trembling Critical Appraisals* (Alabama, 1981), pp. 1–9; S. Spero, 'Is There a Morality Independent of Halakha?', *Morality, Halakha and the Jewish Tradition* (New York, 1983), pp. 167–8; M. Kellner, 'Jewish Ethics', in P. Singer (ed.), *A Companion to Ethics* (Oxford, 1993), pp. 82–90.
2. J. Levy, *Worterbuch uber die Talmudin und Midraschim* (Leipzig: F. A. Brockhaus, 1876–89) understands this word, which occurs frequently in the Talmudic literature (e.g. of the menstrual cycle in Mishnah *Niddah* 1:1) to be the Greek word *ethos*, but only in the sense of a regular happening, not in the sense of ethics. See also Jastrow, Dictionary, who gives a different etymology from the Hebrew.
3. The two minor tractates, *Derekh Eretz Rabba* and *Derekh Eretz Zuta* are Geonic but contain material going back to Talmudic times; see H. L. Strack and G. Sternberger, *Introduction to the Talmud and Midrash* (Edinburgh, 1991), pp. 250–1.
4. *Tractate Derekh Eretz Rabba*, for example, opens with a statement of the laws governing religiously forbidden marriages.
5. See Midrash Genesis Rabbah 6:16, ed. Theodor-Albeck, p. 42 that the reason why the Roman calendar is solar and the Jewish calendar lunar is that it is *derekh eretz*, that the descendants of Esau, the older brother, should reckon the years by the greater luminary, and the descendants of Jacob, the younger brother, by the lesser luminary, the moon.
6. Thus the oft-quoted mazim '*Derekh Eretz* is prior to the Torah' does not refer to the relative significance of the two but only to precedence in time, i.e. in history.
7. *Avot* does contain maxims both religious and ethical, but the thrust of the

tractate is to describe the 'chain of tradition', the teachers of the Mishnah of which the tractate is part, and it is totally incorrect to call it a 'Treatise on Ethics'.

8. See, however, *Kiddushin* 33b where Rabbi Ezekiel is described as 'a master of deeds', *baal maasim*.

9. It is astonishing that the great Talmudic scholar, J. B. Soloveitchk (*Ish Ha-Halakha*, Jerusalem, 1979, p. 36; English translation by L. Kaplan, 'Halakhic Man', Philadelphia, 1983, p. 30) should quote the passage in *Avot* 4:7 as if it read 'Torah and *mitzvot*' in support of a thesis that is, in fact, contradicted by the correct reading, as in all texts of *Avot*.

10. This is in accord with Nahmanides' famous discussion of the command to be holy (Leviticus 19:2), which he understands to embrace separation from the licit which, if not followed, can lead a man to be 'a scoundrel by permission of the Torah'.

11. A comprehensive work on the *Musar* movement is D. Katz, *Tenuat Ha-Musar* (Tel-Aviv, five vols 1956–63), and the same author's *Pulemos Ha-Musar*, (Jerusalem, 1972).

12. Luzzatto's *Mesillat Yesharim* (translated as 'The Path of the Upright', by M. M. Kaplan (Philadelphia, 1936) is a much-favoured text among the latterday *Musarists*.

13. The solo reference to *middot tovot* in the Babylonian Talmud is *Hagigah* 9b, but there the meaning is simply 'all good things' and has nothing to do with dispositions of character.

14. God's attributes are frequently referred to in the Talmud as *middot* and this is relevant to the whole question of *Imitatio Dei*, but the term *middot tovot* as referring directly to human beings is not found until post-Talmudic times.

15. The biblical writers always assume that the nations around Israel are not different from the Israelites so far as the possession of the basic human qualities are concerned; see, for example, Jeremiah 6:2, where the prophet castigates the people of the north country who 'lay hold on bow and spear, they are cruel, and have no compassion', and witness the prophet Amos's denunciation of the various non-Israelite peoples for their wanton cruelty.

16. An attempt was made in the nineteenth century by Menahem Abraham Treves (Dreifus), in his *Orah Mesharim* ('The Way of the Upright Ones', Jerusalem, 1969) to apply *Halakhic* categories to ethical questions. The subtitle of the work is, in fact, 'A *Shulhan Arukh* of Character Traits' (*Shulhan Arukh Le-Middot*) but for all its learning the work fails, as it was bound to do, since the majority of its sources are Aggadic and these are inapplicable to Halakhah. See L. Jacobs: 'Halakhah and Ethics', in *A Tree of Life: Diversity, Flexibility and Creativity in Jewish Law* (Oxford, 1984), pp. 182–92.

17. *Torah Temimah* to Exodus 24, note 30.

18. See D. Katz, *Tenuat Ha-Musar*, vol. 5 pp. 138–9, that the *Musarists* debated whether to recite the Kabbalistic formula: 'For the sake of the unification' (*le-shem yihud*) before carrying out ethical precepts. There were those who objected to this on the grounds that benevolence and acts of kindness ought to stem spontaneously from the character and should not require the spur of religious intention. And the effect on the recipient ought to be taken into account. He will be humiliated if he overhears his benefactor saying that he helps him not because of any regard for him but because he is obliged to do so because of the religious imperative.

19. Berakhot 13a.
20. *Bet Yitzhak. Orah Havvim* (Przemysl, 1875).
21. See C. Taylor, *Sayings of the Jewish Fathers* (Cambridge, 1877), pp. 41–2 for other interpretations and variant readings.
22. See Rashi to the passage that 'unto thy neighbour' may mean literally, the human neighbour, or, more fancifully, this is not an ethical maxim at all but a religious one, the 'neighbour' being God!
23. *Damasek Eliezer* (Pietrikov, 1905). On Perlmutter, a scholar whose work has unfortunately been overlooked, see *Encyclopaedia Judaica* (ed. C. Roth), Jerusalem: Encyclopaedia Judaica, vol. 13, pp. 297–8.
24. Maimonides, *Guide*, I, 54, holds that it is illegitimate to speak of God as Merciful if the intention is to describe His true nature. We're only permitted to 'call' God Merciful in that such acts of care as protecting the embryo and bringing it to birth, if they could be performed by humans, would be because they are merciful.
25. The little ethical treatise by Moses Cordovero (1522–70), *Tomer Devorah*, describes the Kabbalistic understanding of *Imitatio Dei*; see the Introduction to the translation by L. Jacobs, 'The Palm Tree of Deborah' (London, 1960), pp. 18–37.
26. It is, of course, true that the religious attitudes are bound to have an influence on the ethical so that any attempt to divide the two into neat categories is bound to be too sweeping.
27. In Judaism, too, divorce is seen as objectionable, though allowed, but this opposition is based on the idea that in divorce the wife has been betrayed; see *Gittin* 90b.
28. It is incorrect to state categorically that Judaism knows nothing of celibacy as an ideal; see the well-known case of Ben Azzai, whose 'soul was in love with the Torah', *Yevamot* 63b, and the permissibility granted to others as well in *Shulhan Aruk, Even Ha-Ezer* 1:4.
29. See D. M. Feldman, *Birth Control in Jewish Law* (New York/London, 1968).
30. The same may be said of such matters as the just war and vegetarianism.
31. But see the discussion in *Kiddushin* 40b whether study (*talmud*) or deeds (*maaseh*) is the greater. Typically the conclusion reached is that study is the greater *because it leads to deeds*!

6

Leopold Stein: A Liberal Master of Prayer

ERIC L. FRIEDLAND

When one thinks of *Yom Kippur*, one almost instinctively recalls the enduring *Kol Nidrey* chant with its weighty and warm associations. It was not always so. In 1844, at the First Rabbinical Conference held in Brunswick, Liberal-leaning European Rabbis debated, for good reason, whether the ancient legal formula calling for the release from vows should be retained. As the majority consensus was that the Aramaic text exacerbated the distrust of Jews and added fuel to anti-Semitism, it was considered advisable to excise it from the High Holy Day prayerbook, replacing it with a psalm (e.g. 130 or 103), a rewritten version of *Kol Nidrey* (whether in Hebrew or in Aramaic), and/or a new prayer wholly in the vernacular. One of the participants at the Rabbinical Conference, Rabbi Leopold Stein (1810–82), had already jumped the gun and taken it upon himself to compose a three-strophe chorale in German, '*O Tag des Herrn*' ('Day of God'), set to the music of *Kol Nidrey*. First appearing in his *Rosh Hashanah* and *Yom Kippur* supplementary volume of hymns, poetic translations/adaptations of *piyyutim* and contemporary prayers, *Chizzuq ha-Bayit* (1840),[1] Stein's stately and solemn – if to our ears somewhat bathetic – hymn, in three strophes to correspond to the traditional threefold chant of *Kol Nidrey*, was to find its way into many a non-Orthodox rite in Germany and one in Great Britain as well as in several American Progressive *machzorim*, in any one of the hymn's several English renditions. Because of its significant place in the history of Reform liturgy, we print it here in its entirety, in its original[2] and in the slightly wobbly English by Marcus Jastrow.[3]

(I)
O Tag des Herrn!
Du nahst –
Und das Herz erhebt,
Und Schauer fassen die Seelen.
Sie gedenket ihrer Missethat,
Sie gedenket, dass ihr Richter naht
Und zittert. –
Sie bangt, sie zagt; sie klagt
Und vergeht in Thraenen.

Fasse Muth, o belastet Herz!
Schau' du nur trostvoll himmelwaerts!
Guetig ist dein Herr,
Gern giebt Er Gewaehr,
Naht, sich auszusoehnen.
Herr! Gott, sieh',
Sieh' meines Herzens Wehen,
Und neig' Dein Ohr!!
Herr, vernimm,
Vernimm mein heisses Flehen,
Oeffn' uns dein Thor!
Nimm weg die Missethat,
Oeffn' uns das Thor der Gnad',
Und zieh' uns empor.

(II)
Horch! die Stimme des Herrn!
Er ruft
Mit des Abends Wehen
Und Andacht waltet und Stille.
Brueder hoert, wie mild die Stimme toent!
Menschen, ruft sie, Kinder, o versoehnt,
Versoehnt euch!
O folgt dem Ruf! o gebt Gehoer!
Trocknet alle Thraenen.

Brueder, kommt, o kommt heran,
Schliesset, Schliesst euch uns liebend an!
Herz soll morgen rein,
Rein vom Hasse sein;
Eilt, euch auszusoehnen.

Horch, wer weint? –
Es weinen gekraenkte Freunde –
Schliesset neu das Band!
Horch, wer klagt? –
Es klagen verfolgte Feinde –
Hass sei verbannt!
O liebt, wie Gott euch liebt!
Vergebt, wie Er vergiebt!
Reicht euch treu die Hand.

(III)
Nun, Tag des Herrn!
So nah!
Und fuelle die Herzen,
Und fuelle mit Wonne die Seelen.
Von dem Abend bis zum Abend hin
Heiliget vor Gott den Erdensinn
Und betet.

Empor zu Gott, zu Gott empor
Schwingt euch, Erdensoehne!
Stimmet an Gebet, Gesang!
Folget, folget dem Himmelsdrang!
Schwinget euch empor!
In der Engel Chor
Stimmen uns're Lieder.

Tag des Herrn
O sei ein treuer Bote!
Fuehr' uns zurueck!
Tag des Herrn!
Komm' mit dem Abendrothe.
Hell strahl' dein Blick!
Bis wieder Abend naht
Fuehrst du auf lichtem Pfad
Uns zu Heil und Glueck.

(I)
O DAY OF GOD!
Thou com'st,
And my heart is alarmed,

My soul is stricken with terror:
She remembereth her evil deeds,
She remembers that her Judge proceeds,
And trembles.
She sighs and moans, she cries and groans,
And repines in anguish.
  Gather faith, my heart depressed,
  Heavenward look, thou shalt be blessed.
  Pardon is the Lord's;
  Pardon he affords;
  Thou shalt no more languish.
Lord, behold,
Behold my heart's contrition!
In care I wait.
Lord, give ear,
Give ear to my petition;
Hear me supplicate.
Blot out my sin, efface
My guilt, and in thy grace
Open to me thy gate.

(II)
HARK! THE VOICE OF THE LORD!
He speaks
In still evening whispers,
Inviting solemn devotion.
Brethren, hear his voice, how kind, how mild!
'Children,' calls he, 'be ye reconciled
In friendship!'
O, lend your eyes, and wipe all tears;
Soothe each woe and sorrow.
  Brethren, near and nearer move,
  Join your hands, your hearts in love;
  Banish every grudge
  Ere ye meet the Judge;
  Cleanse your hearts ere tomorrow.
Hark, – who weeps?
A brother thou hast offended.
Win back the friend!
Hark, – who moans?
A brother thy hate has wounded.

Let hatred end;
O love like God above;
Forgive, as he forgives;
Faithful hands extend!

(III)
NOW, DAY OF GOD,
Come down,
And fill us with gladness,
And thrill us with comfort from heaven.
From this eve till eve sinks down again,
Brethren, cleanse your souls from all that's vain,
Through prayers.
Rise up to God, to God on high,
Rise on wings of praises.
   String your hearts to prayers and songs,
   Turn to God in sacred throngs!
   Heavenward aspire,
   Join the angels' choir,
   Singing Hallelujahs!
Day of God,
O, lead us back to heaven,
Be thou our guide!
Day of God,
Come with the calm of even,
In lustrous pride.
Till evening come again,
We shall, released from pain,
In God's light abide.

STEIN'S *SEDER HA-AVODAH*– ITS TWO EDITIONS

Leopold Stein published his *Seder ha-Avodah for Sabbaths and Festivals* in 1860 to coincide with the rededication of Frankfurt-am-Main's *Hauptsynagoge* (Main Synagogue), which had been demolished in 1854 because of its poor physical condition and subsequently rebuilt. The historic congregation had meanwhile endured its share of rifts between the Orthodox and Reform parties within its membership. Rabbi Samson Raphael Hirsch led his followers in the formation of a dissident, Neo-Orthodox congregation, the *Israelitische Religionsgesellschaft*, in the 1850s. During his pastorate from 1844 until 1862, Leopold Stein – a moderate Reformer with a deep-seated affection for time-honoured usages and texts – sought to provide a ritual that would be acceptably innovative to the Reform element without offending the *halachic* sensibilities of the observant faction within his congregation. He drew upon his extensive experience in the area of liturgy as formulator of prayers and hymn-writer, as chairman of the Liturgy Committee at the Second Rabbinical Conference (at Frankfurt-am-Main) in 1845 and of similar committees at the Wiesbaden and Giessen Conferences during the 1850s, and as the compiler of recent liturgical efforts by colleagues throughout Germany. The outcome is a basically traditional service in Hebrew with a wealth of supernumerary material in German in the form of hymns, anthems, chorales, poetic renditions of the Psalms, readings, prayers and meditations. The *Seder ha-Avodah* of 1882 is another story. It was edited years after Stein resigned from the aforesaid synagogue, became director of a girls' school, wrote dramas, edited journals, authored religious works, served for a year as spiritual head of the Westend-Union Synagogue in Frankfurt, and kept up his other literary activities. As his last major effort shortly before his death, he re-edited his *siddur* in a more daring direction. While never partaking of the unrestrained radicalism of either the Berlin *Reformgemeinde*'s super-lean, all-but-unilingual rite or the non-conformism of a few of the concurrent American prayer-books, this latest edition constitutes the clearest liturgical expression of Stein's brand of moderate Reform: independent and cutting-edge, yet respectful and fond of traditional forms. While his 1860 prayerbook was intended for public worship on Sabbaths and Festivals (with volumes two and three planned for the High Holy Days and for the home), his 1882 edition was designed to serve as a virtual *kol-bo*, an all-purpose prayerbook.

Some textual emendations

Stein showed ingenuity in his handling of the Hebrew language as he reworked prayers so as to mesh with his Progressive theology. Solely for brevity's sake, only a small sampling of such readjustments will be adduced here. The Morning Benedictions 'Blessed are You, O Lord, our God, King of the universe, who has not made me a heathen' (or, in the 1860 edition of *Seder ha-Avodah* 'Who has made me an Israelite') and 'Blessed are You … who has not made me a slave', are, in effect, compounded and reconfigured as 'Blessed are You … who has made me in order to serve Him' (*she-'asani le-'ovedo*), thus making explicit the underlying religious import of the older formulations, namely, the overriding purpose of being Jewish as carrying out God's will in the world.[4] The *chatimah*, or benedictory ending ('Blessed are You … who bestows lovingkindness upon His people Israel') of the *yehi ratson … she-targilenu* prayer is universalized in the 1882 edition to 'Blessed are You … who bestows His lovingkindness to all His creatures' (*gomel chasadim tovim le-khol beriyyotav*). Within the *yotser* section, many Liberal prayerbooks simply excised the martial description of God as 'Master of wars' or 'Lord of battles' (*ba'al milchamot*) in the rhapsodic finishing paragraph *le-el barukh ne'imot yittenu*. In a brilliant stroke, Stein took as his inspiration verse 10 in Psalm 46 ('He makes wars to cease [*mashbit milchamot*] throughout the earth') and, with the change of a single word, shifted the mood profoundly, recasting the expansive line '[God] who performs mighty deeds, and makes new things; He makes wars to cease [*mashbit milchamot*]; He sows righteousness, causes salvation to spring forth, creates cures …'

Zion and Jerusalem

Unlike the overwhelming majority of his fellow religious Liberals in the nineteenth century, Leopold Stein made room for Zion and Jerusalem in his liturgy, and not just out of compromise with the traditionalists in his congregation. He took seriously Isaiah's vision of a Temple restored in Jerusalem that would embrace all peoples (Isaiah 2:1–4) and one that would exercise its benign influence on all the world. His universalist, spiritual brand of Zionism is clearly eschatologically oriented. It is of the sort that would, however, in no way entail uprooting his fellow Jews from the lands of their dispersion in the here and now or their turning disloyal to the Fatherland. How this messianic Zionism expresses itself liturgically in the 1882 *Seder ha-Avodah* excites interest since, virtually alone in his views, Stein had to create his own idiom.[5] As there are examples aplenty, we will confine ourselves to four. In this vein, the fourteenth benediction in the weekday *Amidah*, the *Shemoneh Esreh*, that contains the petition for God's dwelling again in Jerusalem and rebuilding it as an 'everlasting building' is retained, short of the re-establishment of the Davidic monarchy. However, the tenth benediction, which speaks of the Ingathering of the Exiles, is reworded and given an entirely new meaning. Translated, the Hebrew and the German would read something like 'Sound the great horn for our freedom, and lift the banner to unite our dispersed people around You. O may all peoples form a bond with us, to serve You in truth. Praised be You, O Eternal, who assembles about Him the dispersed of His people Israel.'[6] Stein is the only liturgy-writer in the nineteenth-century Liberal camp known to us who uses the *Kaddish itchaddata*, the customary funeral *Kaddish*, after burial. As might be recalled, this special *Kaddish* comprises the additional phrases, in Aramaic, '[the world] that is to be created anew, where He will revive the dead and raise them up to eternal life; will rebuild the city of Jerusalem and establish His Temple in its midst; and will uproot all idolatry from the earth and restore the worship of Heaven to its place'. It is surprising enough that Stein, undoubted Liberal that he is, leaves the opening paragraph untouched, but, no less astonishingly, he makes sure the Reform insert *al yisrael ve-'al tsaddiqaya*, going back to the Hamburg Temple *Gebetbuch*, stays put. As for Zion's ultimate spiritual impact on all humanity, he had this to say in the Intermediate Benediction of his Festival *Musaf Amidah* about the reconstructed Sanctuary:

Oro techaddesh, kevodo tegaddel, u-veytekha beyt tefillah le-khol ha-'ammim yiqqare.

Sein Licht erneuere, seine Herrlichkeit vergroessere, und ein Bethaus fuer alle Voelker moege Dein Haus genannt werden.

(Renew its light, increase its glory, and may Your House be called a house of prayer for all peoples.)

In the light of the foregoing it is easy to see why Stein would have had no hesitation in including the much-controverted 'Cause a new light to shine upon Zion that we may soon be worthy to enjoy its splendour', towards the end of the *yotser* benediction.

A new liturgical creation

Throughout his rabbinical career Leopold Stein thought the practice of Second Day of *yom tov* totally redundant. Even in the earlier edition of *Seder ha-Avodah*, which on the whole reflects the editor's respectful stance towards his traditionalist members, he does not hide his opposition to the practice.[7] To forestall any confusion as to when the holiday is over, Stein introduced in the Appendix of the 1882 edition a new ceremony of his own devising to mark the official conclusion of Passover, at the end of the Seventh Day. In his *Zur Begruessung des Brotes* ('Welcoming of Bread', pp. 483–4), we read, in selections from Jakob J. Petuchowski's translation:

> *Ha-motsi lechem min ha-arets.* Who causest bread to sprout from the earth.
>
> How great is the goodness of God, who causes the blade of grass to grow, from which we obtain bread! Centuries, perhaps millennia, had gone by ere man obtained bread from the blade of grass – bread, the staff supporting the heart. Behold it, behold it with amazement, that field of grain – bowing like a pious congregation before the Heavenly Giver of Bread ... Looking upon this bread, we celebrate Judaism, we celebrate our cherished ancestral doctrine (*unsere theure Vaeterlehre*), which so simply and reasonably brings the highest truths close to our thinking mind and to our feeling heart. Rise, then, and lift up your hearts in prayer:
>
> *Baruch attah, adonay eloheynu, melech ha-olam, ha-motsi lechem min ha-arets.* Praised be Thou, O Eternal our God (Master of the world – *Herr der Welt*), Who causest bread to sprout from the earth. Amen. Amen.[8]

STEIN'S INFLUENCE ON AMERICAN LITURGIES

Benjamin Szold's and Marcus Jastrow's Abodath Israel

Stein exerted a multiple influence on both sides of the Atlantic that has yet to be fully recognized.[9] The proto-Conservative[10] *Abodath Israel*,[11] edited by the scholarly European-born Rabbis Benjamin Szold (1829–1902) and Marcus Jastrow (1829–1903), owes much to Stein. The rite was used not only in Szold's and Jastrow's 'enlightened' immigrant congregations, in Baltimore and in Philadelphia respectively, during their rabbinical tenures, but in several Conservative synagogues as well, up to the appearance of the unifying *Sabbath and Festival Prayer Book*.[12]

Not only did *Abodath Israel* reproduce Stein's *'O Tag des Herrn'* in its first German edition,[13] and a rendition of it by Marcus Jastrow in its English editions, as noted above, but it duplicated, in varying degrees, *Seder ha-Avodah*'s fusion of the preliminary *Shacharit* prayers,

1. *Yehi ratson ... she-targilenu* and *yehi ratson ... she-tatsilenu ha-yom*
2. *Attah ad she-lo nivra ha-'olam* and *attah hu adonay eloheynu*

In both rites, *ribbon kol ha-'olamim*, after 'the pre-eminence of man over the beast is nought, for all is vanity', tags on the Sephardic 'except the pure soul which must hereafter render an account before the throne of Your glory'. Moreover, for the Sabbath *Amidah*'s summit benediction, the Sanctification of the Day, the American rite repeats *Seder ha-Avodah*'s preferred penultimate phrase, 'May Israel who love Your Name rejoice in You' (*ve-yismechu vekha yisrael ohavey shemekha*) over the more ingrained 'May Israel who hallow Your Name rest thereon [i.e. on the Sabbath]' (*ve-yanuchu vah yisrael meqaddeshey shemekha*). Stein and his liturgiographical disciples in the United States were relying on old variants appearing in *Seder Rav Amram* and *Machzor Roma*.[14] We find, too, *Abodath Israel*'s all-German (or all-English) *Aleynu* and concluding benediction to be hospitably patterned after *Seder ha-Avodah*'s. The newly American editors also made a point of appropriating in their one-volume *siddur-machzor* Stein's capping prayer for *Ne'ilah*. Hereunder are Stein's German and Jastrow's English for the middle portion from the zenith, as it were, of the Atonement Concluding Service:

> *Der Tag ist dahingegangen. Morgen, morgen da geh'n wir wieder an uns're alltaeglichen Werke; die Sorgen des Lebens werden uns wieder umringen; die Beduerfnisse des Leibes werden wieder in Anspruch nehmen, – o wenn wir da wieder in die Fehler verfielen, die wir heute bereut; wenn wir das Unkraut in unserem Herzen nur oberflaechlich entfernt, nicht mit der Wurzel ausgerissen, so*

dass es morgen und uebermorgen wieder an das Tageslicht hervortreibt; wenn wir bald wieder hingiengen, und entweiheten Deinen heiligen Namen, und thaeten, was missfaellig ist in deinen Augen; wenn wir morgen giengen und entweiheten unsere menschliche Natur durch ausschweifende Begierde, durch Suenden und Laster verschiedener Art; wenn wir morgen wieder hingiengen und feindeten an den Naechsten und haeuft Unheil ueber Andere und verlaeumdeten Andere und verkuerzten-Anderen Ehr' und Gut und Leben – wehe! wehe! – Was haette uns denn der heutige Tag genuetzt? Dass Du Dich wieder mit uns ausgesoehnt; dass wir unsere Natur geheiligt, dass wir in Eintracht, unter Deines Hausesdecke verweilet haben, was nuetzte es uns, wenn wir uns nicht wirklich besserten? wenn wir es nicht morgen und alle Tage bewiesen, dass dieser, Dein heiliger Tag, Heil und Segen in uns bewirkt hat.

Now the pregnant prayer in Jastrow's translation:

The day is passing! – Tomorrow we shall again resume our ordinary vocations; we will again be surrounded by the cares and anxieties of life; our bodily wants will again claim our care and attention. O, suffer us not to fall again into the error of which we have today repented; let us not again walk in the path of thoughtlessness, desecrating thy Name by doing what is evil in thy sight, and detracting from our dignity by falling into vice and iniquity. Banish from our hearts ill-will towards our neighbours, so that we bring not harm, grief or loss to them either in their life, their character, or their possessions. Of what avail, O God, will have our long abiding in thy House, if we amend not our ways? Of what benefit will this day have been to us, if we are given no evidence of other days, that it has wrought salvation within us?

On the practical plane, Szold and Jastrow borrowed, too, from their senior colleague an eminently user-friendly device that deserves our attention, and that is the numbering of each of the prayers so as to make them easier to locate and thereby avoid unnecessary repetition in print of the same prayers. Naturally this feature resulted in reducing the *siddur*'s bulk and rendering the tome easier to manage and hold than most prayer

manuals, then or now. We know of no other prayerbook that
has copied this procedure.

Max D. Klein's Seder Avodah

After enjoying a long duration, *Abodath Israel* was succeeded in
Philadelphia during the 1950s by *Seder Avodah* (to be distinguished from Stein's *Seder ha-Avodah*), edited by a latitudinarian
Conservative rabbi, Max D. Klein. It was produced first and
foremost for his devoted Congregation *Adath Jeshurun*, which
he served for fifty years. Klein expressed the hope it would be
adopted by other like-minded congregations. Structurally and
textually, *Seder Avodah* leans heavily on *Abodath Israel* while
taking on a slightly more traditional cast than the older rite. In
his Acknowledgments at the end of the 1960 High Holy Day
volume, Klein tells the reader that the English prayers during
the final service on *Yom Kippur* are based on Jastrow's version,
which in turn were taken from the *Ne'ilah* Service composed in
German by Leopold Stein of Frankfurt-am-Main. Klein's one-
of-a-kind handling of *Kol Nidrey* deserves special mention. He
provides:

1. The wonted Aramaic formula with the climactic verse in its
   Sephardic wording, *Mi-yom kippurim she-'avar ad yom kippurim
   zeh ha-ba aleynu le-tovah*, for vows made since last Yom Kippur
   that have not been fulfilled.
2. A newly composed Hebrew *Kol Nidrey* by Klein himself,
   which may be sung to the melody of *Kol Nidrey*.
3. An adaptation of Stein's '*O Tag des Herrn*'.

In effect, *Kol Nidrey* in *Seder Avodah* is repeated thrice, as
mandated by tradition, but each time under a different guise.
The Liturgical Notes (p. 881) inform us:

> As to the Hymn, 'O Lord, our God' – the words are based
> on the hymn '*O Tag des Herrn*' ('O Day of God'), written
> by Leopold Stein of Frankfurt-am-Main and adopted by
> the Reform Liturgy. Originally used in full, the latest
> Reform Prayer Books have reduced the hymn to a few
> sentences. The Jastrow Prayer Book (*Abodath Israel*) had
> retained the entire hymn in the early editions in the

original German, and in the later editions in a complete, faithful English version.

The editor of the *Seder Avodah* has utilized two stanzas of the hymn, having rewritten them and changed the salutation from 'O Day of God' to 'O, Lord, our God'.

It is interesting to see how Klein modified the *retseh* prayer in the *Amidah*, and one may wonder whether Stein had any influence at all. The first of the last three benedictions of the *Amidah* is traditionally an entreaty that God accept the prayers of Israel, restore the service to the Temple, and receive 'favourably and lovingly' their fire-offerings (*ishey yisrael*) and prayer. In the 1860 edition of *Seder ha-Avodah*, Stein replaces the term for fire-offerings with freewill offerings – in Hebrew, *nidvot [yisrael]*; in German, *Israels Gabe*. (In the 1882 edition the term *nidvoteynu*, i.e. our freewill offerings, is used instead, in a curtailed version.) He leaves the rest of the prayer unimpaired. Unlike Szold and Jastrow but like Stein, Klein keeps the entire benediction intact while changing one word only, from *ishey* to *shirey [yisrael]*, with its near-alliterative affinity, yielding 'Accept there [i.e. in Zion] in thy gracious love Israel's songs and prayers'.

In conclusion, what this word study discloses is that both liturgiographers favoured a Temple rebuilt in a Zion restored, but, in accordance with Progressive Jewish doctrine, barring animal sacrifices.[15] After the elevation of the Torah (*hagbahah*) and during its dressing, Klein's *siddur* features a hymn that reads:

All praise to thee we bring,
  To thee our fathers' God,
For all the teachings of thy Law,
  The way all Israel trod.

Our fathers loved thy word.
  They went through fire and flame.
Thy law they kept in life and death,
  And sanctified thy name.

For prophet and for sage,
  Who led us on the way,
And gave all Israel strength and light,
  We thank thee, God, today.

To us the will impart,
    That we as firm may be,
To live our lives as they lived theirs,
    For Israel and for thee.

O Israel's Guide and Shield,
    Uplift us through thy Law;
Unveil our eyes that we may see
    The wonders which they saw.[16]

Now we discover to our pleasant surprise that Jastrow had a similar paean to the Torah, 'This is the Torah', designated, however, for *Simchat Torah*, in his 'Songs of Divine Services' placed at the end of the 1873 edition of *Abodath Israel*. We reproduce the first two and last stanzas:

This is the Torah, this is the word
    Our fathers did inherit;
Intact it was to us transferred
    Intact we will transfer it.

Uplift the Scroll, unfurl it wide,
    Let all the world look on it;
Show it, O Judah, show it with pride,
    And tell the price that won it.

...

To God be thanks, the combats rest;
    Oh, may they rest forever!
But we will watch our sires' bequest,
    And leave our standard never.

As we pick up Stein's *Seder ha-Avodah* and turn to its psalm and song section, we come across his German original, *Wesoss hattora (Ve-zot ha-torah) Hagbahah*, which is sung by the cantor and its antiphon by the choir. The uncluttered verse flows effortlessly:[17]

Choir:
Dies ist die Tora, dies das Wort,
Das Gott uns hat gegeben,
Dass wir's bewahren fort und fort
Und tragen durch das Leben!

Reader (*Vorbeter*):
Weis' auf, Volk Juda, hoch sie auf,
Du darfst mit Stolz sie zeigen,
Sie ist gekauft um hohen Kauf,
Um hohen Preis dein eigen.
Du gabst ja hin fuer dieses Gut,
Was nur der Mensch besitzet;
Glueck, Habe, Freiheit, Ehre, Blut
Hast du darum verspritzet.

Choir:
Dies ist die Tora ...

...

Reader:
Drum heben wir sie freudig auf!
Wir duerfen kuehn sie zeigen,
Sie ist gekauft um hohen Kauf,
Um hohen Preis uns eigen.
Die Kaempfe ruh'n; doch wuerden sie
Je wieder uns erreichen,
Sie sollen finden, dass wir nie
Von unsrer Fahne weichen,

Choir:
Die ist die Tora, dies das Wort,
Das Gott uns hat gegeben.
Dass wir's bewahren fort und fort
Und tragen durch das Leben!

The haggadah *in the preliminary edition of* The Union Prayer Book

Stein's sway is detected in another American rite, a late-nineteenth-century Passover *haggadah*, by the dedicated, fecund and still wrongly undervalued Reform liturgy-maker and editor, Rabbi Isaac S. Moses (1847–1926). *The Domestic Service for the Eve of Passover* is contained in a precursory edition of the *The Union Prayer Book*, which, revised, eventually became the standard worship manual of the Reform movement in the United States until displaced by *Gates of Prayer* in 1975.[18] A close examination of the *haggadah* reveals that it is none other than Stein's endearing

Seder-Hagada translated into English.[19] Stein essentially re-created the *haggadah* so as to make it altogether user-friendly, by paraphrasing the Passover narrative in contemporary German idiom and by providing a generous supply of songs at various intervals throughout the *seder*. The only portions retained in Hebrew are the *Kiddush*, two *Hallel* psalms, the midpoint *asher ge'alanu* prayer, the blessings over the *matsah* (with none, how-ever, for the *maror!*), *birkat ha-mazon*, and a totally revamped *shefokh*. The rest, including the familiar *seder* melodies, is in German. The *Maggid* section is conspicuous for its use of indi-vidual verses from the traditional narrative portion *arami oved avi* (Deuteronomy: 26.5–9), to be recited by the youngest in lieu of the Four Questions and followed by Stein's discursive expla-nation read by the leader of the *seder*. To give a taste of his dis-sertational method, here is his comment to 'With a strong hand …':

> *Der Juengste:*
> *Be-yad chazaqah – Mit starker Hand*
>
> *Der Hausvater:*
> *Wenn die Unschuld unterliegt; wenn die Bosheit triumphiert, da erscheint Gott, nimmt Antheil am Streite, und sein ist der Sieg. Also zersprach er mit starker Hand Fesseln Aegyptens und befreite seine Kinder von der Macht ihrer Draenger.*

Which Isaac S. Moses translates (minus the Hebrew phrase) as follows:

> *The Youngest:*
> With a strong hand
>
> *Leader:*
> When innocence is about to succumb; when wickedness triumphs, then God appears and takes part in the struggle, and His is the victory. Thus He broke the chains of Egypt with a strong hand, and delivered His children from the power of their oppressors.

While the ephemeral American *haggadah* was monolingual – except for the *kiddush*, the blessings over the unleavened bread and the bitter herbs and the *birkat ha-mazon* – it is patently clear that Stein was attached to the Hebrew language, no less than to the German.[20] One further proof lies in his own simple yet successful transformation, utilizing Biblical phraseology, of the retributive 'Pour out Thy wrath' (*shefokh chamatekha*) verses, struck out in most Reform *haggadot*, upon opening the door for Elijah.

> *Shefokbh ruchakha al kol basar, ve-yavo'u kol ha-'ammim le-'ovdekha shekhem echad ve-safah achat. Ve-hayetah l-adonay ha-melukhah.*

> Pour out Your spirit upon all flesh, that all peoples may come to serve You in one accord and in one speech. And the kingdom shall be the Lord's.

Although it is true that Moses' *haggadah* faded quickly, certain of his more winning translations for Stein's lyrical renditions of old-time Passover favourites held out. The following 'Praise the Lord! One accord', set to the melody of *addir hu*, is a very close rendition of Stein's *Lobt den Herrn/Nah und fern* in seven stanzas.[21]

Praise the Lord!
  One accord
Sound through all creation!
  Laud and sing!
  Honour bring
Him without cessation!
  And His fame
  Loud proclaim
Every land and nation!

Which Stein first had, even more genially, as:

Lobt den Herrn
Nah und fern
Alle Schoepfungsheere!
Lieder singt!
Preist und bringt
Ihm allein die Ehre
Alle Welt,
Treu gesellt,
Seinen Ruhm vermehre!

The comely, cross-denominationally popular *New Union Haggadah*[22] embraced selected verses of Rabbi Henry Berkowitz's 'And It Came to Pass at Midnight', headed up with the first and last stanzas, in Hebrew, of the sixth- or seventh-century Palestinian *payyetan* Yannai's *va-yehi ba-chatsi ha-laylah*. Berkowitz is erroneously identified here as the translator of the historicizing *piyyut*. Isaac S. Moses made a notable attempt to translate Stein's mellifluous German broad paraphrase – all twenty-two stanzas – and, unfortunately, did not make the grade. What Berkowitz did, conceivably at the prodding of the Central Conference of American Rabbis for its official 1908 *haggadah*, was to rewrite Moses' stilted effort, and he took the prize. Remarkably enough, Berkowitz's reworking of the Stein/Moses themes in an unlaboured and felicitous nineteen-stanza poem has persisted from the first edition of *The Union Haggadah*[23] to the 1982 *New Union Haggadah*. The (British) Union of Liberal and Progressive Synagogues has a commendable record of producing quality *haggadot*. The *Haggadah shel Pesach: Passover Eve Service for the Home*,[24] edited by John D. Rayner, contains all nineteen stanzas, but the current *Haggadah shel Pesach: Passover Haggadah*,[25] co-edited by John D. Rayner and Chaim Stern, *zikhrono li-verakhah*, drops Berkowitz's paraphrase, based on Moses' almost literal translation of Stein's new-look paraphrase, in favour of Yannai's *piyyut*. The early mediaeval poem is accompanied by a smooth English translation.

STEIN'S INFLUENCE ON SUBSEQUENT GERMAN LITURGIES

Caesar Seligmann's prayerbooks

Leopold Stein exercised his posthumous influence additionally in another direction, on his former congregation, the famed *Hauptsynagoge* in Frankfurt-am-Main, by way of one of his successors and a creative liturgiographer and poet in his own right, the prolific Rabbi Caesar Seligmann (1860–1950). The latter's prayerbooks for the Sabbath, Festivals and the weekday[26] and the High Holy Days[27] adhere largely to the contours of the traditional *siddur*[28] and *machzor*, but the contents are predominantly in German paraphrase, for the most part written by Seligmann himself in appealing and fluent literary style. There are, to be sure, exceptions here and there. For example, appropriated is Stein's poetic rendition of *mi khamokhah* and *Adonay yimlokh*, sung (in the Seligmann rite) by the choir and the congregation during Sabbath and Festival Evening Services:

Wer unter Maechtigen,
Ew'ger, dir gleich?
Wer so verherrlicht,
Heilig wie du?
Herrlich im Lobe,
Wundervollbringer!

Gott nur ist Koenig,
Sein ist das Reich.
Er wird regieren
In Ewigkeit.
Hoch sei gepriesen
Unser Erloeser!

Caesar Seligmann followed Stein's tactic of furnishing metric renditions of psalms so that they might be sung in the vernacular. Residues of Stein's prosody can even be spotted in Seligmann's *Gebetbuch*, as in the German choral refrain for *lekhah dodi*: '*Kommt und heisset den Sabbath willkommen!/Freudig werde er aufgenommen!*' For the rest of the hymn, however, Seligmann supplies his own versification to replace Stein's. The 1882 edition of *Seder ha-Avodah* has special services for the eve of *Hanukkah*,[29] *Purim* and *Tish'ah be-Av*, all discharged with pomp and circumstance. In like manner Seligmann accords each of these technically minor holidays (and fast day) the dignity of a full-fledged service with cantor, choir and sermon. To illustrate, he equips his public observance for *Hanukkah* with his regular opening hymn '*Froh nah' ich dir*' sung by the choir; the cantor's solo chanting of Psalms 116–17, with the choir joining in for *hodu l-adonay ki tov* (verses 1–4) and *odekha ki anitani; anna, adonay hatslichah na* (verses 21–5);[30] a two-page-long rabbi's prayer; the opening stanza of '*Gott, mein Licht, Schutz und Hort*' ('God, My Light, Refuge and Shield' – the beloved German equivalent of *ma'oz tsur*)[31] sung by the choir and congregation; the three blessings before kindling the menorah sung by the cantor; the fourth stanza of '*Gott, mein Licht*'; a reading out of I Maccabees, chapters 1–4;[32] a sermon; and the sixth and last stanza of '*Gott, mein Licht, Schutz und Hort'*, followed by Seligmann's adaptation of the weekday Evening Service. Stein's earlier version is quite similar, albeit with significant differences, e.g. the recitation of *Ma'ariv* depends on local usage and the entirety of the German version of *ma'oz tsur* is sung on the heels of the prefatory *mah tovu*. After the candle-lighting a slightly modified *ha-nerot hallalu* (minus the proscriptive 'During all the eight days of Hanukkah … it is forbidden for us to make profane use of them') is said. Also, Stein does not call for an actual reading from the Book of Maccabees *per se*; an apt summary of the *Hanukkah* story based on the apocryphal book in the form of a meditation (*Betrachtung*) suffices. Otherwise, all is as Seligmann was later to pattern his service, along with a reprise of *'Gott, mein Licht, Schutz und Hort'* (stanzas 4–6).

The Einheitsgebetbuch

A quick perusal of the *Einheitsgebetbuch*, 'the last great monument to the striving for Reform and to the liturgical creativity of German Judaism' (Petuchowski), shows what may reflect the influence, however direct or indirect, of *Seder ha-Avodah*, aside from the obvious *'O Tag des Herrn'*. The choice of elegies for the Ninth of Av are the same:

1. *Eli tsiyyon ve-'areha;*
2. *Shomron qol titten;*
3. *Sha'ali, serufah ba-esh.*

One further elegy is added: *Tsiyyon, ha-lo tish'ali*. The *Einheits-gebetbuch*'s abbreviated Hebrew *Tachanun* with its paradoxically detailed rubric as to all those dates on which it is not to be recited is substantively identical with Stein's all-German version, accommodating just *rachum ve-chanun, chatati*, Psalm 6 and *va-anachnu lo neda*. More careful study will undoubtedly reward us with further evidence of Stein's influence.

AN ASSESSMENT OF THE MAN

Leopold Stein was 'a sweet singer of Israel' who somehow got lost in the shuffle. When he left his rabbinical post at the *Haupt-synagoge* in 1862, the prominent Jewish scholar and exponent of

Reform, Rabbi Abraham Geiger (1810–74), filled the vacancy. He had his reservations about what Stein had done in his *Seder ha-Avodah* and promoted at the Frankfurt synagogue the liturgical changes introduced in his previous congregation at Breslau.[33] Both men had very different personal and operational styles, theological approaches and pastoral concerns. Geiger understood the Judaism of his day to be evolving towards a thoroughly denationalized, de-ethnicized, spiritual kind of Judaism.[34] Thus, his prayerbooks were largely traditional, with a verbal emendation here and there or an occasional, sometimes barely noticeable, textual omission consistent with Reform theology and always with the newly envisioned Judaism in mind – accompanied by a very loose German paraphrase or an idea intimated by the Hebrew prayer text. The *sancta* of Jewish identity were essentially eclipsed in the ethereal, theologically correct renderings by Geiger. Because of their pronounced gradualism when it came to liturgical change, however, Geiger's prayerbooks won the day, both in the *Hauptsynagoge* in Frankfurt-am-Main and, decades later, in the *Einheitsgebetbuch*. Stein had no such qualms. He was uninhibited in his spontaneous love of the Hebrew language and of German letters, his espousal of Jewish tradition and his fearless adoption of Reform when seen as reinforcing that tradition. He was able to embrace Jewish particularity, wholeheartedly, within the context of a redeemed humanity. Always historically grounded, *Wissenschaft-des-Judentums*-style, Geiger's liturgiography was, to be sure, altogether proper, but lacking in the emotional sphere or in collective sentiment. Continually inspired, Stein seized every possible opportunity to allow his prayerbook, on virtually every page, to make music and sing, in Hebrew and in German. When Seligmann took the helm of the Frankfurt synagogue, he forged a new rite that was in many ways animated by Stein's work, but, for whatever reasons,[35] never sufficiently acknowledged his debt to his predecessor. No doubt Seligmann's prayer manuals came to overshadow *Seder ha-Avodah* and obscure its memory. In their time Stein's prayers and hymns indeed took flight, but his wings were clipped before they could reach their full height.[36] All the same, it took a 'master of prayer' with the soul of a musician like Leopold Stein to say, with warmth and gratitude, in the Preface to his last liturgical effort, the product of a lifetime:

So fahre wohl, du geliebtes Buch, und habe Dank fuer die vielen heiligen Stunden, welche du beglueckend mir in Fuelle geschenkt hast.
Ehre sei dem Namen Gottes in Ewigkeit.
Amen We'amen.

So, farewell, beloved book, thanks for the many holy hours you sent bringing me abundant joy.
Glory be to the Name of God forever.
Amen and amen.

NOTES

1. *Gebete und Gesaenge zum Gebrauche bei der oeffentlichen Andacht der Israeliten. Oder: Bausteine zur Auferbauung eines veredelten Synagogengottesdienstes. Erste Lieferung: Neujahr und Versoehnungstag* (Erlangen: Verlag von Ferdinand Enke, 1840).
2. Chizzuq ha-Bayit, pp. 81–4.
3. B. Szold, *Abodath Israel*, Israelitish Prayer Book, rev. M. Jastrow (Philadelphia, 1873), pp. 346–7. Another translation may be found in J. Krauskopf, *The Service Manual*, 2nd edn (Philadelphia: Press of Edward Stern & Co., 1892,) pp. 297–8.
4. For his *Seder Tefillah Devar Yom be-Yomo, Israelitisches Gebetbuch fuer den oeffentlichen Gottesdienst in ganzen Jahre* (Breslau: Verlag von Hainauer, 1854), Abraham Geiger uses the precise same wording in his *Preliminary Benedictions*. Here Stein may well be the debtor.
5. In his Preface to the 1882 edition Stein makes plain his view: 'As far as Israel's exalted hopes are concerned, we have devoutly retained his holy place for the Messiah, bearer of our ideal future. Thereby we have established the validity of the great promise that, one day, mankind will give concrete expression to its unity in God by a great temple of peoples [*Voelkertempel*]. That Temple will find its eternal place in Jerusalem. Where else? Not in Berlin, capital of German Protestantism. Not in Rome, center of the pagan world of the past, and of the Catholic world of today. But in Jerusalem, the Holy City, in which all nations and religions have an equal share [*an welcher alle Voelker und Religionen gleich grossen Antheil haben*].' (Trans. by J. J. Petuchowski, *Prayerbook Reform in Europe* [New York: World Union for Progressive Judaism, 1968], p. 179).
6. Appropriately enough, the rubric for this benediction in *Seder ha-Avodah* is *Freiheit und Einheit*. Stein may be happily guilty of inconsistency for preserving in his nuptial Seven Blessings the one that invites Zion to rejoice 'when her children are gathered within her in joy'.
7. In a footnote to the *she-hecheyanu* blessing recited over the *lulav* on the Second Day of Sukkot if the First Day falls on a Shabbat, Stein is fairly explicit: 'The Second Day of the Festivals is not biblical and really has no longer has any festive meaning in our time. Religious habit in our congregations is still not about to remove their observance from the synagogue.'
8. *Prayerbook Reform in Europe*, p. 315.
9. It is a crying shame that the current *Encyclopedia Judaica* does not have an entry on Leopold Stein.

10. My term for traditionalist Reform in nineteenth-century America that eventually identified itself with Conservative Judaism, which came into its own at the end of the century.

11. The transliteration nowadays would be on the order of *Avodat Yisrael*.

12. *Sabbath and Festival Prayer Book* (New York: The Rabbinical Asssembly of America and the United Synagogue of American, 1946); E. L. Friedland, 'Were Our Mouths Filled with Song', *Studies in Liberal Jewish Liturgy* (Cincinnati: Hebrew Union College Press, 1997), p. 66.

13. B. Szold, *Abodath Israel, Israelitisches Gebetbuch fuer den oerfentlichen Gottesdienst im ganzen Jahre* (Baltimore, 1864).

14. S. Baer, *Seder Avodat Yisrael* (Roedelheim, 1868; Tel Aviv, 1957 [reprint]), p. 188.

15. Stein explains in the Preface to the 1860 edition that in those sections where a prayer is recited aloud communally, every effort would be made to keep it as traditional as possible and hold the verbal alterations at a minimum (*die alte Formel moeglichst unveraendert beibehalten*). In the case of prayers said silently, if textual changes are seen as necessary to reflect the Reform view, the older formula would be placed in smaller print along the revised wording. The doctrinal view expressed here is remarkably similar to that formulated in the Sabbath, New Moon, Shabbat-Rosh Chodesh and Festival Additional Services in the Israeli *Masorti Siddur Va-Ani Tefillati* (Jerusalem: The Rabbinical Assembly in Israel and the Masorti Movement, 1998), pp. 120, 388, 414 and 528.

16. This admittedly plodding lyric found its way, as Hymn #203, into the American *Reform Union Hymnal: Songs and Prayers for Jewish Worship* (Central Conference of American Rabbis, 1936), and is set to music by P. Jassinowsky. Klein did something out of the ordinary in that he himself provided a reasonably decent rhymed Hebrew translation for 'All Praise to Thee We Bring'.

17. Again, only the three stanzas are reproduced here, roughly matching Jastrow's abridged English.

18. *Gates of Prayer – Sha'arey Tefillah – The New Union Prayerbook* (Central Conference of American Rabbis, New York, 1975).

19. The home celebration appears in the 1882 edition *Seder ha-Avodah*, and its full title is *Seder-Hagada: Vortrag fuer den Pesach-Vorabend (Familienfeier)*.

20. It is to be recalled that at the Second Rabbinical Conference, in Frankfurt, Stein sided with Zacharias Frankel on the indispensability of Hebrew in contemporary Jewish worship. M. A. Meyer, *Response to Modernity: A History of the Reform Movement in Judaism* (New York/Oxford: Oxford University Press, 1988), p. 137.

21. Union Hymnal, Hymn #130, p. 137.

22. H. Bronstein (ed.), *A Passover Haggadah: The New Union Haggadah*, rev. edn (New York: Central Conference of American Rabbis, 1982), p. 90.

23. Cincinnati: Central Conference of American Rabbis, 1908.

24. London: ULPS, 1962.

25. Hertford: ULPS, 1981.

26. *Israelitisches Gebetbuch, Erster Teil: Sabbat, Festtage und Werktag* (Frankfurt: Selbstverlag der israelitischen Gemeinde in Frankfurt a. M., 1910).

27. *Neues Gebetbuch fuer Neujahr und Versoehnungstag* (Frankfurt: M. Lehrberger & Co., 1904).

28. Like Stein, Seligmann starts his prayerbook with Sabbath services. The weekday services appear in the latter part of the volume, indicating its intermittent use.

29. See 'Service for Hanukkah' in *Union Prayer Book*, I (Central Conference of American Rabbis, 1940), pp. 85–92.
30. These psalms of course constitute the latter half of the Hallel, the recitation of which is traditionally prescribed for the Morning Service throughout *Hanukkah*.
31. My guess is that this hymn is a composition of Stein's, as there were several other adaptations to the tune of *ma'oz tsur*, as may be found in the Appendix to the lamented *Einheitsgebetbuch* [= C. Seligmann, I. Elbogen and H. Vogelstein, *Gebetbuch fuer das ganze Jahr, Erster Teil: Werktag, Sabbat und Festtage* (Frankfurt: M. Lehrberger, 1929)], pp. 108–13. Its simplicity, directness and grace typify his hymnody.
32. It should recalled that I and II Maccabees are books from the non-canonical Apocrypha and not normally part of the Scripture of the Synagogue.
33. *Devar Yom be-Yomo*, 1854; Petuchowski, *Prayerbook Reform*, pp. 165–7.
34. J. J. Petuchowski, 'Abraham Geiger, the Reform Jewish Liturgist', *New Perspectives on Abraham Geiger: An HUC Symposium* (Cincinnati: Hebrew Union College Press, 1975), pp. 42–54.
35. It is possible during his rabbinate there were congregants, or descendants of congregants, who had unhappy recollections of the unfortunate sequence of events that led to Stein's resignation. For an insight into the background of Stein's stepping down from the pulpit of the *Hauptsynagoge*, see R. Liberles, 'Leopold Stein and the Paradox of Reform Clericalism, 1844–1862', Leo Baeck Institute Year Book XXVII (1982), pp. 261–79. An older account of Stein's life may be found in H. W. Ettelson, 'Leopold Stein', Yearbook of the Central Conference of American Rabbis XXI (1911), pp. 306–27.
36. In *Prayerbook Reform in Europe* (p. 178), we are told that in 1917 R. Gruenfeld adapted *Seder ha-Avodah* for the Augsburg Jewish community.

7

Baruch and *Berachah*: Blessing in Judaism

WALTER HOMOLKA

THE ROOT *'BRK'* AS THE FOUNDATION OF A JEWISH UNDERSTANDING OF FAITH

Berachah in the Hebrew Bible means 'blessing'. *Baruch* also means 'the one who is blessed'. The words *baruch* and *berachah* are both derived from the Hebrew root *bet-resh-kaf*, which means 'knee'. This refers to the practice of bending one's knee and bowing as signs of respect. In the understanding of the Hebrew Bible it is not only God who blesses human beings, but humans praise God through blessings as well (see for example Psalms 16:7, 34:2, 63:5).

Baruch, therefore, is the attribute which describes God as the source of all blessing.[1] When one recites a blessing, one does not bless God, but expresses astonishment and wonder about God's acts of blessing towards us humans.

BLESSING AS GOD'S PROMISE

As one of the first promises God gives to Abraham, God says: 'And all the families of the earth shall bless themselves by you.' (Genesis 12:3).

Blessing and curse are not simply about the provision of information or the relation of a wish, but they intend to bring about what they promise. In the Hebrew Bible the result is dependent on God and does not happen as if by magic. Blessing and curse are therefore related to prayer and magic, but they are not identical with them. While blessing is given a central role, magic is not approved of in the Bible.

Blessing promises what humans have asked of God. In the Hebrew Bible, promises are generally related to concrete things, such as descendants, fertility, prosperity, a good harvest, afflu-ence. Promises, however, can also refer to more abstract concepts such as peace and happiness. The overarching category com-municated through blessing is participation in God's saving action. Blessing is thus an expression and concretization of the relationship of Jews with God.

Most important is the distinction between blessing and wish. Blessing is different from wishing, since it promises more. Bless-ing is also more than strength derived from positive thinking. As an expression of faith, blessing lives in the relationship of human beings to God and receives its power and reality as well as its framework and limitations from this relationship. A blessing promises what is received in faith from God. Trust against all reason is shown by Job, who even in his suffering does not curse God (Job 1:11, 2, 5, 9), but continues to praise him (1:21).

Blessing has a high status in the Hebrew Bible, often becom-ing a legacy (Deuteronomy 33). The patriarchs bless their chil-dren, in particular before they die (Genesis 27:49ff.). Here, a blessing is very concrete, *it exercises authority*. Once pronounced, a blessing cannot be taken back, even if based on an error: in Genesis 27 Jacob obtains the blessing of the firstborn by devious means and hangs on to it even after Isaac discovers his error.[2] Thereby the younger brother, Jacob, receives authority and power over the older brother, Esau.[3]

The priestly blessing

The classic biblical blessing is Aaron's blessing (Numbers 6:24–6) which has been used widely in its present format since the seventh century BCE. The evidence for this widespread use are engravings in silver jewellery found in graves at Ketef Hinom, south-west of the Old City in Jerusalem, which use the blessing almost in its biblical wording. Even the dead need blessing. Since earliest times, the priestly blessing closed the Temple service (eg,. Leviticus 9:22ff., Numbers 6:23–7, Psalms 118:26, II Chronicles 30:27).

This usage of the priestly blessing continues in the service of the synagogue. It is used in Liberal services primarily at the end of the prayer service, after *kaddish* and the final hymn, in Orthodox communities in the morning service on *Shabbat* before the last *berachah* (*Sim Shalom*) of the *Amidah* and on the Day of Atonement during *musaf, mincha* and *ne'ila* (*Ta'anit* 26b). In Orthodox communities, the descendants of priests, the *Cohanim,* are sometimes called up to recite this blessing. Conservative and Liberal communities do not adhere to this practice of distinguishing between *Cohanim,* Levites and Israelites.

The same wording of the blessing is used on Friday night during *kiddush* and on the eve of the Day of Atonement when parents bless their children, and it is also part of the blessings said under the *chuppah* during a Jewish wedding.

From getting up to lying down: a hundred blessings

The Mishnah – the codification of Jewish religious law edited around 200 CE – begins with a tractate about blessings (*Berachot*). This underlines the importance blessing has in particular in post-biblical Jewish tradition. In early Judaism, as well as in contemporary Chassidism, receiving a blessing from a famous and admired *zaddik* or *rebbe* is significant. More widespread, however, is the frequent saying of a blessing.

Berachot, blessings, are a particular form of prayer and are said frequently in everyday life. Jewish tradition appeals to every Jew to say one hundred blessings every day.

The thrice-daily recitation of the *Shemoneh Esreh*, with its nineteen petitions, already amounts to fifty-seven *berachot* on every weekday. And there are plenty of opportunities to complete the hundred blessings.

At the beginning of the morning service one says the *Birchot ha-Shachar*. Historically, upon awaking, Jews began their day with these blessings, which were incorporated into the formalized morning service in the ninth century by Rav Amram. The Babylonian Talmud, in particular *Berachot* 60b, contains a whole list of blessings.

A blessing accompanies many daily recurring occasions and events. Jewish religious life is a way of interpreting daily life through blessings.

From this develops a culture of blessing which extends

beyond the confines of the prayer service. Thus it can be concluded that blessing is of central importance in Jewish practice.

BLESSINGS AS ACCEPTANCE OF GOD

Three types of blessings can be distinguished:

1. those which are said before enjoying a physical pleasure (*birchot ha-ne'henin*);
2. those which are said before fulfilling a commandment (*birchot ha-mitzvot*);
3. hose which refer to a particular time or a specific event (*birchot hoda'ah*).

Blessings before enjoying a physical pleasure (for example: eating, drinking, wearing new clothes) praise God as the creator of the things we are about to use. The blessing over bread honours God as the one who brings forth bread from the earth. The blessing before wearing new clothes describes God as the one who clothes the naked. By using this *berachah* we are accepting God as the creator of all things, whose permission we need before we enjoy God's creation. In practice, the *berachah* asks God for permission to use something which originates – like everything – not from us but from God.

The blessings we say before fulfilling a commandment praise God as the one who makes us holy through God's commandments and who instructs us to do that which we are about to do. The recitation of the *berachah* belongs to the act of fulfilling the commandment. Jewish tradition knows no hierarchy of *mitzvot*. There is no greater merit in performing a *mitzvah* because one is commanded to do so than performing one by chance or on a whim. By saying the *berachah*, we are concentrating on the fact that we are responsible to God for this religious obligation we are about to fulfil. It is important to say blessings over all the *mitzvot* we do, whether the blessing is derived from the Hebrew Bible or formulated later by the Rabbis. The interpretation of Jewish tradition by the Rabbis is almost as highly regarded as the biblical text itself and therefore binds us with similar force.

Blessings said at a particular time or on a specific occasion (witnessing events in nature such as a rainbow, sighting a king or head of state, upon hearing good or bad news, encountering unique beauty, etc.) acknowledge God as the origin of all good and bad in the universe.

Berachot are not only recited about good things but also about bad things. In the latter case, God is praised as the 'just Judge', underlining that even when we cannot understand it, bad things happen for a just reason.

Strangeness and closeness as a paradox of faith

Many of the blessings used today were formulated about 2,500 years ago by Ezra and the Great Assembly. All *berachot* use the formula '*Baruch atah adonai elohenu melech ha-olam* – Blessed are you, Eternal God, Sovereign of the universe.' Our closeness to God and our intimate relationship with God is expressed through the use of the familiar '*atah*' as informal personal pronoun in the second person singular.

Immediately after this opening formula, the *Berachah* switches to the third person singular. A good example may be taken from the *birchot ha-mitzvot* which are formulated according to the following format: 'Blessed are you, Eternal God, Sovereign of the universe, who sanctified us with his commandments and commanded us ...' In Hebrew the third person singular in an address expresses great respect and high praise. Thus a blessing combines the suggestion of particular closeness to God with the expression of transcendental distance and inaccessibility. The Jewish relationship with God is characterized by this paradox of simultaneous nearness and infinite distance.

1. The blessing after the meal: Birkat ha-Mazon[4]

One of the most important Jewish prayers is already commanded in the Hebrew Bible. This prayer is never said in the synagogue, but it is particular to the table, the altar of the home. The blessing after the meal is based on Deuteronomy 8:10: 'When you have eaten and been satisfied, praise the Eternal One your God who has given you this good earth.'

This commandment is fulfilled by the blessing after the

meal.[5] The *birkat ha-Mazon* is recited after every meal at which the staple is bread. In Yiddish, this prayer is called *benschen*, a word derived from the Latin *benedicare*, 'to bless'.

The blessing after the meal is preceded by three blessings before the meal. The *birkat ha-Mazon* consists of four groups of blessings, three of which were formulated at the time of Ezra and the Great Assembly. The fourth was added after the destruction of the Temple.

1. The *birkat hazan* (blessing for food) thanks God for the provision of food.
2. The *birkat ha-aretz* (blessing for land) thanks God for leading us out of Egypt, for giving us the covenant and for granting us the land of Israel as an inheritance.
3. The *birkat Yerushalaim* (blessing for Jerusalem) brings to mind a rebuilt Jerusalem as God's throne and the advent of the messianic time.
4. The *birkat ha-tov ve'ha-metiv* (blessing the person who is good and does good deeds) emphasizes God's kindness as the origin of all that is good. This is an old thought, but added here after the destruction of the Temple.

To complete the blessing after the meal, verses from Psalms and the Book of Proverbs may be added, depending on the occasion.

Blessing as a recurring obligation

The ubiquity of blessings is central to Jewish religious practice. Through blessings Jews experience that their lives in the face of God are blessed, and acknowledge that their actions, which originate in God's creative power, should become a blessing for all humanity.

Tikkun Olam – the repairing of the world – can come about only if we allow God's salvation to work in the world through bringing God's blessing into the world.[6] Through every blessing we turn anew to the world and its creatures, relate with them and gain a new perspective on the world. *Blessed are You, Eternal God, Sovereign of the universe who has not created us to be strangers to You.*

NOTES

1. K. H. Richards, 'Bless/Blessing', *Anchor Bible Dictionary* 1, D. N. Freedman (ed.) (New York, 1992).
2. C. A Keller, 'Segnen', *Theologisches Handwörterbuch zum Alten Testament*, E. Jenni and C. Westermann (eds) (Munich/Zurich, 1984) pp. 353–67.
3. J. D. Rayner, 'Esau's Kiss', *An Understanding of Judaism* (Providence/Oxford: Berghahn, 1997), p. 34.
4. A. Böckler and W. Homolka, *Tischdank* (Berlin, 2002), pp. ix–xxiv.
5. J. Romain and W. Homolka, *Progressives Judentum: Leben und Lehre* (Munich, 1999), p. 142.
6. R. Hirsh (ed.), 'Tikkun Olam: Theory and Practice', *The Reconstructionist – A Journal of Contemporary Thought and Practice* 68 (1).

8

The Challenge of Genetic Research

MARGARET JACOBI

The last few years have seen rapid advances in genetic research. What was science fiction only a few years ago is now science fact. Each advance offers the promise of progress but also raises difficult ethical and theological questions. The science of genetics challenges our understanding of ourselves as human beings. The questions it raises are not necessarily new, but recent research has led to increased public debate about key philosophical and theological issues. Among these are questions about how far our genes determine our nature and our actions, and to what extent we are 'playing God' by altering the fundamental building blocks of our being.

I shall begin with a review of some of the recent advances in genetics and their implications, and then consider how Jewish sources can help us respond to the challenges.

BACKGROUND AND RECENT ADVANCES IN GENETIC RESEARCH

In February 2001, the first draft of the human genome, the chemical message along the DNA[1] of a human being, was made public. This was less than a decade after the project began. The publication represented a further milestone in the acquisition of knowledge about our genetic makeup, and therefore in our ability to control it.

Modern genetics could be said to have begun in 1953, when Francis Crick and James Watson published the structure of DNA. Since that discovery, there has been rapid progress in the analysis of the function of DNA and the application of the findings in humans, animals and plants.

In certain cases, the gene for a disease has been located and this has made it possible to identify the biochemical defect that causes the disease. For example, cystic fibrosis is a disease with widespread effects, particularly in the lungs and bowel. The gene has been identified from the DNA of those suffering from the disease and their families.[2] The hope is that eventually it will be possible to alter the gene in order to treat the disease.

Gene therapy has already been effective in rare cases. The first effective treatment was for the disease adenosine deaminase (ADA) deficiency,[3] in which the sufferer is unable to overcome infection because certain white blood cells are damaged. In 1990, the gene for producing ADA was inserted into the affected cells, enabling children suffering from the disease to lead relatively normal lives.

At present, most applications of genetic therapy are for the treatment of cancer.[4] In cells that cause cancer, one or more of the genetic mechanisms that regulate cell multiplication fail, so cells multiply without the normal controls and invade the surrounding tissues. The aim of gene therapy is to prevent this uncontrolled multiplication.

While gene therapy has, as yet, been applied only to a few rare diseases, other aspects of genetics have had more widespread applications. For example in bacterial cloning, the gene for a particular protein is inserted into a bacterium and as the bacterium reproduces itself (the process of cloning), so the protein is produced too. Human insulin was the first human protein to be produced by this process, so that diabetes no longer needs to be treated with insulin from pigs. Similarly, haemophilia can now be treated with genetically engineered Factor VIII. Previously, it was treated with Factor VIII obtained from human blood, which led to some sufferers being infected inadvertently with HIV.

One of the most controversial advances is genetic modification. A gene is inserted into an organism in order to confer on it different properties. For example, the gene for the production of a human hormone may be inserted into a cow so that the hormone is produced in milk. Genetic modification of crops has been hotly debated, but is outside the scope of this chapter. Another controversial advance was made in 1997 when a sheep named Dolly was born. Dolly was a clone of her mother. A clone means an identical copy, as in the bacteria mentioned above. Normally, mammals have DNA from both parents. In the case of Dolly, DNA was from one only.[5] The cloning of a mammal represented a considerable technical achievement, but raised questions about the possibility and desirability of cloning a human being.

Finally, the deciphering of the human genome by an international team has represented a major advance in our understanding. As the authors are keen to point out, however, their findings are very much a first draft, and provide more questions than answers. One of the most striking findings is how few human genes there are – about 31,000 compared with 6,000 for a yeast cell and 13,000 for a fly. Clearly, there is far more to the development of human beings than can be attributed simply to our genes, which as the authors of a paper in *Nature*[6] point out, provides us with a major challenge to work out how a human being can develop from so few genes.

A JEWISH APPROACH TO GENETICS

In exploring a Jewish approach to genetics, I draw on sources from a time when there was no knowledge of modern genetics. There are, however, some passages in the Bible and Rabbinic literature which show understanding of plant and animal breeding and of human inheritance. For example, an incident is related in the book of Genesis in which Jacob selectively breeds sheep.[7] In the Talmud, hereditary diseases are considered, including probably the first recorded description of haemophilia. There is a ruling that if two male sons have bled to death as a result of circumcision, a third son should not be circumcised. There seems to have been a recognition that the disease was sex-linked (inherited through the mother and passed on almost exclusively to sons). Maimonides makes this explicit in his ruling that if a father has two male children who died at circumcision and he remarries and has a son by another woman, this son should be circumcised.[8]

Later *halachic* literature also recognizes a hereditary component to disease and legislates accordingly. For example, although according to the Talmud it is a virtuous act for a man to marry a niece,[9] R. Elijah Klatzkin rules that because niece marriages are more likely to lead to the birth of defective offspring than marriages between genetic strangers, they should be avoided.[10]

These illustrations demonstrate the concern of Judaism for the preservation of life, to the extent that established law and custom may be overturned if there is a perceived threat to life.

A PROGRESSIVE JEWISH APPROACH

As Progressive Jews, we find these examples helpful in our exploration of the Jewish approach to genetics. In common with Orthodox Judaism, we look to traditional texts for guidance. Our approach differs in important respects, however. Most fundamentally, we differ in our view of revelation. For Orthodox Judaism, the Torah is the word of God, directly revealed to Moses at Sinai. It may be interpreted according to certain fixed rules, which were also revealed to Moses, but it must not be contradicted. Thus, an Orthodox approach to genetics would draw on the traditional texts and, where no parallels can be found, attempt to draw analogies with contemporary situations. It would be bound by the rulings of the past and would not challenge them. Orthodoxy would also have some concerns which we do not share, for example the implications of genetic research for priestly lineage[11] or the status of the *mamzer* (the child of a forbidden union, Deuteronomy 23:3).

Progressive Jews accept the view of modern Biblical scholarship that the Torah represents writings from different times and places over a period of centuries, and as such reflects an ongoing attempt by human beings to understand God's will. We respect and value the wisdom of the past, but we also recognize that sometimes the Torah reflects the understanding of its time, which we would now regard as erroneous. Thus we reject both the role of the priests and the concept of the *mamzer*, which we consider unjust.

As Progressive Jews, we attempt to take some of the underlying values of Judaism, which have continuing validity for us, and to apply these to contemporary problems. This approach requires knowledge of our tradition and the application of our own intellect and conscience. Thus we make ethical decisions in the light both of enduring Jewish values and of the knowledge of today. In doing so, we must avoid hubris, realizing that knowledge is provisional and that our understanding is incomplete.[12]

A number of Jewish values and beliefs can help us in approaching the ethical problems posed by genetic research. Among these are:

The duty to save life (pikkuach nefesh)

This is one of the most fundamental Jewish values. The duty to save life outweighs virtually all others, so that one may break all but three of the commandments in order to save a human life. If genetic research can help towards the saving of life, it would generally be welcomed.

Human beings are created in the image of God (b'tselem Elohim)

At the beginning of the Torah it is stated: 'God created human beings in the Divine image.'[13] Each human being therefore has intrinsic worth and is infinitely precious. This is emphasized in the Rabbinic statement: 'Whoever sustains a single human being is as if they sustained an entire world, and whoever destroys a single human being is as if they destroyed an entire world.'[14] Each person is therefore deserving of care and no one is to be viewed as a means to an end, to be used for another person's benefit.

The duty to procreate (p'riyyah u-r'viyyah)

The first commandment in the Bible is: 'Be fruitful and multiply.'[15] We would endorse the importance of procreation (though also being aware of the problem of overpopulation) and also emphasize the blessing of children. Where genetic research can help enable couples to have children, it would therefore be encouraged in principle, while taking the welfare of any potential children into account.

Partnership in creation

For Jews (in the words of Edmund Fleg) 'the world is not completed, human beings are completing it … humanity is not created, human beings are creating it'.[16] Human beings are partners with God in the process of *Tikkun Olam*, repairing the world. We are enjoined to undertake any task that will help to make the world a better place. Scientific and medical research is seen as part of this endeavour and therefore to be encouraged.

Justice (Tsedek)

The concept of justice is central to Judaism. Deuteronomy commands: 'Justice, justice shall you pursue,'[17] and commandments concerning just conduct permeate the Hebrew Bible. Justice demands that all should be treated fairly, irrespective of income. The poor should not be at a disadvantage, but everyone should share society's benefits equally. This has important implications for genetic research, which is costly but may bring great benefit. We need to ensure that money spent on such research is not at the expense of helping the poor by other means, and that the results of this research are available to all, whatever their ability to pay. There also other implications, for example in the areas of patenting and insurance, which I will deal with later.

Free will

Judaism emphasizes that human beings have free will. We have a good inclination (*yetzer tov*) and an evil inclination (*yetzer hara*). Although we are commanded to choose life and good, ultimately we have the freedom to choose for ourselves. The products of scientific research are usually morally neutral and it is up to us whether they are used for benefit or harm.

The obligation to heal

In the Bible, illness is generally seen as a punishment from God and healing is regarded as a sign of divine forgiveness. Therefore it could be expected that healing should be left to God. The Talmud, however, maintains that human beings have been given permission to heal, citing as proof Exodus 21:19: 'He shall cause him to be thoroughly healed.' Later *halachists* went further and considered healing not only to be permitted, but *demanded* of human beings. It was recognized, however, that only those with the necessary skills (i.e. trained physicians) should undertake this work. The obligation to heal is based largely on the duty to save life, though the textual proof often cited is Deuteronomy 22:2: 'You shall return it [a lost object] to him.' Here health is seen as being equivalent to a lost object. To some extent, the Jewish emphasis on the obligation to heal has developed in parallel with the ability of human beings to heal. Now that more diseases are amenable to medicine, the obligation to heal has greater force.

These beliefs and values from our tradition can guide us in our decision-making as we approach some of the difficult ethical issues posed by genetic research.

ETHICAL ISSUES – SOME EXAMPLES

Genetic screening

A large number of genetic diseases occur in human beings, for example haemophilia, muscular dystrophy and Tay–Sachs disease. The genes for such diseases are transmitted by a parent who may be unaffected but is a 'carrier'.[18] It is estimated that there are some 4,000 diseases caused by a fault in a single gene. Each individually is rare, but collectively they affect 1 to 2 per cent of all live-born babies. It is possible to detect carriers for a number of diseases. In some cases, for example Huntingdon's chorea (a neurological disease fatal in adulthood), it is possible to detect individuals who carry the abnormal gene and so will develop the disease, but do not yet have symptoms. With one or two rare exceptions, however, the diseases are still incurable, and it is therefore important to be clear about what, if any, benefits screening might bring.

In the case of parents who are carriers of a recessive disease, it may be possible by pre-marital screening to avoid the marriage of two carriers. This is the path that has been advocated for Tay–Sachs disease and implemented by some Orthodox groups.[19] Testing is also open to non-Orthodox couples of

Ashkenazi descent. It is less likely they will want to break off their relationship, but they can be advised as to the risks, and screening for affected fetuses may be carried out, followed by termination of pregnancy if desired.

It is also now possible to fertilize eggs outside the body and then screen them for a genetic disease before they are implanted in the uterus, so that only embryos unaffected by the disease are implanted (pre-implantation genetic diagnosis). By making a diagnosis before implantation, the termination of an established pregnancy is no longer called for, and a difficult, traumatic (and, to some people, ethically unacceptable) procedure is avoided.

Pre-implantation genetic diagnosis is not free from ethical problems, however. Apart from the issue of research using embryos, discussed below, the selection of embryos is morally problematic. It is one case where 'playing God' can be said to apply, in that there is a decision as to which embryos have the chance of life and which do not. If embryos are screened for a disease such as Tay–Sachs, or severe chromosomal abnormalities, then this would seem to be justified by the prevention of suffering. The arguments are similar to those for abortion, which has been extensively discussed in Jewish sources, and is considered below. There is, however, room for greater leniency in pre-implantation diagnosis, since Judaism considers the sanctity of the fetus to increase gradually with development and therefore the status of the pre-implantation embryo (up to fourteen days) to be less than that of the fetus.[20] Nevertheless, pre-implantation diagnosis should not be seen as a means for the parents to select whatever desirable characteristics they want for their future offspring (though most characteristics are in any case not determined solely by a gene or genes).

If it is possible to make a diagnosis only once pregnancy is established, this raises questions about the ethics of 'therapeutic' abortion. Although I shall not discuss this in detail, it can be briefly stated that Judaism places a high value on the embryo and fetus as potential human beings. The fetus, however, does not have the status of a full human being. Rather, it is considered a part of its mother (*ubar yerech immo*, B. Hullin 58a) until the head appears at birth. If there is a risk to the mother's life during pregnancy, her life takes precedence over that of the fetus.

Some Orthodox authorities, for example Rabbi Moshe

Feinstein, have forbidden abortion for diseases such as Tay–Sachs. They consider that abortion is justified only in cases of serious risk to the mother, which does not apply in this instance. Others, notably Rabbi Eliezer Waldenberg, have stated that abortion may be permitted up to the seventh month of pregnancy because of the 'great need', the mental anguish to the mother of knowing that her child will suffer terribly and die within a few years.[21] In general Progressive Jews would agree with this view, considering that the anguish of the parents and the suffering of the child, who will live only a short time, justify the abortion of an affected fetus. 'Therapeutic' abortion, however, cannot be said to be a cure.

Abortion also raises the question of where to draw the line. In permitting abortion of a fetus for Tay–Sachs disease, for example, are we starting on a 'slippery slope' to permitting abortion of any child likely to be disabled in any way? This is a concern that has been expressed by groups representing the disabled and is especially emotive since for some it recalls the Nazi programmes of eugenics (i.e. the production of an 'improved' population through genetic engineering).

We would endorse screening for genetic disorders in fetuses if it is carried out with appropriate safeguards. Although the fetus is valued as a potential life, the life of a child with a disease such as Tay–Sachs is not a life in the fullest sense. It would be cruel to both the child and its parents to insist that the child lives its short life in terrible suffering. Even where the suffering of the child would be less, the life of the parents comes first. For example, if their mental health is likely to be threatened, they are entitled to choose to terminate the pregnancy.

We do not consider that abortion in such cases warrants comparison with Nazi eugenics programmes. First, it is a recognition that the parents of the child are ultimately responsible for the child. If, given the emotional and physical suffering that may be entailed, they feel unable to care for it, then that choice must be respected. Second, where it is known that an infant will suffer for most of its brief life, it could be argued that it is less humane to bring such an infant into the world than to abort it.

This is not to dismiss concerns about eugenics. It has been argued that there are features of pre-implantation diagnosis which are eugenic, and there is evidence that clinical geneticists tend to think in terms of eugenics, particularly in making a presumption of termination rather than listening to parents' views.[22] It is important that we continually question practice with regard to genetic screening and abortion to ensure that such programmes are not carried out for the 'benefit' of society, but rather are carried out with respect for the feelings of the parents and with the aim of reducing suffering. The basis of any such programme must be respect for the potential human being, and the value of human life, even where the decision is ultimately made that a particular life should not develop.

Screening of potential sufferers from genetic disease carries different problems. Screening may have psychological consequences and also has financial implications. It is important that there should be sufficient provision for counselling and psychological support, and that screening should be focused on likely carriers to reduce the costs – both financial and psychological. It is also important to be aware of the accuracy levels of the screening process. For example, on the basis of present knowledge, it is possible to detect cystic fibrosis with an accuracy of about 84 per cent. This means that 16 per cent of carriers will remain undetected, and those screened cannot be definitively assured of a negative result.

In the case of a disease such as Huntingdon's chorea, where sufferers may be informed that they will develop the disease some years hence, the need for psychological support is even greater. There is evidence that those who screening indicates will develop the disease can benefit from this awareness by making future provision. Equally, some people will be reassured that they will *not* develop the disease. Screening may therefore be of value if appropriate support is offered. Where a condition is curable or preventable, for example in the case of familial polyposis coli (a predisposition to cancer of the bowel), screening may even be a positive obligation, as Dorff suggests.[23]

An issue of debate is the age at which it is appropriate to carry out screening. Legally, young people aged under eighteen are permitted to consent to a medical procedure if they are considered competent to understand the implications. Yet genetic counselling units often refuse testing. Young people who have a family history of Huntingdon's chorea, for example, occasionally express the desire to be tested for the disease. In such circumstances, they may have a far more mature grasp of the issues than their contemporaries.[24] On the other hand, further research is needed if we are to have a clearer idea of the benefits and burdens of screening young people.[25]

Traditional Judaism recognizes the majority of a child at the age of twelve or thirteen. While Progressive Judaism does not recognize this as the age of legal majority, arguing that a young person is not yet sufficiently mature, it does recognize that by this age the transition to adulthood is beginning. Some teenagers below the age of eighteen may be sufficiently mature to make 'adult' decisions, and if this is the case, their decision should be respected.

Gene therapy

Gene therapy falls into two categories: somatic and germ cell. In somatic therapy, the cells of the body are treated, for example the cells of the lung in Alpha-1 antitrypsin deficiency (a disease where the lungs lose their elasticity and therefore cannot exchange oxygen efficiently). In germ cell therapy, the DNA of sperm or eggs is altered, resulting in a change that can be passed on to subsequent generations. The Clothier Report in 1992[26] concluded that somatic cell gene therapy posed no new ethical problems. As with any new treatment, there was a need for careful assessment and long-term monitoring, and the report recommended a new supervisory body be established to undertake these roles. This became the Gene Therapy Advisory Committee.

We would agree with these conclusions. Somatic gene therapy involves the alteration of human genes to a limited extent. Altering the chemical composition of cells within the body is part of many therapeutic processes, for example hormone replacement. Although the processes involved in gene therapy may be new, the effect is essentially similar, in that a defect in the chemical processing of cells is corrected. If effective somatic gene therapies can be developed, then this would be in accord with the Jewish obligation to heal and to save life, and would be viewed positively.

Germ cell treatment, on the other hand, poses greater ethical problems, which led the Clothier Committee to recommend that it should not be carried out at present. Germ cell treatment involves altering the sperm or eggs of a man or woman who carries a genetic disease. If such a treatment were successful, this would obviate the need for treatment throughout a person's life and the parents could give birth to children knowing they would be free of the treated genetic defect. *Halachah*, with its emphasis on saving life, is open to the idea of germ cell therapy. Rosenfeld, for example, has argued that it is permitted, 'assuming, of course, that the surgical procedures are reliable and safe'.[27] This is the crux of the matter. It is particularly hard to determine the reliability and safety of germ cell therapy since the corrected gene is passed on to subsequent generations and there is little control over it. Any problems may not come to light until the gene is already passed on to the second, or even third, generation. The Clothier Committee has therefore recommended that germ cell therapy should not be carried out at present.

Even if treatment were successful, altering a gene on a widespread basis may have unforeseeable problems. One such possibility is that a gene may have unknown beneficial effects, which would also be lost. For example, whereas sickle cell disease in homozygous sufferers (those who carry two abnormal genes) results in severe illness, in heterozygotes (those who carry one abnormal and one normal gene), it offers some protection against malaria. It is hard to predict what effect the widespread elimination of a gene may have in a population.

A further problem with germ cell therapy is that the ethics of testing is unclear when the subject is not so much the parents as their unborn children, who may not discover the side effects until they themselves reproduce. Although we recognize the right of parents to place their children at risk if it is for their welfare, for example by consenting to their undergoing a surgical procedure, both *halachah* and British law take the view that there must be a known benefit that clearly outweighs the risk. There would therefore have to be a clear benefit before such treatment became acceptable. This would be difficult to assess without subjecting unborn offspring to risk, given that the therapy is at an experimental stage. Unless there is overwhelming evidence that germ cell therapy could be successful and relatively free of risks, it should not be considered at present.

The problem of assessing the risk to offspring in new techniques also applies to a recently developed treatment for fertility known as intracytoplasmic sperm injection (ICSI). ICSI was introduced in the early 1990s. By 1998, 5,000 'ICSI children' had been born across the world. The technique allows a man who has either too few sperm or a high proportion of abnormal sperm to have genetically related children by injecting one of his sperm directly into an egg. Although the technique has resulted in a number of apparently normal pregnancies, concerns remain.[28] Most seriously, little is known about the long-term health of the children. The sperm which are used in the technique are sometimes immature or ageing, and the latter have acquired relatively high levels of DNA damage. This may mean that children will be at risk of disease later in life, especially leukaemia, which is linked to the presence of damaged DNA.

ICSI promises short-term benefit in enabling a couple to have a child who is genetically related to both of them, but as yet the long-term risks are unknown and may be serious. Only long-term follow-up will enable us to know what these are. In such circumstances, there should be pre-clinical studies (including animal studies) to assess the risk as far as possible before a new technique is introduced. The implications should be discussed carefully with the potential parents before using the technique so that they can balance the pros and cons and consider alternative treatments. There should also be close long-term follow-up of any children born as a result of the technique.

There will always be uncertainties in using new medical treatments, but in the case of ICSI and gene therapy the risk is for future children, perhaps at a distance of more than one generation. We should therefore be especially cautious before introducing such techniques.

Cloning

Cloning denotes the production of genetically identical organisms or cells. Some cloning techniques, e.g. bacterial cloning, have been carried out for some years with little controversy. At the other end of the spectrum, reproductive cloning of human beings has now become a realistic possibility and has consequently attracted considerable publicity.

A distinction may be made between reproductive cloning, which produces genetically identical individuals, and techniques which do not have this result but may have therapeutic benefits. Non-reproductive cloning has been termed 'therapeutic cloning'. A variety of techniques are covered by the term. They have not yet resulted in any therapy but have the potential for developing treatments for human disease. In particular, it is hoped that they would allow the development of cells to replace those that have degenerated in diseases such as diabetes and Parkinson's disease. If cells from the patient can be made to develop into the required cells, this would avoid the problem of rejection when cells are transplanted. It is thought the best way of developing such treatments is by research on 'stem cells' (cells which are not yet specialized and have the potential to develop into any of the specialized cells in the human body). Although research is possible on adult cells, at present it is considered that the best hope of success lies in research on early embryonic cells.

Embryonic cells may be created by *in vitro* fertilization and may either be 'spare embryos' which are not implanted during fertility treatment, or else may be created specifically for research. Embryonic cells may also be created by inserting the nucleus from an adult cell into an egg with its nucleus removed – known as cell nuclear replacement or cloning. The ethics of creating embryonic cells for research are discussed below.

A recent report by an expert group of the Chief Medical Officer recommended that stem cell research be permitted.[29] Its findings have been generally been accepted and passed into legislation. Embryo research remains regulated by the Human Fertilization and Embryology Act 1990. The report recommends that the permitted use of embryo research under the Act should be expanded to increase understanding about human disease and disorders. Permission is only to be given, however, if there appears to be no other means of meeting the objectives of the research. There are also strict guidelines with regard to the consent of donors to the use of embryos and appropriate monitoring and review. The mixing of human cells with genetic material from other species is not permitted and neither is any attempt at reproductive cloning.

Reproductive cloning presents different ethical issues. It makes more immediate the issue of 'playing God', since it bypasses the normal method of human reproduction. In this, however, it is no different from other treatments for infertility which involve *in vitro* fertilization. Like those treatments, it raises the question of the mechanization of human reproduction. The major difference is that the genetic material from only one individual need be involved. In theory, one parent might wish to create a copy of him– or herself, or of a child they have lost. It is important to realize, however, that if a person develops from a cloned embryo, he or she will still be an individual, in the same way that identical twins, though genetically identical, are different and unique. Even physically, they are not absolutely identical, and their personalities are quite distinct. In cloning an individual, one would not be creating a carbon copy.

The issues concerning reproductive cloning are complex, but there has been a surprising degree of agreement across the Jewish religious spectrum. For example, Dorff[30] (Conservative) and Broyde[31] (Orthodox) both consider that human reproductive cloning may be permissible in certain circumstances. At present, however, there are too many dangers, both ethical and practical, and most scientists working in the field consider human reproductive cloning should not yet be attempted. When sheep and other mammals are cloned, a large number of malformed embryos are produced and a high proportion of the offspring die within a few days of birth. The same is likely to apply, probably to a greater extent, in humans. Such a cost would be unacceptable. There has been less discussion among Jewish scholars of 'therapeutic' cloning, perhaps because it has received less publicity and perhaps because it is less controversial. The issue of *pikkuach nefesh* comes to the fore. If adult stem cells were used, there would be no fundamental ethical problem other than the general problems of medical research. The use of embryonic stem cells is more problematic. Since embryonic cells do not have the same status in Jewish law as fully developed human beings, however, and the saving of human life takes priority, these techniques would be permitted with appropriate safeguards, or even welcomed, if they were likely to lead to the saving of human life.

An eloquent personal voice makes an important contribution to the debate. Leah Wild suffers from a rare genetic disorder and has therefore received infertility treatment with pre-implantation diagnosis to discover which embryos are free from the genetic disorder. Of eight embryos formed using her eggs, two have been found to be free of disease. Of the others she writes:

I regard my rare ability to donate a part of my body to science with similar sorrow, perhaps, to that of a family donating a relative's kidney, heart or eyes. I wish it wasn't like this. But given that it is, some good should come of it ... Infertility treatment will always produce 'spares'. It is deliberately designed that way, to maximise the chances of conception ... To object to the use of my embryos for research and therapeutic cloning is, in essence, to be against infertility treatment itself ... There is little that is positive about being infertile, but the possibility that the embryonic byproducts might help to cure disease is a compensation.[32]

With regard to therapeutic cloning, we would echo those words. Given that 'spare' embryos are produced in the treatment of infertility, their use for research into therapeutic cloning, with the potential for curing disease, represents some hope of good that may come out of a difficult and traumatic procedure.

It is, however, appropriate to draw a distinction between embryos which already exist as a result of fertility treatment and embryos created *specifically* for the purpose of research. The latter case is problematic, in that embryos are created for a utilitarian purpose, as a means to an end. Although embryos do not have the same status as a full human being, they are still accorded sanctity as potential human beings. Using them as a means to an end can be seen as diminishing their sanctity. Here, the *halachic* categories of *lekhat'chillah* (to begin with) and *bedi-abad* (after the event) are helpful. These distinguish between what is desirable in principle (*lekhat'chillah*) and what is permissible given that certain circumstances have occurred (*bedi-abad*). *Lekhat'chilla*, to begin with, one would be concerned about creating embryos solely for research purposes. *Bedi-abad*, after the event, once the embryos exist, it would be as ethical to use them for research as to discard them.

As for reproductive cloning, although it may offer hope for treatment of infertility in the distant future, the vast majority of those involved in the field are agreed that the time is not yet. There are too many technical and ethical problems to make it acceptable at present. Even if the technical problems could be overcome, the enormous ethical problems associated with reproductive cloning should be fully explored before it is allowed to become a reality, and as with research on human embryos, a legal framework to regulate it should be established.

GENES AND JUSTICE

One major area of concern when considering genetic research is the financial issues that arise. These affect the justice of genetic research. We will consider three issues which pose problems: patenting, insurance and the cost of research.

Patenting

The ethics and legality of patenting are hotly debated. The discovery of the human genome reflected this. It was published simultaneously in two journals: *Nature*, where it was the result of an international collaboration of scientists who felt the results should be openly available; and *Science*, where it was published by a commercial company which had been researching in parallel and which hoped to sell the information.

In theory, a patent should be for something original – an invention, not a discovery of something already present in nature. The Douglas principle in the United States and the European Patent Convention both reflect this belief. Both in the USA and Europe, however, a number of genes have already been patented. This seems to many people to be intuitively wrong. As D. and A. Bruce put it, patenting what is already found in nature is a 'violation of life as a gift' from God.[33]

The biotechnology industry argues that patenting is necessary so that a company is able to invest in biotechnology research, knowing that some of the enormous costs involved will be recouped. To some extent this may be true. Only larger companies, however, can afford the legal fees incurred during the patenting process. For smaller companies, these costs may be prohibitive. Those companies least able to afford to invest large sums in research are therefore also least able to reap the benefits of their investment through patenting.[34]

We would tend to agree with the concerns of D. and A. Bruce about patenting what is already in nature. It seems unjust that a part of God's creation should be appropriated by patenting so that it is not freely available to others. It also hinders openness, and consequently holds back further progress for the benefit of others. On the other hand, it has to be recognized that companies need to recoup their investment. One helpful way to consider this, as Peters suggests, is to draw a distinction between patenting the *application* of findings and the findings themselves. Thus, a patent may be acquired not for the structure of a gene, which is a discovery and on its own has little meaning, but for the way it can be applied by altering the gene or using it in other ways.[35] Such a distinction is helpful in maintaining a balance between the need to ensure fair reward for investment and the need to ensure that genetic research does not result in exploitation for financial gain.

Insurance

With the availability of genetic testing has come the problem of its use by insurance companies. Premiums might be increased or insurance refused to individuals testing positive. In the United States, the problem is even more acute, since medical treatment is often dependent on private health insurance and employment. As a result, thousands or even millions of people may find themselves uninsurable or unemployable on the basis of a genetic test rather than actual illness. On the other hand, it has been estimated that if genetic testing is not taken to into account there may be an increased cost to insurance companies, of about 10 per cent, due to increased uptake of insurance by people at risk.[36]

It is a matter of ethical concern that healthy individuals might be refused certain forms of insurance on the basis of a genetic test. There is further concern that they might be deterred from undergoing a medically desirable test because they feared being refused insurance, as has occurred with HIV testing. We would suggest that the most just solution would be for the risk to be shared by all members of society so that individuals should not suffer because of their genetic backgrounds. If the cost of any increased risk were shared in this way, the cost to each person would be small, whereas refusal of insurance to individuals would result in considerable harm to them.

The cost of research

Genetic research is expensive, and although great potential benefits have been claimed, they are are generally distant. Those genetic diseases that are now treatable, such as adenosine deaminase (ADA) deficiency, are very rare: there are about fifty individuals born with severe combined immune deficiency in the USA each year.[37] Eventually, it is hoped there would be effective cures for more common diseases such as cystic fibrosis. This may result not only in health benefits but financial savings, since the cost of treating a cystic fibrosis patient was estimated in 1994 as more than £125,000.[38] But as yet the enormous investment in genetic research has resulted in relatively little public health benefit. Indeed, Lewontin has described how much current research is commercially driven, with a close link between genetic research and private profit.[39]

The resources devoted to genetic research may be better spent in other areas. There is not only a financial cost but an 'opportunity cost' to genetic research. If the effort devoted to genetic research were applied to basic health prevention issues, such as poverty reduction and the provision of clean water, the impact in terms of saving life and improving its quality would be far more significant for millions of people. As Neil Holtzman puts it: 'Exaggerating the importance of genetic factors as determinants of health stops people thinking about the need to clean up the environment and tackle socio-economic inequity.'[40]

It might, of course, be possible to fund both. Long-term investment in genetic research may indeed provide great benefits. Investment in basic (non-applied) research in other disciplines has provided diverse benefits, for example in the treatment of heart disease, which could not have been envisaged at the outset. In addition, applied genetic research is likely to provide some healthcare benefits in the developing world, such as the development of new vaccines for the infectious diseases that now kill one child in five in some countries.[41]

We consider it important to ensure that spending on genetic research is not undertaken at the cost of spending more likely to benefit those worst off in the world. On the other hand, investment in genetic research may have diverse and unforeseen benefits in the future. Spending on one area need not, therefore, preclude research in another, but it is our responsibility to see that the benefits are made available to all, independent of their ability to pay or where they live.

GENETICS AND FREE WILL

Genetic research has raised the question of determinism – that is to say, do we have free will, or is our behaviour determined by our genes? Some geneticists and evolutionary biologists, such as Richard Dawkins,[42] have painted a picture of human behaviour as directed solely towards evolutionary ends. Other biologists are equally certain that environmental and other factors are at least as important as our genes. I shall not go into the arguments in detail here, but rather attempt to assess their implications and their relationship to Jewish teaching about free will.

Even at the level of determining structure, which is generally attributed to genes, it is clear that genes are not the only determinants. As Cohen and Stewart point out,[43] a caterpillar and a butterfly have the same genes. In a butterfly egg, a caterpillar develops; in a pupa, a butterfly develops. Genes are switched on or off depending on circumstances.

The role of DNA in disease is even less clear. For example, although a genetic component has been implicated in some forms of coronary heart disease, environmental factors such as stress and diet are thought to be more important in most cases, as well as other unknown factors. When we come to non-physical characteristics, such as intelligence, the role of DNA is highly debatable. This is complicated by the fact that it is hard to define intelligence and IQ tests give a measure only of ability to perform IQ tests! The argument is further complicated by its being highly politicized, particularly with regard to questions of 'race' and intelligence.[44] In studies of 'nature' and 'nurture' it is hard to disentangle the two, but the evidence seems to be that both play a part. A favourable environment can help children attain their potential and an unfavourable environment can hinder this.

Genetics alone rarely determine what a human being becomes. However, this does not necessarily lead to the conclusion that human beings have free will. Both our genetic make-up and our environment are factors outside our direct control.

How much control do we, ourselves, have over what happens to us?

Judaism has always affirmed that human beings *do* have free will. Right at the beginning, Adam and Eve were offered a choice: they could choose to obey God or disobey by eating the fruit of the Tree of Knowledge of Good and Evil. They chose to disobey, and some see this as what God intended, just as parents know that their child is likely to do exactly what they forbid. So human beings were given knowledge of good and evil and told to choose good. As Deuteronomy tells us: 'I call heaven and earth to witness against you this day, that I have set before you life and death, the blessing and the curse; therefore choose life, that you may live.'[45]

The Rabbis of the Talmud talked of human beings as having a *yetzer ha-ra*, an inclination towards evil, and a *yetzer tov*, a good inclination. We have the choice as to which predominates. As Moses Maimonides, the greatest mediaeval *halachist* and philosopher, put it: 'Every person has been given free will. If you wish to turn to the good way and be righteous, you have the power to do so; and if you wish to turn to the evil way and be wicked, you are free to do that. Every person is capable of being righteous like Moses or wicked like Jeroboam, learned or ignorant, merciful or cruel, mean or generous.'[46]

Philosophically, the issue of free will remains open. The complexity of the argument is summarized succinctly in the title of a chapter on the subject by Cohen and Stewart: 'We wanted to have a chapter on free will, but we decided not to, so here it is.'[47] Suffice it to say, most of the time we feel as if we have free will. We feel as if we are in control of what we do and have the ability to choose whether we act for good or evil. This is in itself evidence that we do have free will, for what we know is inevitably based on our own perceptions. It may be that ultimately, this sense of free will is an illusion. But as Cohen and Stewart point out, to say that free will is 'just' an illusion is to imply that it is insignificant, whereas that sense of free will may be crucial to how we act and interact with others.

Peters also points out a paradox in our thinking about genetics and free will, which he encapsulates in the contrasting concepts of 'puppet determinism' and 'Promethean determinism'. On the one hand, genetic researchers imply that we are like puppets, whose actions are determined by our genes without our having any control over them. On the other hand, by researching into our genes we are seen as interfering with creation – 'playing God' – just as Prometheus did when he stole fire from the gods.[48] Although Peters resolves the question in terms of Christian theology, some of his conclusions are helpful for us. He suggests our paradoxical view of free will is bound up with a twofold image of ourselves – of soil and of spirit. Our destiny is to rise above the soil and realize our full potential as human beings. Judaism, too, sees us as created both of the earth (Adam comes from the Hebrew *adamah*, meaning 'earth') and of the divine spirit, and so we have the potential to behave in a godlike way.

Ultimately, the important question for us here is a moral one, as Judaism would affirm. Whether or not free will is an illusion, we have to act in accordance with our sense of free will and use our freedom to choose good. We cannot blame what we do on circumstances or say that that is how we were made. If we abandon a sense of responsibility for our actions, then we should be held accountable. Whatever our genetic inheritance, we *do* have a choice as to what we make of it and a duty to act responsibly and for good.

PLAYING GOD? CONCLUSIONS

Our obligation to act responsibly and for the good is crucial to the way we approach genetic research. As indicated above, the accusation is often made that those engaging in such research are 'playing God'. This is compounded by a sense that we are 'playing' with the building blocks of creation and attempting to usurp God's role.

The issues in genetic research are generally similar to other aspects of research into human cells and tissues although there are some more far-reaching implications. But power over life and death is more frequently exercised by doctors working in intensive care every day, who decide whether or not to continue treatment. It is generally accepted, both in Judaism and modern society, that the ability to heal and save life gives doctors permission to use this power, though not without appropriate controls.

We can go further. Judaism considers human beings to be

partners with God in creation, and we are not only permitted but obligated to work with God to make the world a better place. To do this is not to 'play God', to usurp God's role, but to act as God intended us to do, and so to 'play human'[49] in the fullest sense.

It is up to us to use the abilities we have been given with wisdom and compassion. Genetic research carries potential for good and for harm and it is not always easy to know what will be for good. We can only try to discern what we can, using the best of our knowledge, and to act in humility, recognizing our responsibility to God and for our fellow human beings and our world. Genetic research threatens our sense of the sanctity of human life. We must ensure that research upholds that sanctity by treating human beings and potential human beings with respect and safeguarding the dignity of each person.

We must also ensure that the benefits of research are shared with justice. We must not allow such research to increase the gap between the affluent few who are able to benefit from its advances and the many who need help. Rather, we should aim to help especially those who are most vulnerable.

The challenges posed by genetic research are likely to continue and to become increasingly complex in the years to come. Jewish tradition can help to guide us through the maze. It tells us that we are partners with God in creation and have the ability to help to create a better world – a world where the dignity and value of every human being is respected, and all human beings can fulfil their unique potential. We have been given freedom to choose how to use that ability. Let us choose to use it for good and blessing, so that we and our children may live.

NOTES

1. Deoxyribonucleic acid, the chemical that encodes genetic information. DNA is found within the chromosomes of human cells.
2. W. Bodmer and R. McKie, *The Book of Man: The Quest to Discover Our Genetic Heritage* (London: Abacus, 1995), pp. 311–12.
3. Ibid., pp. 287–95.
4. Gene Therapy Advisory Committee Fourth Annual Report (Draft), Health Departments of the UK, 1998.
5. The nucleus from a cell in the udder was inserted into an egg from the same animal, from which the nucleus had been removed. The egg was then re-implanted and developed into a sheep.

6. D. Baltimore, 'Our Genome Unveiled', *Nature* 2001, 409, pp. 14–15.
7. Genesis 30:25–43.
8. Mishneh Torah, Laws of Circumcision 1:18.
9. BT Yev. 62b–63a; San. 76b.
10. D. Sinclair, 'Genetics and Jewish Law', *L'Eylah* 1996, pp. 39–44.
11. DNA analysis has produced some fascinating insights into priestly lineage. Those Jews who consider themselves *cohanim* do in fact show similarities which suggest descent from a common ancestor.
12. For more about a Progressive approach to Jewish Law, see J. D. Rayner, *Jewish Religious Law: A Progressive Perspective* (New York and Oxford: Berghahn Books, 1998).
13. Genesis 1:27.
14. Mishnah Sanhedrin 4:5.
15. Genesis 1:28.
16. *Siddur Lev Chadash* (London: ULPS, 1995), p. 190.
17. Deuteronomy 16:20.
18. In some cases, the disease will be transmitted only if both parents are carriers (recessive inheritance); in some if the mother is a carrier (sex-linked inheritance) and in some if either parent is a carrier, even if the other does not carry the gene (dominant inheritance).
19. J. D. Bleich, *Judaism and Healing: Halakhic Perspectives* (New York: Ktav, 1981), pp. 103–9.
20. Technically, the conceptus is termed an embryo for the first twelve weeks of gestation, and a fetus thereafter.
21. Sinclair, *Genetics and Jewish Law*.
22. D. King, 'Pre-implantation Genetic Diagnosis and the "New" Eugenics', *Journal of Medical Ethics* (1999), 25, pp. 176–82.
23. E. Dorff, *Matters of Life and Death: A Jewish Approach to Modern Medical Ethics* (Philadelphia and Jerusalem: The Jewish Publication Society, 1998), p. 158.
24. D. L. Dickenson, 'Can Children and Young People Consent to be Tested for Adult Onset Genetic Disorders?', *British Medical Journal* (1999), 318, pp. 1063–4.
25. G. Geller, 'Commentary: Weighing Burdens and Benefits Rather than Competence', *British Medical Journal* (1999), 318, pp. 1065–6.
26. Report of the Committee on the Ethics of Gene Therapy, HMSO, 1992.
27. A. Rosenfeld, 'Judaism and Gene Design', in F. Rosner and J. D. Bleich (eds), *Jewish Bioethics* (New York: Sanhedrin Press, 1979), pp. 401–7.
28. G. M. W. R. deWert, 'Ethics of Intracytoplasmic Sperm Injection: Proceed with Care', in P. Devroey, B. Tarlatzis and A. Van Steirteghem (eds), *Current Theory and Practice of ICSI, Human Reproduction* (1998), 13, Supplement 1, pp. 219–27.
29. *Stem Cell Research: Medical Progress with Responsibility*, Department of Health, June 2000.
30. Dorff, *Matters of Life and Death*, p. 322.
31. M. J. Broyde, 'Cloning People and Jewish Law: A Preliminary Analysis', *Journal of Halacha and Contemporary Society* (1997), 34, pp. 27–65.
32. *Guardian*, 16 August 2000.
33. D. Bruce and A. Bruce, *Engineering Genesis: The Ethics of Genetic Engineering in Non-Human Species* (London: Earthscan Publications, 1998), pp. 228–9.
34. Ibid., pp. 235–7.
35. E. Peters, *Playing God? Genetic Determinism and Human Freedom* (New York and London: Routledge, 1997), p. 130.

36. Ibid.
37. Bodmer and McKie, *The Book of Man*, p. 289.
38. Ibid., p. 334.
39. R. C. Lewontin, *The Doctrine of DNA, Biology as Ideology* (London: Penguin Books, 1991), pp. 73ff.
40. N. Holtzman, 'The Cautious View', *British Medical Journal* (2001), 322, p. 1017.
41. B. R. Bloom and D. D. Trach, 'Genetics and Developing Countries', *British Medical Journal* (2001), 322, p. 1006.
42. R. Dawkins, *The Selfish Gene* (Oxford: Oxford University Press, 1989).
43. J. Cohen and I. Stewart, *Our Genes Aren't Us* (*Discover*, 1994), pp. 78–84.
44. The concept of 'race' is itself highly dubious, even more so in the light of research on the human genome which has shown far more variation among individuals within a so-called racial group than among 'races'.
45. Deuteronomy 30:19.
46. Mishneh Torah, *Hilchot Teshuvah* 5:1.
47. J. Cohen and I. Stewart, *Figments of Reality: The Evolution of the Curious Mind* (Cambridge: Cambridge University Press, 1997), pp. 227–42.
48. Peters, *Playing God?*, pp. 27–62.
49. Ibid., p. 177.

9

Judaism and Today's Asylum Seekers

JULIA NEUBERGER

In the earliest days of the Jewish Religious Union, the Hon. Lily Montagu, child of the so-called Anglo-Jewish aristocracy, was already involved in her Girls' Club. She was not alone of her class among the Jewish community; the various 'settlements' set up by Oxford and Cambridge colleges, encouraging their students to undertake social work among the underprivileged of London (and to some extent, though a little differently, in the other great cities) were already well established. Young women of good breeding who had not been to the universities were nevertheless expected to play their part among the less fortunate. The kind of philanthropy and social endeavour expected of them was akin to that piloted by the Anglican philanthropists such as Josephine Butler and Octavia Hill, though vestiges of the Quaker approach, particularly in the idea of settlements, can also be discerned.

The clubs – many of which were transformed into a syna-gogue or a church group in later years – relied on a social structure so highly stratified that it would appear to us to be peculiar and snobbish. The girls would call Lily Montagu 'Miss Lily'; she, on the other hand, would have addressed them by their first names. She was older than most of them, but in some of the clubs there were members who were older than the helpers. Titles went by rank, rather than age. The assumption was that the wealthy young people from Bayswater, St John's Wood, Hyde Park or South Kensington could help in the East End, where their fellow Jews had recently arrived and were experiencing considerable hardship and poverty.

This has to be set against the fact that many 'West End' Jews were not wholly appreciative of the arrival of tens of thousands of Eastern European Jews between 1881 and 1905, fleeing pogroms and poverty. Some of the 'West End' Jews supported the passing of the Aliens' Act in 1905, one of the most disgraceful pieces of immigration legislation this country has ever known, made law within days, in panic at the large numbers coming into the country. The Act was designed particularly to keep out the hordes of Jews pressing for entry in the wake of the two Kishinev massacres of 1903 and 1905.

It was these people, first-generation immigrants or their children, that the better-off young Jews were sent to assist. Many did it willingly, with enthusiasm. They wanted to help. They felt a kindred spirit with the young whose life experience had been so different from theirs. Others were moved to help for less commendable reasons. There was undoubtedly a concern that these new Eastern European Jews would get Jews in general in Britain a bad name; in the eyes of the new Jewish middle class they were dirty, noisy and ill-educated. The more that could be done to teach them English ways, the better. So there was a curious alliance of people wanting to help and support, with very mixed motives.

Lily Montagu's motives were not mixed, however. She simply wanted to help, as did Basil Henriques and many others. The West Central Girls' Club (which still holds its reunions) and the Oxford and St George's Club (the Settlement, where, until its recent merger with South West Essex Reform Synagogue, the synagogue still continued at Beaumont Grove, in Stepney) were among the clubs particularly associated with the early Reform and Liberal movements in Britain.

Those who formed the Jewish Religious Union, and those who were the Reform and Liberal Jewish leaders of the early twentieth century, were among the best leaders of the young people's clubs. They motivated many, of both their helpers and their members, with a passion for Judaism, and gave them opportunities for learning.

There were classes in all sorts of activities and skills, as well as holidays away in the countryside, with a mixture of Boy Scout-type activities and celebrations of the Sabbath under canvas and by starlight. There were musicals and outings, literacy classes for the few, and accountancy classes for girls who wanted to become more advanced book-keepers. The shop girls, who made up the majority of the members of Miss Lily's club, themselves became sponsors of other children and young people. And the clubs often provided help to young German Jewish refugees when they came to Britain, though their favoured haunts were their own clubs in Hampstead and at the West London Synagogue.

It is important to remember, in looking back at the early days of Liberal Judaism, that there was a social conscience deeply ingrained in its early members, a sense of duty towards fellow Jews and towards others less well off. One can read of it in the accounts of the various clubs, and one can hear about it from the surviving members. It was based on a concept of obligation, which also extended, among some, to work for the German Jewish refugees who started coming in the early 1930s and for whom real activity and help was organized from about 1936 onwards. Not all members of Liberal synagogues were wholly welcoming, but the clubs, and some individuals in the congregations, made a huge effort.

One can see that same strain at work in the efforts for Soviet Jewry which occupied much of the late 1970s and 1980s, led by Margaret Rigal, a member of the Liberal Jewish Synagogue, and others. This was a Jewish social conscience in action. There are countless other examples – of young Jews involved, as Jews, in JONAH (Jews Organized for a Nuclear Arms Halt), a more overtly political movement, or young Jews working with people with AIDS. There are collections of food for the needy and for asylum seekers in many synagogues, particularly at Sukkot, and almost all congregations have a social action programme of some kind, varying from active participation in a local project, often alongside a local church, to the more casual giving of financial help to needy causes. There are soup kitchens for the homeless, and soup runs carried out by Jews over Christmas. Young Jews help to staff all sorts of projects over Christmas, and relieve Christian staff in old people's homes. The LJS's 'Out and About Club' has catered for people with disabilities for decades.

Social Action, the successor to the original Social Action Forum set up in the early 1990s under the chairmanship of Steve Miller, united the Union of Liberal and Progressive Synagogues (ULPS) and the Reform Synagogues of Great Britain (RSGB) in a variety of activities, including those above. Most noteworthy were the drop-ins for the homeless which in one case – Finchley – grew into a separate charity, and the Kings Cross Furniture Project, which started as a lecture theatre converted into a warehouse by volunteers, providing recycled furniture to those in need across north London. It grew so rapidly that it became a separate charity, though Social Action volunteers continue to staff it and to be involved. It is the major supplier of this furniture across the whole of north London and beyond. In addition, ULPS young adults have organized parties for children in temporary accommodation, toys have been collected for Kosovar refugees, and there are dozens of other projects large and small, from soup runs and conferences to campaigns on human rights and a Disability Advisory Group which seeks to make our synagogues more aware of disability issues. It adds up to a not inconsiderable contribution, although still not involving enough of the synagogues' membership.

Yet I often wonder whether, in this arena, we have done as well as we should as Liberal Jews. After all, we regard ourselves as prophetic Jews, the ones whose motivation comes from the prophetic tradition. We quote to ourselves and to each other:

> Is this the fast I have chosen, a day of mortification such as this? ... Is this what you call a fast, a day acceptable to the Lord? Is not *this* what I require of you as a fast: to loose the fetters of injustice, to untie the knots of the yoke, to snap every yoke and set free those who have been crushed? Is it not sharing your food with the hungry, taking the homeless poor into your house, clothing the naked when you meet them, and never evading a duty to your kinsfolk? (Isaiah 58:5–7)

But we tend to use it as a quotation to denigrate the love of our more Orthodox brethren for the minutiae of Jewish ritual, while we get the 'big picture'.

Yet the question remains: have we actually got the big picture? We certainly have a credible record of involvement in social issues. Various members of our synagogues carry out wonderful works of lovingkindness. Our achievement stands comparison with many. But there is no area of social action which we could point to and honestly call our own, as Liberal Jews. There is not among us the kind of person frequently thrown up by our non-conformist cousins in Christianity (for we are the non-conformist Jews) – people such as the Reverend Adele Blake-borough, founder of the Kaleidoscope Project for heroin addicts, or the Reverend Andrew Mawson, founder of Community Action Network. You do not see young Liberal Jews setting up modern settlements and clubs, for example for asylum seekers whom the state partly wishes to disown and certainly to discriminate against. You rarely see young Liberal Jews involved, as Jews, in regenerating the inner city or in working with people with long-term mental health problems (except as psychiatrists, and, of course, that classic Jewish growth area, as psycho-therapists!) Where Christians are strongly involved in Third World issues, Jews have been slow to tread. And, where they have trodden, it has been by no means with a particularly Liberal Jewish voice. We do now have *Tzedek*, a Jewish voice seeking social justice, particularly in Third World issues. And Social Action gives an opportunity to those in the two non-Orthodox movements who want to do something. But to make social action universal in our congregations would be an uphill task, for it does not appear to come naturally to us any more. And yet it was our origins. The needs may be different now-adays but they are no less.

I want to hazard a guess at some of the reasons for this. Knowing that I am deliberately contentious, let me say that this may raise hackles, but I believe it to be a necessary debate for us to have, as we enter our second century. For if we are not all here to serve others, to work as prophetic Jews, then where is the difference between us and any other Jews of whatever degree of observance, for whom membership of a synagogue is more a social and comfort matter than a stimulus to the conscience? If we are not moved to carry out activities on behalf of others, then what point is there in us being Liberal Jews as opposed to any other kind of Jews, or for that matter any other kind of people?

There are two particular trends which have made our social justice activities less strong than once they were. The first is the women's movement which has been taking place within non-Orthodox Judaism itself. Some of those who might naturally have drifted towards social action have been caught up in the women's movement both within and outside the Jewish community. Such an injustice appears to have been done to women that the righting of that injustice has taken precedence for many young women. The struggle for women to become rabbis was merely a first stage. There has been the search for a genuine women's spirituality in Judaism, and for a recognition of a different voice for women, as relevant in Liberal Judaism, which thought of itself as non-discriminatory but prayed in a male language, as in other forms of Judaism. There has been the struggle to achieve some measure of Jewish learning for women who felt they were denied it, and the attempt to include women more fully in services. There has been an effort to stop expecting women to do all the catering and make the teas, though that will still take generations. And there has been the recognition that, alongside the desire for more Jewish education for women, there is a greater demand for Jewish education for everyone. The mood of the time has been somewhat internalized, inward-looking and trying to put right injustices within.

Linked to that is a search for a form of spirituality which many of the founders of Liberal Judaism would not have known how to describe. Many of them, however, experienced it. You could not have been in Lily Montagu's presence without the sense that she felt herself talking directly to God, and felt driven by God as well. The reflectiveness sought by many of our young people would have been foreign to the movement's founders, however. And that search for spirituality, almost a search for meaning outside the mundane, practical and material, has also distracted many of our young people from a sense of obligation to others less well off than they are themselves.

But there is another factor. That is the Holocaust. The shock to the Jewish system of the realization of the destruction of such a large proportion of our people in the Holocaust; the discovery of Holocaust denial; the attempts to get back looted works of art; to get compensation for those who never received it in earlier years – all this has taken the place of the fight for social justice for others. The sense is one of an injustice done to us, and that sense, growing exponentially, and paradoxically, as the events of 1939 to 1945 grow more distant, makes it difficult for our young to turn outside their own community and say that they understand what happened to us, but that, however awful, and however constant the injustices still remaining, there is nevertheless a duty upon us to help others who need our succour and support.

That is something that Liberal Judaism could, I believe, achieve in the next century. It could achieve a social justice ethic much nearer its origins than has been the case in recent years. It could, for instance, decide to campaign on behalf of asylum seekers, who seem to have no friends in an increasingly xenophobic country and continent. It could campaign for the Roma, themselves the victims of the Nazis as surely as the Jews were. Our young could become involved with the children of the inner cities whose life chances are so very much worse than their own. And they could throw in their lot with the homeless, whose lives are still bleak, despite countless attempts to provide hostel accommodation for them.

There are any number of other causes, and it would not be right for me to suggest what would be most appropriate. The lot of refugees and asylum seekers, however, is one which Jews would do particularly well to examine. Most of us, in our families, have been refugees and asylum seekers in the not so distant past. We might, even with our very limited resources, be able to do something to alleviate the burden of friendlessness, bureaucracy and indifference. We might even be able to bring some joy into the lives of people who, as we once did, have come to this country as strangers. 'For you know the heart of the stranger ...' (Exodus 23:9).

But if we are to do this, then we have to throw off the shackles of our own inward-looking tendency. We have to question our inclination to function increasingly separately as a Jewish community – a Jewish social life, a Jewish day school education, living in Jewish areas, in a country where those who need our help most severely may not share our narrow identity. Looking outwards, rather than inwards, is what is required. Whereas Liberal Judaism started as an attempt to keep the young within the fold, enabling them to function socially and religiously as modern Jews looking both in and out, we run the danger of looking inwards too much, too worried by questions of identity and the malaise of material well-being, and forgetting to look outwards, and to remember our own history.

If Jewish social action, with a Liberal Jewish label, is to mean anything in its second century, it will require that outward look, that self-critical assessment of what we have actually achieved rather than what we like to think we have done. It will – rightly – drive us out into harsh terrain, certain of our own safe position back in our warm community, but even more certain that those we ought to be helping, in the name of our Jewish faith, have no such security about their future, their material well-being, and their children's fate. 'For you know the heart of the stranger ...' At the beginning of our second century, do we?

10

Liberal Judaism and Mixed Marriage

DANNY RICH

For more than 150 years the Board of Deputies of British Jews has been collecting data on births, marriages, divorces and deaths which take place within the Jewish community in the United Kingdom. According to the Institute for Jewish Policy Research,[1] births fell from 3,300 in 1996 to around 2,500 in 1999, a decline of 24 per cent. Burials and cremations have fallen from an average of 4,900 in 1975–79 to 3,800 in 2000, a decline of 22 per cent. Marriages have also declined in recent years, so that in 2000 there were 907 synagogue marriages, four per cent fewer than the average of 947 for 1995–99. The only statistic to show an increase in recent years is *gittin* (religious divorces).

Marriages between Jews and non-Jews are not recorded in the Board of Deputies' statistics, although it is not denied by any reputable Jewish organization that a reality of modern living is the increasing number of Jews who make their lives with non-Jews.

In its 1992 statement *Affirmations of Liberal Judaism*,[2] the Liberal Jewish movement declares its willingness to 'confront unflinchingly the challenges of our time, welcome gladly all advances in human knowledge, and respond constructively to changing circumstances'. The increasing number of Jews who make their lives with non-Jewish partners is perhaps the greatest change in circumstances faced by Anglo-Jewry, and it is, therefore, hardly surprising that a Liberal Jewish response is both sought and required.

My response will begin with a comment about definition. I will then examine the history of, and Jewish attitudes to, the partnering of a Jew with a non-Jew. Thereafter I will explore a number of myths concerning such partnerships and those who participate in them. Finally I shall discuss an appropriate Liberal Jewish stance.

DEFINITION

The literature uses a number of terms to describe the partnerships between Jews and non-Jews. American sociological material[3] prefers the unfamiliar term 'exogamy'; Sanford Seltzer[4] uses 'mixed marriage' although it suffers from imprecision; Judy Petsonk and Jim Remsen[5] prefer 'intermarriage' although the previous objection remains, and British Reform rabbi, Jonathan Romain,[6] writes of 'mixed faith marriages'. No respectable writer talks of 'marrying out' for reasons that will be set out below. In order not to make any pre-judgement and despite its clumsiness, I will talk of 'partnerships between Jews and non-Jews'. Although even this description suffers from the defect of defining the 'non-Jewish' partner in relation to the Jew rather than understanding his/her own identity, by so doing it avoids assumptions about matrimony, sexuality and whether being Jewish is understood as a religious or cultural description. One further point of clarification is required: I am not concerned with the relationship between a born Jew and a person converted to Judaism since that is, in accord with Jewish tradition, a relationship between two Jews.

The desirability of 'marrying' within one's own group, and the concern for those who look outside it, is as old as the Jewish people. Abraham, rejecting local women, sent his chief servant back to his country of birth to seek a wife for Isaac (Genesis 24:3–4), and Isaac in turn seeks similarly for his son, Jacob (Genesis 28:1). Legislative passages in Exodus 34:15–16 and Deuteronomy 7:3 reinforce the negative view of marrying outside the tribe. Even though one might argue that this referred particularly to the seven pagan nations of Canaan, Rabbinic tradition extended it to all non-Jews (see, for example, Avodah Zarah 36b). The well-known condemnation by Ezra (chapters 9 and 10) and the attempt at rabbinic denial at least of the 'validity' of partnerships between a Jew and a non-Jew (Kiddushin 68b), give a clear indication of the discomfort experienced by the leaders of the community when a member sought a relationship outside the group.

Nevertheless, there are a good number of Jewish heroes and heroines who transgressed the prohibition. Moses 'took' the Midianite, Zipporah (Exodus 2:21), and in the fable of Esther it is her marriage to the Persian King which is crucial in the deliverance of the Jews (Esther 3:9, 7:1–6).

Such examples in all generations and places notwithstanding, the discomfort of the Jewish community found reinforcement from the Church. At about the time that Christianity was becoming the official religion of the Roman Empire, in 306 the Council of Elvira (Spain) forbade Christians and Jews from marrying each other, a ban reinforced by the death penalty in the following century. Further restrictions on where Jews might live, in which trades they might work, and with whom they might eat and drink,[7] coupled with legislation on inheritance and heresy, made the problem of partnerships between Jews and non-Jews more theoretical than practical.

It was the French Revolution, with its physical and ideological breaches of the ghetto walls, that brought the question of a Jew marrying a non-Jew back to the forefront of Jewish minds. Revolutionary ideas of equality and liberty led to what was later to be called 'social mobility' across the religious, rural/urban, and feudal divides. The matter of partnerships between Jews and Christians was specifically addressed in the third question put by Napoleon Bonaparte to the Assembly of Notables gathered in Paris in 1806.[8] The Great Sanhedrin (which succeeded the Assembly) was arguably under duress but declared that: 'Marriages between Jews and Christians which have been contracted in accordance with the laws of the civil code are *civilly* legal, and that, although they may not be capable of receiving religious sanction, they should not be subject to religious proscription.' This response of the Great Sanhedrin was to be the subject of debate at the rabbinic conferences of the 1840s and the 1871 Augsburg Synod. Among the participants was the radical Reform rabbi of Berlin (from 1846), Samuel Holdheim, who declared 'valid such marriages between Jews and such as hold the monotheistic belief'.[9] The debate at Brunswick in June 1884 was wide-ranging. Rabbinic participation, education of children, Jewish–Christian relations and the betrothal vow were all discussed until finally a majority agreed to the motion proposed by Ludwig Philippson: 'Members of monotheistic religions in general are not forbidden to marry if the parents are permitted by the laws of the state to bring up children from such wedlock in the Jewish religion.'[10]

Whatever the number of Jews marrying non-Jews was, it is difficult to assess how this affected the Jewish community. At the time of the rabbinic conferences it was not easy to marry a non-Jew and retain one's Jewishness. 'Conversion would almost invariably have to precede marriage,'[11] since marriage was a religious institution. Civil marriage was not available in England until 1837 or in Prussia until 1846, and thus a Jew who married a non-Jew usually converted to the other's religion and ordinarily disappeared from the Jewish community.

Egon Mayer and Amy Avgar observe (probably reflecting the American experience) that 'In the first half of the twentieth century, the relatively small numbers involved brought sadness to the Jewish community but they were not seen as a threat.'[12] If that was so in the early part of the twentieth century, in its final quarter the mentality of the Jewish community was to undergo a transformation.

Responding to the Shoah (in which perhaps one-third of the world's Jews had perished), in the 1970s respected sociologists and community leaders were talking of the 'vanishing American Jew'. In the continent which then played host to the largest Jewish population of the world, headlines began to talk of intermarriage and attrition leading to a critical decline in the Jewish population. Accurate facts were still hard to come by (civil marriages required no declaration of religion by participants), and it was not until the 1970s in the United States[13] and a decade later in Britain[14] that the statistics became available. The statistical surveys confirmed that the rate of marriage between Jews and non-Jews was increasing. The widest-ranging survey, *The 1990 National Jewish Population Survey,*[15] was conducted by Egon Mayer, Professor of Sociology at Brooklyn College and perhaps the most prolific writer in this area. His two main conclusions transformed American Jewry. As Rabbi Alexander Schindler, then President of the Union of Hebrew Congregations, reported: 'One out of every two marriages involving a North American Jew is now an interfaith marriage; there is a higher rate of conversion from Judaism than to it, and only a third of the children of interfaith marriages are presently being reared as Jews. These statistics cry for an all-out outreach effort by the Jewish community ...'[16]

It did not take a statistician to work out that on these figures the prognosis would be a demographic disaster – and the American Jewish community responded, lamenting its shrinkage and imminent demise. It is not my purpose here to challenge the accuracy of those statistics. In an article in the *Los Angeles Jewish Journal* of December 1999, however, J. Goldberg reported on a recently completed survey, which might lead one to the opposite conclusion, namely that the Jewish community of America was growing. The rate of intermarriage is, the new survey suggests, nearer one-third than the 52 per cent of the 1990 survey, and the number of inter-faith families raising their children as Jews is half rather than the 28 per cent quoted in the 1990 survey. Notwithstanding disputes about the figures, 'intermarriage is here to stay'.[17]

Virtually any rabbi of any part of the Jewish community in any part of the world (excepting the State of Israel) knows personally of families affected in one way or another by a Jewish member of that family making his or her life with a non-Jew. 'Cold statistics, however, are made up of warm people.'[18] I would now like to look at the issues raised by these 'warm' people and offer a comprehensive response in accord with the *raison d'être* of Liberal Judaism, which 'values human need above legal technicalities'.[19]

There are four major myths surrounding the Jew who partners him/herself with a non-Jew:

1. That the Jew has rejected his or her Judaism.
2. That s/he never had much Judaism to worry about in the first place.
3. That s/he comes from a particular part of the Jewish community.
4. That relationships between Jews and non-Jews are of themselves 'inherently dysfunctional'.

There is a limited and incomplete body of evidence concerning these myths. When the rate of partnerships between Jews and non-Jews was low it might have been possible, in the words of Richard Rubenstein, to conclude that such a radical step was indeed 'the principal means of departure from Jewish life'.[20]

Increasing testimony, however, affirms the irony that many Jews in such a situation accentuate their commitment to and practice of Judaism rather than seeking to flee from or reject it.

It is increasingly difficult to measure, and I am unable to find any useful documents concerning, the level of Jewish education and/or commitment to Judaism of those Jews who partner themselves with a non-Jew. Evidence from my rabbinic colleagues within the Rabbinic Conference of Liberal Judaism; from my own congregation, the Kingston Liberal Synagogue, where 20 per cent of family units consist of partnerships in which only one of the partners is Jewish; and the enquiries I have received from couples asking me to 'officiate' at their (marriage) ceremonies (more than 150 so far), indicates that Jews who are partnered with non-Jews have a wide range of levels of Jewish education and experience.

Concerning the third myth, Jonathan Romain, who has run a series of seminars for Jews partnered with non-Jews and their families – the largest initiative of its kind in Europe and outside of the United States – concludes that 'the issue affects Orthodox communities as much as Reform ones [I would include Liberal ones too!], and seminars for Jews in mixed-faith marriages attract equal numbers from both camps'.[21]

The fourth and final myth has also been repeated constantly without supporting evidence. Jonathan Romain declares: 'Some [mixed-faith marriages] do end in tears and there is evidence that such couples have a somewhat higher rate of divorce than do same-faith couples',[22] although he does not give the reader any references concerning the evidence, and qualifies it in the following sentence: 'The current divorce rate in England and Wales is high enough for an observer to draw many inferences.' In the United States some studies in the 1960s and 1970s[23] seemed to show a higher divorce rate among mixed-faith marriages, but divorce is only one index of how well any marriage functions. It is more likely to be true, as Leslie Malamuth and Robin Margolis report, that 'partnerships between Jews and non-Jews do have unique stresses, and that it may be possible that problems which may arise in many types of partnership are exacerbated where dual loyalties are the unexplored background'.[24]

Whatever the research, or lack of it, Liberal rabbis and their communities must be prepared to acknowledge and welcome Jews who are partnered to non-Jews. Those Jews partnered with non-Jews who approach Liberal rabbis and their communities do so for many of the same reasons other Jews do. They are hopeful – that their partnerships will be enduring; they are diverse – coming from a variety of expressions of Judaism; they are educated – in Jewish matters to a greater or lesser degree; and they wish to affirm, and be affirmed in, their Judaism.

A Jew partnered with a non-Jew has much in common with any other Jew, but may also have particular needs at specific times. Potentially the most controversial of these times is the occasion of a public commitment ceremony or marriage. The traditional form of Jewish marriage is the public witnessing of the contract between a Jewish groom and a Jewish bride in which the rabbi has a non-statutory but, in the modern period, increasingly important, role (*masadder/et kiddushin*). The rabbi's role has increased for two major reasons: first, there is increased ignorance of both Hebrew and Judaism among modern Jews, and second, the rabbi is expected more and more to act as a pastor and an overseer of ceremonies, particularly life-cycle events. For most couples, their wedding day is one of the most memorable moments they share. Many couples desire a spiritual element to this 'moment of transition', which for two Jews, or for a Jew contemplating marriage to a non-Jew, may include the presence of a rabbi.

The question of rabbinic participation is not a new one. The Central Conference of American Rabbis (CCAR), the rabbinic arm of American Reform (equivalent to British Liberal) Judaism, declared as early as 1909 that inter-faith marriage was 'contrary to the traditions of the Jewish religion'. It affirmed that position in 1947 and 1993 but it recognized that a number of its members felt differently and provided *de facto* autonomy for members to do as their consciences dictated. In 1989 Egon Mayer carried out a research project on the effects of rabbinic agreement or refusal to officiate at marriages between a Jew and a non-Jew. He concluded that 'rabbinic officiation at mixed marriages has relatively little, if any, connection to the expressed Jewishness in the family lives of non-Jews married to Jews'.[25] Similarly, rabbinic refusal to officiate at mixed marriages seems to have relatively little, if any, connection with large-scale alienation from Jewish activities (in other words, participating in *seder* meals, lighting *Hanukkah* candles, attending synagogue regularly, being a member of a synagogue etc.). Nevertheless, the number of CCAR members willing to officiate at inter-faith marriages – and prepared to be open about officiating – is increasing.

In the United Kingdom the two affiliates to the World Union for Progressive Judaism differ in their stances. The Assembly of Rabbis of the Reform Synagogues of Great Britain insists that 'no member shall participate in any mixed-faith wedding ceremony in any way, whatever the circumstances and wherever the venue'.[26]

On the other hand the Rabbinic Conference of Liberal Judaism has, for some time, permitted its members to 'officiate' at ceremonies involving a Jew and a non-Jew, subject to certain conditions. These conditions sought to:

- protect colleagues who felt unable to participate at such ceremonies;
- promote the priority of conversion leading to Jewish marriage;
- secure the Jewish upbringing of any children of the marriage (by means of an unenforceable pledge); and
- make a clear distinction between Jewish wedding rituals and anything that might occur in an inter-faith ceremony.

In April 2003 the Rabbinic Conference reviewed its approach to 'mixed-faith marriage'. It reaffirmed its 'commitment to prioritise and encourage Jewish marriage' and to stress the 'advantages of conver[sion]'[27] and reiterated the individual rabbi's conscience clause, the Shabbat and *yom tov* (festival day) exclusion, and the distinction between Jewish wedding liturgy and rituals and anything that might occur in an inter-faith ceremony.

The new policy removed the (unenforceable) pledge on securing the Jewish upbringing of any children, but was more radical in two ways: first, it allowed the participation of non-Jewish clergy at such ceremonies, and second, but undoubtedly of more significance, it permitted such ceremonies to 'take place in a synagogue building, or on neutral ground, according to the conscience of the rabbi concerned and with due regard to the [views of the] lay leadership of the synagogue concerned'.

As a member of the conference and a long-time advocate of a 'liberalization' of the rules concerning an 'Act of Prayer following the Marriage of a Jew to a Non-Jew', I am delighted with the April 2003 decision. In my view the conference might have gone further in two ways: first, with an insistence that the couple attend classes on Judaism or satisfy the rabbi that they have an appropriate understanding of Judaism; and second, the conference might have committed itself to advocating a change in English statute permitting rabbis to act as civil registrars at such ceremonies. (Currently rabbis or other designated members of the synagogue may, under the Marriage Act 1949, serve as 'Marriage Secretary', carrying out the civil registration of the marriage provided the ceremony is between two persons both of whom 'profess the Jewish religion'.)

Those rabbis in the United States and in Britain who oppose rabbinic participation do so on three grounds: it is against Jewish tradition; it is not an appropriate task for rabbis; and it appears to condone partnerships between Jews and non-Jews.

Those who support it have usually done so on the basis that acceptance may help to create a Jewish family and rejection may incline the family concerned in the opposite direction. I see the matter in simpler terms. I take the view that when requested a rabbi ought to take each and every opportunity to promote Judaism – its ethics and its way of life. The request to officiate at any ceremony (but particularly one between a Jew and a non-Jew) is a chance to demonstrate the beauty and openness of Judaism. In my opinion it is not the time to pursue hidden Jewish agendas or to extract unenforceable promises.

Accordingly, when I receive a request (currently about two per month) to officiate at a marriage ceremony involving a Jew and a non-Jew, I invite both to meet me in my study at the synagogue. I first must satisfy myself that both parties have an appropriate understanding of Judaism, and if either or both do not, then I arrange for them to attend adult classes at the synagogue. I insist that they meet with me on enough occasions to prepare them for their marriage, and, following a positive decision by the Council of Kingston Liberal Synagogue, the couple may arrange their ceremony in the synagogue building or elsewhere. The couple must join their local synagogue (in whatever capacity is permitted; see further). My restrictions would be only these: that the ceremony should not take place on shabbat or *Yom Tov* (which would show a disregard for Jewish traditions) and that the rabbi and the couple agree a means of demonstrating that the ceremony is not a Jewish marriage in the traditional understanding of the phrase.

Of course, a marriage ceremony is only the beginning, and it makes little sense to be welcoming and supportive of the Jew and his or her partner at this point in their lives and not thereafter. In the United States, the Union of American Hebrew Congregations (the UAHC is the collective body of American Reform Judaism) has produced two booklets, *Defining the Role of the Non-Jew in the Synagogue* (1990 and 1993).[28] The booklets are significant in that they were a public acknowledgement that a Jew and a non-Jewish partner might desire, and receive, a welcome in, and some of the benefits of, the life of the synagogue. The booklets are a movement-wide effort to guide the process rather than an 'attempt to dictate specific policy' in matters of synagogue membership, synagogue governance and leadership, Jewish ritual at life-cycle events and involvement in public prayer.

In the United Kingdom the way was led by Liberal Judaism, which initiated a movement-wide exploration of the role of the non-Jew in the synagogue, and by some of its constituents (the Liberal Jewish Synagogue in St John's Wood, Kingston Liberal Synagogue and Northwood and Pinner Liberal Synagogue, for example) which have Affiliates' or Friends' Schemes. Detailed comment is outside the scope of this particular contribution. What is clear is that we need to explore ways of welcoming and affirming Jews partnered with non-Jews not only at the point of 'marriage' but also at other crucial times, and other ordinary times.

Perhaps Claude Montefiore, the intellectual founder of Liberal Judaism, puts it best when he wrote: 'God's unity and righteousness, the inseparable union of religion and morality, the election of Israel for a religious mission and service, the joy of communion with God – these doctrines [are] the essence of our Judaism today.'[29]

It is in this spirit that Liberal Judaism, its rabbis and constituents, will greet the growing number of Jews and non-Jews who choose to make their lives together.

NOTES

1. *Long-term Planning for British Jewry: Final Report and Recommendations* (London: JPR, 2003), p. 47.
2. *Affirmations of Liberal Judaism* (London: ULPS, 1992).
3. B. Kosmin, N. Lerer and E. Mayer, *Intermarriage, Divorce, and Remarriage Among American Jews 1982–7* (New York: North American Jewish Data Bank, 1989).
4. S. Seltzer, *Jews and Non-Jews Falling in Love* (New York: UAHC, 1976).
5. J. Petsonk and J. Remsen, *The Intermarriage Handbook* (New York: Arbor House, 1988).
6. Jonathan Romain, *Till Faith Us Do Part* (London: Fount, 1996).
7. J. Katz, *Exclusiveness and Tolerance* (Oxford: Oxford University Press, 1961).
8. S. Schwarzfuchs, *Napoleon, the Jews, and the Sanhedrin* (London: Routledge, 1979), p. 69.
9. D. Philipson, *The Reform Movement in Judaism* (London: Macmillan, 1907), p. 90.
10. G. Plaut, *The Rise of Reform Judaism* (New York: WUPJ, 1963), pp. 220–22.
11. S. Schneider, *Intermarriage* (New York: Free, 1989), p. 13.
12. *Conversion Among the Intermarried* (New York: The American Jewish Committee, 1987), p. vi.
13. Ibid., pp. 1–3.
14. S. Waterman and B. Kosmin, *British Jewry in the Eighties* (London: Board of Deputies of British Jews, 1986).
15. E. Mayer, *The 1990 National Jewish Population Survey* (New York: Council of Jewish Federations, 1991).
16. In A. King, *If I'm Jewish and You're Christian, What are the Kids?* (New York: UAHC, 1993), p. ix.
17. G. Glaser, *Strangers to the Tribe* (New York: Houghton Mifflin, 1997), p. 245.
18. S. Jacobs and B. Jacobs, *122 Clues for Jews whose Children Intermarry* (California: Jacob's Ladder, 1988), p. 14.
19. *Affirmations of Liberal Judaism* (London: ULPS, 1992).
20. *After Auschwitz* (Baltimore: Johns Hopkins University Press, 1966), p. 173.
21. J. Romain, *Till Faith Us Do Part*, p. 168.
22. Ibid., pp. 167–8.
23. S. Seltzer, *Jews and Non-Jews Getting Married* (New York: UAHC, 1984), pp. 27–8.
24. L. Malamuth and R. Margolis, *Between Two Worlds* (New York: Pocket, 1992), pp. 136, 156–61.
25. E. Mayer, *Intermarriage and Rabbinic Officiation* (New York: American Jewish Committee, 1989), pp. 7–8.
26. J. Romain, *Faith and Practice* (London: RSGB, 1991), p. 167.
27. Rabbinic Conference, *Ha Madrich* (London: ULPS, unpublished), section G9.
28. *Defining the Role of the Non-Jew in the Synagogue* (New York: UAHC, 1990 and 1993).
29. Claude Montefiore, *The Old Testament and After* (London: Macmillan, 1923), p. 587.

11

Feminist Bible Interpretation

SYBIL SHERIDAN

When Lily Montagu helped to establish the Jewish Religious Union in 1902, she was part of the first wave of religious feminism. In the centuries before, Jewish women had only a second-hand and highly interpreted knowledge of the Biblical text. Such works as *Ze'ena u-Re'ena*, a selection of stories from the Bible written in Yiddish specifically for women, served up a vision of our foremothers that was idealized and often anodyne. But when, during the nineteenth century, women's general education improved, such infantalized visions of Jewish history served only to put the intelligent woman off her heritage. In order to get her sisters to reconnect with their past, Grace Aguilar (1816–47) published *Women of Israel*. In the introduction, she wrote:

> To desert the Bible for its commentators; never to peruse its pages without notes of explanation; to regard it as a work which of itself is incomprehensible, is indeed a practice as hurtful as injudicious. Sent as a message of love to our own souls, as written and addressed, not to nations alone, but as a voice of God to individuals – whispering to each of us that which we most need; thus it is we should first regard and venerate it.[1]

Writing partly as an apologetic against Christian criticism that Jewish women were unfairly subjugated and partly as a rallying call to enthuse and educate the Jewish women of her time, Aguilar presents women from the Bible and Rabbinic literature as role models for her contemporaries to emulate. Undoubtedly, her two-volume work was read by Lily Montagu and could well have been an influence on her life's vocation.

Fifty years later, Elizabeth Cady Stanton (1815–97) published the *Woman's Bible*. Of very different character and background from Grace Aguilar, Stanton – a leading suffragette in the American movement – was brought up as an evangelical Christian. She later rejected these beliefs, demonstrating an ambivalent attitude towards religion while at the same time lecturing and publishing, with a committee of like-minded feminists, her 'Bible'. She saw the Bible as responsible for shoring up institutions inimical to equality – supporting slavery and the subjugation of women, for example – but claimed that it was the interpretation, not the Bible itself, that was responsible for this. Her commentary demonstrated that it was possible for women to read the text directly and derive their own very different interpretations from it. An example is the story of Pinkas, who famously thrust his spear through Zimri and Cozbi – an Israelite man and the Midianite woman with whom he was sleeping at the time (Numbers 25:6–15). Where current commentary tended to focus on the justification of Pinkas, Stanton added her own ironic comment:

> Jewish law forbade a man going outside his tribe for a wife. It was deemed idolatry. But why kill the woman? She had not violated the laws of her tribe and was no doubt ignorant of Jewish law. Other commentators say that Zimri was notorious at the licentious feasts of Baal-peor and that the Midianitish woman tempted the sons of Israel to idolatry. Hence the justice of killing both Zimri and Cozbi in one blow. It is remarkable that the influence of woman is so readily and universally recognised in leading the strongest of men into sin, but so uniformly ignored as a stimulus to purity and perfection.[2]

The mode in which Cady Stanton challenged the cherished beliefs of the male-dominated Judeo-Christian tradition differs little from that of many feminists today. For the past twenty years the focus of feminist Bible interpretation has been to question the assumptions of men – assumptions that the Bible 'is about men and women when in reality it is only about men'.[3]

For example: it is generally believed that in biblical society, the burial of a person would be accompanied by professional mourners who composed lamentations to sing or chant over the dead. These mourners were women. Why then is it assumed that the author of the Book of Lamentations was a man?

For example: the famous list of 'times' in *Kohelet* begins *eit laledet* – translated always as 'a time to be born'. In reality, the Hebrew means 'a time to give birth'. Why the change? The mistranslation may be more inclusive and it parallels more neatly the 'time to die', but I suspect it owes more to an assumption that the subject of the piece is mankind not womankind.

For example: the Hebrew language is a highly gendered language. There are no neuter words and thus the norm for humanity is written in the male gender. This 'male' language includes the female in verb, noun and pronoun – in fact in all aspects except where the female is 'different' or separated. Then the female form is used. Thus whenever the female noun, verb or pronoun is used, we see woman as an exception. Moreover, the traditional Rabbinic Bible has often been read to imply that the male excludes the female. Such is the classic reading of the *Shema: veshinantam levanecha*. 'Teach them diligently to your children' is how our prayerbook translates these words,[4] but *midrash* takes an exclusive rather than inclusive view. *Levanecha velo livnotecha* – 'to your sons, but not your daughters', thus excluding them from the *mitzvah* of Torah study.[5]

This exclusion through language and linguistic assumptions has rendered the women in the Bible marginal or virtually invisible.

This is the reality today's feminist biblical scholar confronts. Whether rejecting, revising, reclaiming or rejoicing in the Bible as it stands, interpreters focus on one of four aspects of the Bible to achieve their ends. These often interconnect, and scholars are prone to use more than one – but for simplicity, they can be divided into:

1. an examination of texts about specific women in the Bible,

2. an examination of texts written by women in the Bible;

3. an examination of texts that throw light on the life of women in biblical times; and

4. an examination of texts that challenge the basic assumptions of women and men in biblical times.

All approaches can be said to use the methodologies of literary criticism.

AN EXAMINATION OF TEXTS ABOUT
SPECIFIC WOMEN IN THE BIBLE

One way of achieving a feminist interpretation is to look at the lives of famous women in the Bible and reinterpret them in the light of modern understanding in order to celebrate them. A pioneer in this field is Athalya Brenner, whose book *The Israelite Woman*[6] looks at the social institutions and literary paradigms that define most of the female characters in the Bible. Thus, she lists queens, wise women, women poets and authors, prophetesses, sorcerers and prostitutes under institutions, and identifies mothers of great men, temptresses, foreign women and the ancestress as literary paradigms.

> Quite a few stories about women in the Old Testament are cast in recurrent moulds. The portraits of female heroines are often drawn in such a fashion that one gets the impression that these extraordinary women are not defined as individuals but, to a large extent, as generalised representatives of their type. These shared features define the figures as recognisable manifestations of the type or concept(s) they supposedly dramatise. The identification of a type which informs a particular story through its affinities with literary conventions within other similarly motivated stories, will therefore enhance our understanding of both the passage under discussion and its parallels.[7]

An example can be made by comparing the wise women of Tekoa and Abel with Abigail, David's second wife.[8]

Joab, David's right-hand man, is trying to persuade him to forgive Absalom after the death of his brother Amnon. To this end, he sends to Tekoa for a 'wise woman' whom he instructs to dress as a widow in mourning and speak to the King the words he prepares for her. The wise woman plays the part so well that David's heart is moved and she convinces him as Joab had hoped she would. What is the wisdom this woman has? The ability to act a part? To use words with particular effectiveness? How much are the words Joab's, and how much her own? She seems to use words prophetically; her story – one of blood, guilt and revenge – mirrors David's own in much the same way as did Nathan's story of the poor man's lamb when condemning David for taking Bathsheva.[9] 'This "wise" woman can be commissioned to manipulate a person to act the way she wants him to. She achieves this by enlisting the person's co-operation instead of arousing his anger or animosity. She can be counted on for sensing undercurrents of emotions and opinions and utilising them, and can adapt easily to changes in atmosphere, improvising as necessary.'[10]

The second story is similar. This time Joab is pursuing a rebel by the name of Sheba ben Bichri, who seeks refuge in the town of Abel. A wise woman appears on the ramparts to talk to Joab, who is about to besiege the town. She argues against violence and negotiates for Joab to receive the head of Sheba. Like the woman of Tekoa, she is called wise. Like her, she negotiates in a tricky situation and like her avoids unnecessary bloodshed. Moreover it is unclear whose words she is speaking here – her own or the townspeople's. 'The woman is widely respected; everybody listens attentively to what she has to say, from Joab to her fellow townspeople. She has authority and influence. After assessing the situation she does not hesitate to comply with Joab's demands and ensures that they are carried out. Therefore it seems that she is no ordinary woman.'[11] Brenner concludes that the wise woman was some kind of professional, known for her skill and possibly wearing a distinctive garment that would render her recognizable as a person with authority.

How different is Abigail who met David in his youth. Having fled from Saul, David organized a protection racket around Maon in order to feed his troops. Abigail's husband refuses to comply with David's request, but Abigail steps in and, dressed becomingly, she enters David's camp. She offers David a carefully constructed speech through which she negotiates the sparing of her husband's land. Though the powers of persuasion are similar to those of the wise women, and likewise her objective is the avoidance of violence, there are notable differences. Abigail's words are her own. She is motivated by self-interest and the situation is a local difficulty, not a matter of state. We realize she is different from the very fact that she is named, and she is called not a wise woman, but an intelligent one – *tovat sekel* – one with common sense.

These and other comparisons highlight Abigail, and define her character more sharply than had her story been told in isolation. Yet she in her turn works as a preparatory character for an even more greatly defined individual: Judith in the Apocrypha, who also demonstrates powers of persuasion and takes matters into her own hands.[12]

AN EXAMINATION OF TEXTS WRITTEN BY
WOMEN IN THE BIBLE

It was a man, Schlomo Goitein, who in the 1960s first high-lighted the fact that women were also authors of the Bible.[13] Goitein made a study of Yemenite society when the immigrants who arrived on 'Operation Magic Carpet' first settled in Israel. Little was known of the Yemenite way of life, and it came as something of a revelation that their society was so different from other Arab-Jewish communities and so – in the term common then – primitive. Goitein and others believed that they had been influenced less than any other society by the culture around them and were in a sense living in a time warp that linked them directly with the communities of Biblical times.

The people on the whole were generally illiterate. They communicated and were entertained by songs, and an elaborate culture of singers and their songs developed as an important means of communication.

> Some of these singers were men, some women. They did not sing together, of course, and the sexes appeared to have different functions. To the men fell the duty to sing of sacred matters. They sang in Hebrew and had a specially honoured place in their society. But the women were equally honoured. Theirs was a quasi-sacral role, requiring a special initiation, that suggested to Goitein a function reminiscent of that of the bands of prophetesses of which we read in the Bible.[14]

The women would sing in the vernacular rather than in Hebrew, and their subjects were current events, local gossip and popular songs. 'They sang of famines and persecution, of great victories in battle, both past and present – they sang of the War of Independence for example.'[15] Compare this with the songs of Miriam and Deborah, for example, or the song of the women that so enraged Saul: 'Saul had slain his thousands, but David, his ten thousands.'[16]

Through Goitein's work several significant areas have been identified as possibly authored by women and many feminist scholars have followed his lead – in particular in examining the *Song of Songs*, which particularly lends itself to this type of appraisal. While it is hard to say for certain what literature is authored by a woman and what by a man, J. Cheryl Exum[17] has pointed out the number of verses that describe the woman's attitude and feelings in the *Song*. In identifying poetic cycles within the work, she makes it evident that the majority of speech is the woman's while the man very often is seen through her eyes. Phyllis Trible suggests that the garden in the *Song* is a deliberate echo of the Garden of Eden. What went wrong there – the inequality of the relationship between the man and the woman – is righted here: 'There is no male dominance, no female subordination, and no stereotyping of either sex.'[18]

A great deal more work is still needed in this field, but the recognition of female authorship has enabled many feminists to look differently at the Bible. Rather than see it as a text whose aim is to keep women subordinate, they recognize the diverse nature of the Bible; some texts speak more to men, others more to women, but both sexes have a share in its rich heritage.

AN EXAMINATION OF TEXTS THAT THROW LIGHT ON
THE LIFE OF WOMEN IN BIBLICAL TIMES

In her book *Discovering Eve*,[19] Carol Myers combines the sciences of social anthropology and archaeology with the tools of critical Biblical exegesis and of women's studies to focus on the person of Eve.

> Eve. We all think we know her and understand what she represents. Few come of age in the western world without having heard of Eden. It would be difficult to find anyone unfamiliar with the primeval couple, Eve and Adam. Nearly all of us have read, or have had read to us, the simple and powerful narrative of Genesis 2 and 3 ... Nevertheless, biblical scholars in recent years have taken on the task of rediscovering the pristine Eve. The woman of Eden is being given her own voice, a voice radically distinct from the one heard through the unsympathetic, if

not misogynist, words of influential figures ... For centuries we have looked at Eve through the distorting lenses of patriarchal, Judeo-Christian tradition. Now perhaps we can examine her in the clear light of her own world.[20]

In her study of Genesis chapters 2 and 3, Myers presents a picture of early Israelite society with Eve as a representative of 'Every Woman'. But, rather than Every Woman as subject to the will of Man – and, from her creation, subordinate to him – there emerges from Myers's studies a strong, independent female whose contribution was vital to the economic survival of the community.

This is a society of pioneer settlements on the barren mountainous regions west of the Jordan, a logical setting for the first Israelite villages, since the fertile plains reaching to the sea were fully occupied and well defended. This explains the description in Genesis chapter 2 (in contradiction to that of the first chapter) of the world before creation as a barren, waterless waste and why the first thing God does for man is to plant a garden.

Myers claims that a pioneer settlement in an unfriendly environment, and dependent on all its labour, male and female, to survive, results in a society where women have more or less equal status with men. It is only with urbanization and increased wealth – when society is no longer economically dependent on all its citizens – that women lose their value. No longer needed to work the fields to ensure the physical survival of the community, they are free rather to enjoy its profits, to spend their time raising their children, to be decorative rather than useful. Their role changes in this sort of society and as a consequence, so does their status.

At the centre of the book lies a close reading of the story of Eve in the Garden of Eden, in particular the oracle in Genesis 3:16:

I will greatly multiply your pain in childbearing;
in pain you shall bring forth children.
Yet your desire shall be for your husband,
and he shall rule over you.

Myers is careful not to call it a curse, but an oracle. The language and context suggest that what happens here is a consequence of the actions in the Garden, not a punishment.

Comparisons of the use of the Hebrew word *heron* in other contexts suggest that in the first line it should be translated not as childbearing, but pregnancy. Yet we know that the pain comes in the actual birth, rather than the nine months before it. Myers explains, then, that the word *issabon* actually does not mean pain in a physical sense, but emotional toil – hard work. Thus her first line reads, 'I will greatly increase your toil and your pregnancies.' In the second line, she claims the root *yld* used transitively in the Bible refers not to the act of giving birth, but to the raising of children. *Esev* again means mental anguish. Thus her second line reads: '[Along] with travail shall you beget children.'

'Travail', according to Myers, reflects 'the stresses of parenting rather than the strains of parturition'. As every mother knows, the pain of childbirth is nothing to the anxiety which accompanies the child's perilous journey towards adulthood. Add to this the ever present threat of dying in childbirth and one asks: why do the women, working so hard on the land, submit to so many pregnancies? The answer lies in the next two lines, translated according to Myers:

For to your man is your desire,
And he shall predominate over you.

Thus we have a picture of Eve as Every Woman in the harsh context of early Israelite settlement. A life of incessant work – and of incessant childbirth. Childbirth is necessary to produce the intensive labour needed to work the farms in the unforgiving landscape; and childbirth is made possible because despite the dangers, despite the anguish, the woman's desire for her husband overrides all other considerations. It is that which has mastery over her – nothing else.

AN EXAMINATION OF TEXTS THAT CHALLENGE THE BASIC
ASSUMPTIONS OF WOMEN AND MEN IN BIBLICAL TIMES

Ilana Pardes in some ways represents the next stage in feminist biblical interpretation. No longer simply attempting to describe the women in the text, to champion them and push their presence back into the minds of the general public, Pardes goes beyond the female characters to look at their relationship to the male and the reasons why the characters are described in the way they are. What is included about them and why? What is excluded about them and why? Along with the narrative and generalized moral purpose of the Bible there are texts that do not quite fit – countertraditions that hint of something else. That is what Ilana Pardes tries to explore in her book *Countertraditions in the Bible.*[21]

> The Bible is a far more heteroglot text than Higher Criticism would have it. The stratification which biblical scholars have offered is a good point of departure, but it does not suffice. What Higher Criticism didn't dream of dealing with … is the gender code, or rather, the possibility of friction between heterogeneous perceptions of femininity. My goal is to explore the tense dialogue between the dominant patriarchal discourses of the Bible and counter female voices which attempt to put forth other truths.[22]

In her Introduction she raises the question of Miriam in Biblical tradition. Most stories about Miriam are positive and affirmative. She first appears as Moses' sister – unnamed, but the agent of Moses' salvation, ensuring he comes to no harm and that Pharaoh's daughter employs his mother as wet nurse. Nothing more is heard of her until the crossing of the Reed Sea. Then, described as Prophetess, she leads the women of Israel in song. 'But her career as a leading poet is curtailed. She disappears from the picture for the rest of Exodus and is never mentioned in Leviticus.'[23]

Miriam reappears in the midst of the wilderness wanderings in a story that 'does not have a prominent status in the collective memory'. It is the story of her complaint, along with Aaron, about the 'Cushite' woman Moses had married. Her punishment for questioning Moses' authority is a bout of leprosy. It is not a pleasant story. The question is, what is its purpose?

On one level, it seems to be yet another story of female rivalry – like that of Sarah and Hagar, or Rachel and Leah. But why then is Aaron involved? A second strand would suggest it to be a 'canonization story', affirming the authority of Moses. But this raises the question, why is Aaron not punished too?

The story does seem to contain within it a certain misogyny not present in the other narratives regarding Miriam. After this story we hear no more of her until her death.

But this picture of Miriam is not the residing image. In Deuteronomy 24:8–9, where the laws of leprosy are described, Miriam is seen as an exemplar. In Micah 6:4 she is described as a national liberator. The fragmentary evidence suggests that there is more to Miriam's story than is recorded.

> One should bear in mind that non-canonical texts such as the Book of the Yashar, the Book of the Battles of Yahweh, and the Chronicles of the Kings of Judea are in fact mentioned in the Bible. These titles may not sound too promising as far as women's histories are concerned, but they serve as evidence for the corpus of ancient Hebrew literature which has been lost.[24]

Add to that the famous legends about Miriam's well, which followed the camp of Israel throughout her life and disappeared at her death; and that of Miriam's tambourine, which caused even the animals to dance – legends that appear in the *Midrash*, but are in all probability of far older provenance. Taken together these present a picture of a woman who may well have been of far greater significance to the early Israelite cult than the text gives credence to.

What Ilana Pardes does is to reverse the givens in the Bible and bring to prominence those countertraditions, with unexpectedly rich results.

> I have tried to show throughout this book that if such a line of inquiry is taken in reading the Bible, if we avoid patriarchalising or depatriarchalising it and defy comfortable categorisings of the biblical stance on gender issues, then unknown reaches of the past may open out before us, revealing faded figures of female precursors who, through their very otherness, have the striking capacity to add much colour and intensity to our own lives.[25]

Colour and intensity have certainly been the hallmarks of feminist biblical critics. Men have had two thousand years in which to study the Bible, make their comments, derive their conclusions. Two thousand years, in which they have absorbed the traditions of their forebears, built upon what was already said, inherited their assumptions. Women have come in at the tail-end of that process, with all the right tools of intellect and training, but without a link to the chain that enables them to build unquestioningly upon the work of their fathers as do their male counterparts. Women come, moreover, with their own experiences of life and of study, experiences that do not necessarily echo those of men. While feminist Bible scholars may not have discovered a new method of studying the text, they have imbued the old methods with fresh insight, and the result is very exciting.

I am not sure what Lily Montagu would have thought of these approaches. I hope she would have approved, for much of the work can be said to parallel Liberal Judaism in its method, and much can infuse Liberal Judaism and its thought.

For a start, nothing in feminist criticism is taken for granted. The text is examined for itself, not through the lens of tradition, nor via any particular accepted method of interpretation. Then, the study involves taking risks and – at times – of going horribly wrong. Yet the process contains a dynamism and an excitement which makes it the only really fruitful area of Bible study happening today. Then again, role models are important. The discovery of women in the Bible who are intelligent, educated and active, returns us to a relationship with the text that is immediate and relevant to our lives. Finally, the fact that after two thousand years we can still find something so new in the Bible, points us to a future of endless possibilities. Likewise, we have not come to the end of Liberal Judaism; after one hundred years, this is only the beginning.

NOTES

1. G. Aguilar, *The Women of Israel* (London, 1845), p. 1.
2. E. Cady Stanton, *The Woman's Bible* (New York, 1895).
3. Ibid., Introduction.
4. Siddur Lev Chadash, p. 15.
5. Sifrey *Va'etchanan*.
6. Athalya Brenner, *The Israelite Woman* (Sheffield: JSOT, 1985).
7. Ibid., p. 87.
8. II Samuel 14; II Samuel 20:14–22; I Samuel 25:2–42.
9. II Samuel 12.

10. Athalya Brenner, *A Feminist Companion to Samuel and Kings* (Sheffield: Sheffield Academic Press, 1994), p. 35.
11. Ibid., p. 36.
12. For a detailed discussion of Judith, see S. Shulman, 'A Woman of Strong Purpose', in S. Sheridan (ed.), *Hear Our Voice* (London: SCM, 1994).
13. S. Dov Goitein, 'Nashim veYotsrto Sugei Sifrut baMikra', *Iyyunim baMikra* (Tel Aviv, 1963) p. 298.
14. S. Sheridan, 'The Song of Solomons' Wife', *Hear Our Voice* p. 69.
15. Ibid.
16. I Samuel 18:7.
17. 'A Literary and Structural Analysis of the Song of Songs', *Zeitschrift fur die alttestamentliche Wissenschaft* 85 (1968), pp. 47–9.
18. 'Depatriarchalising the Old Testament', in E. Koltun (ed.) *The Jewish Woman* (New York: Schocken, 1976), pp. 217–41.
19. Carol Myers, *Discovering Eve* (Oxford: Oxford University Press, 1988).
20. Ibid., p. 3.
21. Ilara Pardes, *Countertraditions in the Bible* (Cambridge, MA: Harvard University Press, 1992).
22. Ibid., p. 3.
23. Ibid., p. 7.
24. Ibid., p. 11.
25. Ibid., p. 155.

12

Compelling Commitments: A Radical Re-think of Liberal Judaism?

ELIZABETH TIKVAH SARAH

Since its inception in 1902 in the form of the Jewish Religious Union, Liberal Judaism has not only acknowledged that Judaism is dynamic and changing, but has also empowered individuals to make choices and take responsibility for their own Jewish lives. What is more, from the outset, the three principal founders and exponents of Liberal Judaism – Claude Montefiore, Lily Montagu, and Rabbi Israel Mattuck – were determined not only that Judaism should progress to meet the challenges of the modern world, and make a contribution to the task of creating an ethical and just society, but also that reason and intellectual integrity should be the hallmarks of this new progressive form of religion.

As early as 1899, Lily Montagu, writing about 'Spiritual Possibilities of Judaism Today', declared: 'Together we must sift, with all reverence, the pure from the impure in the laws which our ancestors formulated in order to satisfy the needs of the age.'[1]

In one of his early sermons, entitled 'Religious Education', at a Jewish Religious Union Shabbat service, Claude Montefiore argued: 'Religion needs the mind; it needs thought and study, as well as ardour and love ... Where Jewish students, or rather Jewish teachers, so often fail is that they learn the answers of past ages to past problems, but hide their ears and envelop their minds from the questions and problems of today.'

Forty years later, Israel Mattuck, who became the rabbi of the newly established Liberal Jewish Synagogue in 1912, wrote:

'Judaism cannot for all time be confined in a form given it in the past. It must develop as life changes and human thought grows ... Judaism ... was always a developing religion. Rabbinic Judaism developed out of Biblical Judaism; the Bible itself records a development of Judaism. Liberal Judaism is its latest development.'[2]

Unlike Orthodox Judaism, which regards the Torah as God's word, pure and simple, *min-hashamayim* – 'from heaven', Liberal Judaism understands the Torah as the work of human beings – that is why the founders of Liberal Judaism felt able to teach about the necessity of adapting our Jewish inheritance to meet the needs of the age. What is more, they taught their co-religionists to look not only to the Torah for guidance, but also to the insights and wisdom of generations of our people from Sinai until this day. And so, in searching for guidance rather than instruction, from the inception of Liberal Judaism, Liberal Jews have made the assumption that it is up to individuals to decide what they will and will not do. God, the creator of the world and the liberator of our ancestors, may continue to address us in myriad ways, but the God Liberal Jews apprehend is neither a dictator nor a commander.

It follows that unlike Orthodox Jews, who bear *ol hamitzvot*, 'the yoke of the commandments', Liberal Jews are free to choose. But is it as simple as that? Some years ago I argued that:

> The Progressive debate on the performance of *mitzvot* seems strangled in a false dichotomy. On the one hand there are God's commands – the preserve of the Orthodox ... On the other hand there is 'personal choice' – the privilege of the Progressive Jew ... But what does 'personal choice' mean? Why do individuals 'choose' one practice or another ... what impels me to perform this ritual and not that one?[3]

In the spirit of the legacy of Lily Montagu, Claude Montefiore and Israel Mattuck, Liberal Jews are required to think, and to rethink, to develop our thinking. But thinking alone is not enough. An appeal to our reasoning faculties alone cannot explain the choices individuals make. When Claude Montefiore argued that 'Religion needs the mind; it needs thought and study, as well as ardour and love', he was not suggesting that 'ardour and love' are unimportant. A holistic approach to religion in general and to Judaism in particular, involves both the mind and the heart. Put another way, Judaism needs us to think and also to feel – to engage the whole of ourselves: our minds, our hearts, and our creative energies.

A narrative text from the Torah illustrates the seamless connection between mind and heart. The story of the Exodus begins, not with the liberation of the slaves, but rather several years earlier with the defiance of the Hebrew midwives, Shifra and Puah, who refused to obey Pharaoh's order to kill the newborn Hebrew baby boys (Exodus 1:15–21):

> The king of Egypt said to the Hebrew midwives – of whom the name of the one was Shifra, and the name of the second was Puah – he said: 'When you are helping the Hebrew women to give birth, and you look at the birthing stones, if it is a son then you shall kill him, but if it is a daughter, you shall let her live.' But the midwives feared God, and did not do as the king of Egypt had said to them; rather they kept the boy children alive. So the king of Egypt called for the midwives, and said to them: 'Why have you done this thing, and kept the boy children alive?' Then the midwives said to Pharaoh: 'Because the Hebrew women are not like the Egyptian women; for they are lively, and they give birth before the midwives are coming to them.' So God dealt well with the midwives; and the people multiplied, and became very mighty. And it came to pass that because the midwives feared God, He made for them houses.

How did Shifra and Puah find the courage to defy the genocidal decree of the mighty Pharaoh? The midwives 'feared God', the text tells us, but how was it that they did not fear the supreme overlord of Egypt? What impelled the midwives to save life, rather than follow orders and kill the newborn baby boys? Where did their courage and that impulse come from?

Rather than respond to these questions directly, let us turn to another text from the Torah, from the *parashah* (portion), *Nitzavim*, which is read in synagogues on the last Shabbat of the year – and then reread in Liberal communities on *Yom Kippur* morning (Deuteronomy 30:11–14):

> For the commandment (*ha-mitzvah*), which I command you today is not too complex for you, nor too remote. It is not in heaven that you need to say: 'Who will go up to heaven for us, and fetch it for us, that we may hear it and do it?' Neither is it across the sea that you need to say: 'Who will cross the sea for us and fetch it for us that we may hear it and do it?' For the matter (*ha-davar*) is very near you, in your mouth and in your heart to do it.

The text speaks of 'the *commandment*, which I command you today', not 'the *commandments*'. According to the mediaeval commentator, Nachmanides (Rabbi Moshe ben Nachman, who was born in Gerona in Spain, in 1194) – 'the commandment' is a specific reference to the command to repent, since the chapter begins with the exhortation to return to God.[4] For the majority of commentators, on the other hand, right up to the present day, 'the commandment' refers to the whole of the Torah, or at least to all of the laws set out in Deuteronomy.[5]

My approach to the text is radically different – and my starting point is the very last phrase: 'For *the matter* is very near to you *in your mouth and in your heart* to do it – *Ki-karov eilecha ha-davar me'od; beficha u'vilvavecha la'asoto.*' Most translations of the text render *ha-davar* as 'the word'. Now *hadavar* also means 'the matter'. My interpretation of the text involves making sense of the singularity of *ha-mitzvah* and the singularity of *ha-davar* in the context of the closing image, 'in your mouth and in your heart'. What is in each individual's mouth and heart? The text may be simply talking about the awareness of the Divine Command, in which case the translation 'the word' is appropriate. Alternatively, it may also be suggesting something about a capacity within each individual, in which case, the translation 'the matter' fits better: 'For the matter is very near to you in your mouth and in your heart to do it.'

Why 'in your mouth and in your heart' and not 'in your heart and in your mouth'? Although animals communicate with one another in various ways, human beings, alone among the creatures of the earth, attempt, using language, to make sense of our existence. Not content simply to live and reproduce ourselves, we want to shape the world around us to our own design. Each one of us has that power within us – a power that we discern as we watch a baby learning to speak; a power that centres on our ability to think and feel: 'The matter is very near you, in your mouth and in your heart to do it.'

To do what? Human beings don't just talk, think and feel. Our talking, thinking and feeling leads to action – and we don't act alone. We are biologically driven. We are also fashioners of culture. We formulate rules and regulations and ethical codes, and impose them on ourselves. We build complex social structures. And alongside all our utilitarian pursuits, our mouths and our hearts crave and create beauty in every place.

We don't know what the author intended, but what the passage suggests, so evocatively, is that the feeling of command comes from within us. It is neither complex nor remote; it is neither up in heaven, or somewhere else across the sea; it is neither the responsibility of God, nor of a leader who will fetch it for us; rather, 'The matter is very near you, in your mouth and in your heart to do it.'

As human beings, we feel compelled to act. But where does acting as Jews come into the equation? While all humanity thinks and acts, the concept of *mitzvot* is Jewish. As Jews, we not only have a love affair with words, we have a very particular sense that we must translate words into deeds, into *mitzvot* – the actions that we feel compelled to perform. But what determines which actions we feel compelled to perform?

The key to answering this question lies in the very next section of text: 'See, I have set before you this day life and good and death and evil ... therefore you shall choose life, that you and your descendants may live' (Deuteronomy 30: 15, 19b). *U'vacharta bachayyim* – 'therefore you shall choose life'. What else can we do? 'The matter is very near you, in your mouth and in your heart to do it.' What could be nearer to us, in our mouths and hearts, than the matter of choosing life? And, of course, it begins in our mouths: for a suckling baby, choosing life is a simple biological urge. So, what does it mean for us to choose life? And what makes choosing life a *mitzvah*, a specifically Jewish compulsion? Perhaps, what makes choosing life Jewish is simply the fact that, having looked death and evil in the face so often, we continue to feel compelled to choose life and good – which doesn't mean that, like everyone else, we don't sometimes choose death and evil instead.

Many of the *mitzvot* we find in the Torah, which have been incorporated into codes of law the world over, originate in a

Near Eastern Code, formulated by Hamurabi, an enlightened king of Babylon, who reigned between 1945 and 1902 BCE, and undertook the codification of Babylonian law. As I indicated earlier, the compulsion to create rules and regulations is common to all humanity. The Jewish version of this universal phenomenon is born of our particular adventures and ordeals as a people. And so, for example, while the Ten Commandments may be shared by humanity, for Jews, there is an eleventh – a specifically Jewish commandment, the *mitzvah* to remember everything: the joy as well as the torment. The *mitzvot* have emerged out of our experience: 'Justice, justice you shall pursue' (Deuteronomy 16:20) because we have known injustice. 'Seek peace and pursue it' (Psalm 34:15) because we have been destroyed many times. 'When a stranger resides with you ... you shall not wrong him... you shall love him as yourself, for you were strangers in the land of Egypt.' (Leviticus 19:33–4). We haven't been strangers in the land of Egypt for millennia. But there have been other furnaces, other houses of bondage. Again: in the face of death and evil, what can we do but choose life and good?

What can we do, but be ourselves? No one is simply a human being. Each one of us is a particular human being, with particular characteristics – and being Jewish is part of our particularity, if we so choose: whatever the circumstances of our birth, we are all Jews by choice today. But it's not a free choice. Liberal Jews are caught between the demands of the world, indifferent to our particular Jewish compulsions, and the demands of Jewish particularity, which seem to require us to see the world exclusively through Jewish eyes.

So what do we feel impelled, compelled, to do as Liberal Jews? If we look back one hundred years to the establishment of Liberal Judaism in Britain, it is clear that the founders of that movement, intoxicated with the gifts of the Enlightenment and modernity, felt compelled, almost exclusively, by the drive to transform society into an oasis of reason, truth, justice, compassion and peace. For them living as a Jew was primarily a matter of acting on the ethical principles of Judaism, set down in key sections of the Torah, and highlighted by the prophets. Ritual was a secondary matter only, and only those ritual acts that 'made sense', or which 'enhanced life' – principally, those associated with study, prayer and the celebration of *Shabbat* and the Festivals – became integral to Liberal Judaism.

But after the *Shoah*, Liberal Jews, in common with our sisters and brothers throughout the Jewish world, felt compelled by other concerns. Not only had modernity catastrophically let us down, but also, tasting the acrid smoke of the ovens in our mouths, and our hearts breaking with grief, we longed to savour the flavour of particularity once more, our hearts beating to a Jewish rhythm all of our own. The compulsion to choose life – to choose Jewish life – after our journey through the 'valley of the shadow of death' became almost overwhelming. We were all survivors now. Jewish ethics were no longer enough to sustain us. Liberal Jews, too, needed to nourish our souls by participating in uniquely Jewish acts.

Almost sixty years have elapsed since the *Shoah*. During that time, the Jewish world has been undergoing a process of transformation triggered by a number of developments, including the establishment of the State of Israel, the collapse of Communism in the East, and the liberation of women in the North and West. And so, too, Liberal Judaism has been changing. More than that, Liberal Judaism has been in the forefront of change in the Jewish world, because Liberal Judaism acknowledges that Jewish life is connected with the world and our responsibilities as Jews extend beyond the needs of our people to encompass, not only humanity, but God's creation as a whole. Moreover Liberal Judaism recognizes that life makes demands on us now, impels us to continue to work out how we should live today. Liberal Judaism is not only, like Orthodox Judaism, a response to modernity, to the consequences of intellectual Enlightenment and political emancipation. Liberal Judaism provides a framework for working out how to live Jewishly in the modern – and now post-modern – world; an attempt to reinterpret and re-engage with our Jewish inheritance now. We may not feel commanded by an external force, but we do feel compelled not only to cherish our inheritance, but also to engage in recreating it in the context of the needs of the present, and in relation to the world around us.

But Liberal Judaism is not just about what *we* do. In embracing modernity, Liberal Judaism acknowledged the crucial role played by individuals in defining and perpetuating communal life. So, while Orthodox Judaism continued to demand compliance with divine authority, with the dawn of the modern age, in true liberal fashion, Liberal Judaism championed the autonomy of the individual. But if individual Jews are free to choose, what happens when autonomous individuals decide not to make Jewish choices?

Herein lies the fault-line in Liberal Judaism – but not only Liberal Judaism: eleven years ago, Rabbi Tony Bayfield published his second statement on 'Reform Judaism and the Halakhic Tradition',[6] in an attempt to create a framework for ensuring that individual Jews exercise their autonomy in a responsible manner. Drawing inspiration from Franz Rosenzweig, Tony Bayfield presents a 'Star of Jewish Responsibility' – a combination of intra- and inter-relationships, which together encompass the arena of Progressive Jewish life. Focusing first on the particular context of Jewish life, he demonstrates the way in which the Jewish individual stands in the centre of an 'inner triangle', and negotiates his or her personal autonomy in relation to 'Our God', 'Jewish Tradition', and 'Jewish Community'. There is no such thing as absolute autonomy. No one chooses in a vacuum. Modern Jews make Jewish choices by reflecting on the choices they wish to make in the context of the *particular* responsibilities that define Jewish life.

Having explored this inner triangle, Tony Bayfield goes on to acknowledge 'that there is a second, outer triangle reflecting Jewish existence in a larger world and the theology of our relationship to humanity'.[7] So, standing in the centre of an 'outer triangle', the Jewish individual's autonomy is also mediated by *universal* responsibilities in relation to *'Ein Sof'* – the ineffable mystery of the Eternal One, the human family's shared store of 'Wisdom and Knowledge', and 'Humanity'. Taken together, these two triangles form a *magen david* – 'The Star of Responsible Autonomy'.[8]

Tony Bayfield's 'Star of Responsible Autonomy' is an excellent attempt from the perspective of Reform Judaism to work out how the individual negotiates his or her autonomy in the context of the external demands of Jewish life. In addition to these external demands, I would argue that it is essential to explore the internal dynamic within each individual that propels individuals to act. Which brings us back to that passage in Deuteronomy: the 'you' that the text addresses is the people as a whole – 'For the commandment which I command you today', etc. And yet, the image with which the passage closes suggests that 'you' also means the individual: 'For the matter is very near to you in your mouth and in your heart to do it.' Within the Biblical universe, the feeling, thinking individual is subordinate to communal demands and dependent on communal structures. By contrast, in both the modern and post-modern realms of contemporary existence (excluding the numerous traditionalist societies that still exist the world over), not only has the individual taken centre-stage – politically, economically and culturally – but situating the individual in the context of the complex nexus of primary family relationships, the disciplines of psychology and psychoanalysis have helped us to recognize the ways in which each individual is both determined and determining, motivated by their own complex inner world, and negotiating their needs and desires in relation to significant others.

'For the matter is very near to you in your mouth and in your heart to do it.' If it is, indeed, in each individual's mouth and heart to act, then the central task of Liberal Judaism is to create a framework for that action, which acknowledges not only that the individual Jew will make 'choices', but also that these choices are constrained by internal and external factors. To distinguish this framework from that of both Rabbinic Judaism, rooted in divine commandments, and Classical Liberal Judaism, rooted in the principle of informed choice, I prefer to speak of compelling commitments emerging out of our ongoing experience (including the ongoing interplay between external and internal forces) framing the choices individual Jews make.

So what are these compelling commitments? For the committed Liberal Jew, they not only revolve around God, Torah and the People Israel, but also connect our lives as Jews with the lives of other peoples, and embrace concern for the world as well as concern for Jewish life.

Compelling commitment one: embracing Jewish teaching and engaging with knowledge in the wider world

The commitment to nurture and cultivate our own Jewish lives and the life of the Jewish people as a whole, by continuing to learn and engage with the Torah, with our Jewish stories, teachings and traditions, and by participating in the various ritual acts, which celebrate life with Jewish flavours, colours and tones.

And:

The commitment to engage with the accumulating wisdom of the world, to study and to learn about the major developments in human knowledge, and to find ways of ensuring that the developing wisdom of humanity in all its dimensions connects with and informs Jewish teaching.

Compelling commitment two: sustaining the Jewish community and repairing the world

The commitment to honour both those who have gone before us and those who are yet to be born, by becoming links in the chain of the generations of our people, and by maintaining, restoring and re-creating Jewish communal life in Britain, in Israel, and throughout the world.

And:

The commitment to love not only our neighbours, but also the stranger in our midst; to liberate the oppressed, protect the vulnerable, and support the fallen; to pursue justice and to seek peace; to participate in the great task of *Tikkun Olam*, the repair of the world.

Compelling commitment three: the Eternal is our God and the Eternal is One

The commitment to explore the meaning of existence, to journey, to search, and to *listen* out for the voice of the Eternal, who calls each Jew to become part of *Am Yisrael*, the people of Israel who 'struggle with God', and to strive to sanctify life each day through our actions and our relationships.

And:

The commitment to acknowledge that the Eternal is One, and to work together with all the peoples of the world to recognize the essential unity of existence in all its diversity.

As Liberal Jews face the complex, contradictory challenges of life in the twenty-first century, including the increasing diversification of life patterns and choices, it is becoming increasingly necessary for Liberal Judaism to articulate a holistic approach to living as a Jew that acknowledges and encompasses all the dimensions of our humanity – the intellectual, the spiritual, the ethical, the emotional and the physical. In the *parashah*, *Va'etchanan*, in Deuteronomy chapter 6, we find the verses that form the first paragraph of the *Shema* (6:4–9) – because it begins with the imperative: '*Shema Yisrael!*' – 'Listen Israel!' The principal statement of the *Shema* opens with the words: '*V'ahavta eit Adonai Elohecha bechol-levavecha u'vechol-nafshecha, u'vechol me'odecha*' – which is usually translated along the lines of, 'You shall love the Eternal One your God, with all your heart, with all your soul, and with all your might.'

Translation from one language to another is always tricky, and this translation is a little misleading. Starting with the phrase *bechol-levavecha*, it's important to acknowledge that within the biblical worldview, the word *leivav* denotes mind more than heart – so 'with your entire mind' would be more precise.

If we then turn to the phrase, *u'vechol-nafshecha*, we find that in the biblical context, where there is no distinction between 'body' and 'soul', a better translation of *nefesh* would be 'being'. In the accounts of Creation we find, in Genesis chapters 1 and 2, the expression *nefesh chayyah* – 'living being' – is used not only to describe the first human being (2:7), but also the living creatures (1:20, 21, 24): each creature, both human and animal, is *nefesh chayyah*, a living being. Not surprisingly, the English word 'being' is much more nebulous than the Hebrew word *nefesh*. The physicality of *nefesh* is brought home in Genesis chapter 9, which focuses on the aftermath of the flood. Previously vegetarian, after the flood humanity is permitted to eat flesh – *basar* – but not to eat blood – *dam* – because the blood is the *nefesh* of the animal (9:4). So, the *nefesh* is the stream of life that flows within each one of us, and what makes each one of us palpably alive.

And what of *u'vechol me'odecha*? The translation, 'might', conveys the physical energy and abundance associated with *me'od*, but because it's so familiar, we don't often pause to explore the implications of the word. If *leivav* connotes the 'mind', the centre of understanding, and *nefesh*, 'being', the pulse of life within us, *me'od*, 'might', expresses the power to act on and shape the external world around us.

The key to unlocking the significance of the use of the three words, *leivav*, *nefesh* and *me'od*, lies in the very first word of the passage – in the imperative, '*Shema!*', 'Listen!' The people Israel are exhorted first to listen, then to think about and make sense of what we hear, then to experience it within our whole being, and finally, to act. In the account of the aftermath of revelation in the *parashah Mishpatim*, Exodus chapter 24, the text tells us that the people responded to Moses' reading of the Book of the Covenant by saying, '*na'aseh v'nishma*', 'We will act and then we will listen' (24:7). This phrase, *na'aseh v'nishma*, has become the central catchphrase of Orthodox Judaism. For Liberal Judaism, on the other hand, the process is reversed: *nishma v'na'aseh* – we listen first, and then we act. But it is not enough to listen, think and act: the challenge of living as a Jew involves all of who we are – all our mind and heart, all our being, all our capacity for creativity and action. Moreover, while the text of the *Shema* addresses the singular collectivity of the people Israel, ultimately, it is individuals, individual Jews, each one of us, who are challenged to listen, to think, to engage, to experience, to act: 'For the matter is very near to you, in your mouth and in your heart to do it.'

Let us now return to the story of those defiant midwives. Who were they? The Hebrew with which the tale opens is '*Vayomer melech mitzrayim lameyalledot haivriyyot*' – 'The king of Egypt said to the Hebrew midwives' (Exodus 1:15). This suggests that Shifra and Puah were Hebrews themselves, not simply, midwives of the Hebrews. If the latter were intended by the text, the Hebrew would be *l'meyalledot* (preposition only) – not *lameyalledot* (preposition plus definite article). So, these Hebrew women chose to defy the command of the mighty tyrant, Pharaoh. Moreover, although the midwives 'feared God' (1:17), neither God, nor any other power told them to save the baby boys – the matter was in their mouths and their hearts to do it. Despite the order to kill, what they felt compelled to do was save life.

With their hands, midwives bring new life into the world. When we speak about 'taking action', we often use the metaphor of 'hands'. The story of Shifra and Puah's defiance transforms a striking image in *parashat Nitzavim* into a profound truth: compelling commitments begin in our mouths and hearts and become manifest in the work of our hands. The time has come for Liberal Judaism to reconfigure our completely appropriate emphasis on intellectual integrity and right conduct within a holistic approach to Liberal Jewish action that attempts to engage every dimension of our complex humanity, as we grapple with the challenge of ensuring that Judaism lives in our lives: 'For the matter is very near to you in your mouth and in your heart to do it.'

NOTES

1. L. Montagu, 'The Spiritual Possibilities of Judaism Today', *Jewish Quarterly Review* (1899), p. 226.
2. I. Mattuck, *The Essentials of Liberal Judaism* (London: Routledge & Kegan Paul, 1962), p. 140. First published in 1947.
3. E. I. Sarah, 'Wearing My Tallit: Thoughts on the Hidden Agenda', in *Women and Tallit*, Working Party on Women and Judaism (London: RSGB, 1987), p. 27. Second edn, with a new introduction by D. Eimer and E. Sarah, 1997.
4. *Mikra'ot Gedolot*, the compendium of mediaeval commentaries.
5. E.g., J. H. Hertz (ed.), *Pentateuch and Haftorahs* (London: Soncino Press, 1956).
6. T. Bayfield, 'Reform Judaism and the Halakhic Tradition', in *Sinai, Law and Responsible Autonomy* (London: RSGB, 1993).
7. Ibid., p. 21.
8. Ibid., p. 23.

13

A Religion for the Future

SIDNEY BRICHTO

Human beings are religious animals. Since civilization has been recorded, people have had what we today would call a religious outlook. Our earliest ancestors felt dependent on powers beyond their grasp or control. They believed that, like humans, the gods could be placated and seduced by presents and flattery. Sacrifices, hymns and ritual dances were employed to win over their divine masters. The world was 'peopled' with gods who were responsible for drought and floods, heat and cold, fertility and barrenness. Those who were 'capable' of reading divine omens were the scientists of their day. In the eyes of the populace, they could predict events and so influence them.

Religion provided the foundation of law and order, however absolute and ruthless it may have been. Sovereigns based their authority on the will of the gods. Both natural blessings and catastrophes were at the divine behest and therefore viewed as reward or punishment for obedient or erring kings and people. In Judaism, God's prophets anointed the kings of Israel and Judah. The priests, and not of Israel alone, insisted that the rule books were given by their gods. In certain cultures, the rulers claimed divinity for themselves. Generally, however, arrogance was considered to be the greatest human sin. *Hubris* led to the fall of the Greek heroes.

Religious rituals helped individuals cope with birth, maturity, sex and death. Transitions through life were accompanied by acknowledging that supernal beings were the masters of all, because without their blessings there could be no security. The sources for human procreation and mortality were established by a mythos which provided reconciliation to the human condition of birth, decline and death. An example of this is the story of Eden when Adam and Eve are pictured as sacrificing physical immortality in exchange for divine intelligence. Besides the gift of knowledge, the compensation for the loss of physical immortality is sex and children, who give their parents a sense of eternity of a different kind.

When our ancestors became more aware of the workings of nature and understood the alternations of the seasons and the influences of the heavenly bodies, there still remained a pressing need for religion to establish the sources of human authority and to help the individual cope with nature's cycle. For example, barren women needed the opportunity to appeal to someone to give them fertility so that their lives could have a purpose. The seasons would sometimes go awry, and people needed to believe that their priests could successfully intercede on their behalf if the rains did not arrive when expected, causing drought and famine.

Even today, when it would be considered irrational to expect divine intervention to end drought or floods; even when our future physical and mental health is made the responsibility of scientists, doctors and pharmacologists; even today, when our rulers do not rule through divine right but through the democratic process – there is still a need for religion. Science answers the 'hows' of life but not the 'whys'. While scientists have not found the cure for cancer, they know why it is pernicious and in certain cases how to arrest its development. But they cannot explain why, as I recently read, one child before his *Bar-mitzvah* should be fated to suffer in quick succession the death of both his mother and father from this disease. Of course, religion cannot explain it either, but one of its purposes is to maintain the faith of its believers in the face of these tragedies.

No one can doubt that in the Western world the three monotheistic religions – Judaism, Christianity and Islam – are losing ground. This is so first and foremost among the educated but also among the growing number of prosperous people whose minds and bodies are so 'distracted' by the pleasures on offer, that they feel no need to ask questions about life's meaning or purpose and do so only if struck by personal tragedy. Adherence to the three faiths is more and more based on the desire for identity and the desire to hold on to old values in an age of rootlessness. Mobility, materialism and relativism, however, have been welcomed by most of the new generations.

Those steeped in tradition and the past may want to hold on to religion, but even they are beginning to doubt its efficacy in meeting their 'spiritual' needs.

In Judaism, the desire for identity is the most powerful force for keeping Jews within the fold, even though their synagogue attendance is rare and their observances minimal. Jews who do not observe the Day of Atonement, the holiest day of the Jewish year, may still want a synagogue wedding and a burial plot in a Jewish cemetery. The intense need for some kind of Jewish identity is especially surprising when one considers the strength of anti-Semitism, which should discourage one from wanting to retain a distinctive Jewish identity. The very opposite is the case – there are many who affirm their Jewishness *only* when there is a threat of anti-Semitism.

Equally, there will be non-believing and non-practising Christians who want a church wedding. The symbolism of the sacrament gives the couple a sense of emotional warmth and the security of permanence in their marital state, even if they do not believe in the Christian basis for marriage. Christenings have the same popularity for the non-observant. Ministers, recognizing this, are seeking to increase their active members by rationing the privileges of baptism and christenings to individuals who are involved in their churches. In doing so, they will be following the pattern of the demands made by certain synagogues on Jewish families who wish their children to be *Bar* or *Bat-mitzvah*.

If identification with a group has become the primary reason for belonging to a faith community, it can minimize the importance of that faith's intellectual and spiritual content. This has in fact happened. Nor is this surprising, for how can religions postulated on the faith in a supernatural and intervening God have credibility with modern or post-modern humanity? Ancient Judaism was the creation of the prophets as was Christianity the creation of the apostles and the church fathers. But few rational Christians today believe that Jesus was bodily resurrected and is waiting for his Father's instruction to usher in the Final Judgment at the end of days. Nor are there many Jews who believe in bodily resurrection when they will rise from their graves and march to Jerusalem for *their* final judgment.

The belief in an apocalypse is, I maintain, rooted in the realization of the 'powerlessness' of God to redeem His people in the material world. Some two thousand years ago when the Jews believed in the Messiah, it was possible to envisage a man of flesh and blood, perhaps from the family of David, who could restore independence to the Jewish state. The Jews were not the only nationality who had rebelled against Rome. The odds for victory were not good, but had they not been told that their ancestors had been redeemed from Egypt and had wrestled independence out of the Syrian Hellenists? As God had helped them them in the past, He could help them now. The catastrophic destruction of Jerusalem as the Jewish centre in 70 CE followed by the crushing of the Bar Kochba rebellion, with the martyrdom of the great rabbis who supported his campaign, forced even the most pious Jews to surrender any hopes for achieving independence through an earthly human agent.

It was then that, ironically, Jews were compelled to take the view accepted by their Christian counterparts over a century earlier, namely, that salvation could come from God *without* the human mediation of a Moses or a David. The apocalypse prophesied by the post-exilic prophets was taken literally as the only 'realistic' hope. If there was a God who had the power to save and could no longer do so through his human heroes, then He would, in His own good time, do it on His own. The Christians waited for a divine Jesus – the Son of God – to return triumphantly. The Jews waited for a supernatural messenger of God sent on a white charger to usher in the messianic age – the end of days.

Of course, these religious fantasies arose out of legendary histories which became acts of faith: God had miraculously delivered the Israelites from Egypt, God had conquered Canaan for them and through His divine power, their greatest King, David, achieved an empire. None of this actually happened in this way, but the prophets affirmed this faith to persuade the Israelites to worship Yahweh, the supreme moral God, and to impress upon them that only by worshipping Him would He protect them as part of the covenant – the mutual defence treaty – between Him and them.

The prophetic theology was simple. The Jewish God rewards and punishes His people in accordance to their loyalty to His moral laws. The Jews did not give up this faith even when their behaviour could in no way justify the calamities, climaxing in the Holocaust, which befell them. Deep in their hearts, Jews knew that God had broken His part of the treaty. He has ceased to be their personal saviour. No longer did He send heroes such as Moses and Joshua and David to win His victories for Him. But what could they do? How could they let go of their faith in an almighty, redeeming and loving God of Israel? If they did, they would have to deny His salvation in the past and what would they have left? Without God in their hearts, what would unite them with their past glories, with their fellow Jews in the present, and with their hopes for the future? The Jewish leadership and pious Jews did not let go, but most Jews did. They ceased to believe. Some were happy for the sake of Jewish identity to keep the Jewish norms. A growing number, however, have decided that without faith, the customs and practices have also become meaningless, and are not prepared to keep them merely out of filial piety.

The Christian scenario, even without a Holocaust to confront, is not all that different. Religious wars, internecine struggles within religions, anti-feminism, homophobia and a reactionary or irrelevant approach on most personal issues such as birth control and the scientific ability to assist in the creation of children, has led to disenchantment. I do not know enough to express a view on the attitude of Muslims, but from what I read and hear, it would also appear that Islam is having a decreasing impact on the younger generation in countries of the West, where the goals and pleasures of secular culture leave little time for attention to religious belief or practice.

In an age where God has become irrelevant to human concerns and interests, religious extremists focus on the importance of common modes of behaviour which unite their religious communities and which exclude the 'pernicious' secular influences which threaten their value systems. But this very desire to bind a religious community closer together by insisting on obedience to literalism and atavistic codes, alienates those who, while wishing to retain their identity as part of a community, also have no intention of withdrawing from the larger society of which they are a part. The literalism and parochialism of the ultra-orthodox groups of all organized faiths make liberal religious thinkers of different faiths feel greater sympathy for each other than for members of their own community. A Liberal rabbi is more able to communicate with a liberal Christian minister on matters of faith and religious values than with a Lubavitch rabbi. It is obvious that Jewish university students will feel more at home with Christian students than with Jews who could not join them in drinking a pint at the Students' Union bar. Thus the tension between religious demands and secular tolerance is even diminishing the attraction of shared roots and a common faith identity.

Over lunch, I was discussing the challenge of the subject of this essay with a friend, Christian Tyler, who was then a distinguished features writer for the *Financial Times*. He told me that as the consequence of an Israel Diaspora Trust meeting which he, the editor of this volume and I attended, he was inspired to contribute a piece on religion to the paper's Millennium Day issue. The meeting to which he referred consisted of representatives of the three Abrahamic faiths who had met to discuss fundamentalism and religious extremism. With his permission, his spoof is printed below:

From the *Encyclopaedia Galactica*
CHRISTIANITY
Usually known as Christianity, Old Tradition (OT), to distinguish it from the New Tradition (NT), one of the constituents of Universal Monotheism (UM). UM was the religious federation created at the Conference in Cairo in 2025 of the Common Era, under the chairmanship of King Charles III of England, part of the Isles (see O'Doherty, Padraig). UM emerged as a reaction to the rise of secularism and materialism, the fall in attendance at public worship and the 'privatization' of religious doctrine.

It satisfied demands for married clergy, women ministers, and a 'democratic' liturgy. A decisive factor was the 2020 discovery of apparently intelligent – and therefore potentially redeemable – beings elsewhere in the galaxy. Christianity (OT) continued to be practised mostly in rural areas, alongside literal versions of Islam and Judaism. Adherents of UM understand God to be a spiritual ambience of cosmic force, a concept owing much to modern animism, Ecoism and New Ageism.

Financial Times, 1 January 2000

Smiling aside, there are insights here on the challenges facing traditional religions. To summarize, the role of religion in the past has been:

1. the explanation of natural phenomena (science);
2. the desire to influence natural forces (magic, sacrifice, prayer);
3. the provision of a book of rules for human society (divine law and the divine right of kings); and
4. an emotional structure for the human condition (the life cycle from birth to the separation of death).

The role of religion in the present appears to be limited to the fourth category. In addition, it can still offer a sense of community and security in the face of modern alienation, which is the consequence of the growth of cities, sophisticated technology, the abundance of choice and the autonomy of individuals to decide their own destiny.

It is the freedom of the individual in modern society which provides the greatest opportunity for the religion of the future. Human beings in the Western world now have opportunities for fulfilment beyond the wildest dreams of past generations. There is so much wealth, that, were it not for the competitive instinct fuelled by the urge for greater productivity and material consumption, most men and women could be spending most of their time on leisurely interests; and taking advantage of their unique human gifts, which is what distinguishes us from the rest of the animal world, namely, the intelligence to look beyond our immediate needs and desires, to become co-creators with God in the worlds of art and culture.

The religion of the future – be it a confederation of like-minded individuals from various religious traditions capable of modernizing their ancient beliefs, or the creation of new faiths – will need to provide a moral purpose for our personal existence as members of society. Excluding those 'literalists' to whom Christian Tyler refers (whose piety will enable them to live in the past while the world passes them by) religion will need honestly to reinterpret its traditional theology. Traditional religions will need to accept that the moral foundations of their faiths are based not on historical happenings but on myths created by religious geniuses to impose their moral visions in the brute reality of the human condition.

The role of the religion of the future is to raise humans to their highest level of capacity. It is to fight the rampant materialism which feeds upon itself and which makes intelligent, creative beings slaves to the machines and the service industries which they themselves create. Were Judaism to provide the motivation to stretch human intelligence and creativity, it would be fulfilling the demands of the prophets and rabbis who called on Jews to act like God. In this, it will be no different from a mature Christianity which demands that the followers of Jesus become like him – the Sons of God. The differing myths and images which inspired this common aspiration for a divine future of humanity should not be allowed to divide one religious group from another, but rather should be appreciated as different aspects of religious creativity.

Moving on from the religious challenge of religions to inspire each individual to realize his or her own personal fulfilment, they must *also* inspire a sense of communal responsibility. Individual realization is what Hillel meant when he said 'If I am not for myself, who will be?' The individual seeking to achieve collective fulfilment for *all* men and women is what Hillel meant when he said, 'If I am only for myself what am I?' The religion of the future needs to offer all people the opportunity to achieve their own individuality by transcending family and national barriers to identify with the aspirations of every other human being in the world. This too is nothing more than the vision of the prophets for a world living in harmony, with no one going hungry or fearing for the security of their own lives and families.

An important role for religions of the future will be to inspire governments to shift their objectives from productivity to creativity and from national self-interest to universal responsibility. Many will say that this is an unrealistic hope. That may be so, but religion is about what *ought to be* and not what is. It is, at least, more rational than the expectation of our religious forebears for an apocalypse from heaven. Also, it once again places the responsibility for individual and collective redemption on human rather than supernatural intervention. A mature religious faith must accept that divine intervention was never evident except when God inspired His human creatures to achieve His goal for them – an age of universal peace and justice.

As a participant of a group of Progressive rabbis to the Vatican in January 1999, we were received by the President of Italy. I was somewhat taken aback when I was chosen, without notice, to respond to his desire for an explanation of Progressive Judaism, but a spirit inside me came to the rescue. 'Mr President,' I said, 'In science and in the arts, we all believe that we stand on the shoulders of the geniuses of past ages, and so we progress into new creativity. Progressive Judaism believes that for religions also the future is more important than the past, that we too should be open-minded to spiritual needs created by the challenges of modern life. If there can be progress in science and art, there can be also progress in religion.'

The founders of our movement set those standards of intellectual integrity which put us in a unique position to follow their example in being at the vanguard of radical religious thinking. Only by doing this will we keep our ancient faith as a beacon of light in our own lives and be able to share with our own community and all humanity.

14

Immortality and Resurrection: Maimonides and the Maimonidean Controversy

ALEXANDRA WRIGHT

Rabbi Yehudah said: 'When the blade touched his neck, the soul of Isaac fled and departed, [but] when he heard His voice from between the two Cherubim saying to Abraham, "Lay not thine hand upon the lad" [Genesis 22:12), his soul returned to his body, and [Abraham] set him free, and Isaac stood upon his feet. And Isaac knew that in this manner the dead in the future will be quickened. He opened [his mouth] and said: "Blessed art Thou, O Lord, who quickeneth the dead."'[1]

Narrative *midrash* is perhaps the most powerful vehicle of Rabbinic theology. The anonymous eighth-century author of *Pirke de Rabbi Eliezer* narrates his own account of the binding of Isaac, based on earlier *midrashim*, in which the father's knife touches the neck of his son so that his soul departs from his body. The homilist focuses his listener's attention not on the motifs of sacrifice, obedience to God or the relationship between father and son, but on the *chatimah* (the concluding eulogy) of the second blessing of the *Amidah* and its theme of resurrection. Thus Isaac becomes the originator of the *Gevurot* and a scriptural basis is found for the doctrine of the resurrection of the dead.[2]

Maimonides, who lived from 1135 to 1204, takes up the theme of an eschatological future in the *Mishneh Torah*, his great code of Jewish Law, and in the chapter known as *Perek Chelek* in his commentary on the Mishnah. One work, the *Treatise on Resur-rection*, was written in response to an accusation made by Samuel ben Ali, the Ga'on of Baghdad. In each of these works, Maimonides both explores and defends his own position in regard to resurrection, the nature of the soul, reward and punishment and immortality.

In exploring these concepts, in particular the question of resurrection, Maimonides' views underwent severe attack to the extent that he was accused of denying the doctrine of resurrection. It was not so much the eschatological vision that remained the contention between Maimonides and his contem-poraries (although that was always the more explicit issue), as a fundamental understanding of Scripture and its exegesis that was at stake. 'Essentially the problem is one of the possible synthesis or the absolute antithesis between monotheistic revealed faith and intellectually formulated philosophy.'[3] This was not a new problem within Judaism. There had been both encouragement and deprecation of Greek learning and wisdom; mostly, the latter had prevailed, as this *midrash* on a passage from the *Shema* reveals:

> 'And you shall speak of them when you lie down' etc. (Deuteronomy 6:7). That is, make them the main thing, and not something ancillary so that all your business may be with them, and that you do not mix up other things with them, or say, 'I have learnt the wisdom of Israel; now I will go and learn the wisdom of the nations of the world.'[4]

Hellenization frequently stood for apostasy, so that the 'thick darkness' that fell upon Abraham (Genesis 15:12) alluded to Greece, 'that darkened the eyes of Israel with its decrees'.[5] While the Bible spoke little about resurrection and indeed immortality, Talmudic Judaism had affirmed a doctrine without necessarily entering into precise terms in order to define it. The area of eschatology known as *Ma'aseh Merkavah* was a subject on which speculation was treated with a good deal of caution. Humanity's intellect was unable to grasp fully the ideas about the next world, and therefore it was preferable to steer clear of defini-tions or descriptions. Where Maimonides fell foul of his critics was when he used and drew on philosophical expressions rather than the Talmudic affirmations more firmly rooted in tradition.[6]

Maimonides' conceptions of the soul were inspired more by Arab neo-Aristotelians than by traditional Jewish teachings on the subject. Avicenna, the Arab physician and philosopher (980–1037), combined neo-Platonic ideas with Aristotelian concepts and theories and posited the immortality of the rational part of the soul by bringing five arguments to prove that the rational soul is a self-subsisting substance and is not dependent on one's physical faculties. Thus, despite the fact that a person becomes more frail with age, the very opposite happens with the rational faculty of the soul. Insight, mental acuity and wisdom remain profound and intelligent.[7]

Given that the rational soul is a self-subsisting substance, does it perish with the body or does part of the soul or the whole soul survive? Avicenna adopts the Aristotelian conception of the human soul, which sees it as being of a purely spiritual substance. Therefore it can exist independently of the body. Both Avicenna and Maimonides called the tenth and last of the 'Separate Intelligences', the 'Active Intellect', and it was this intellect which enabled the rational faculty of a person to change from a state of potentiality to a state of actuality. 'When the human mind acquires the intelligible forms and is capable of comprehending universal concepts, the rational faculty becomes the acquired intellect.'[8] Avicenna divided the soul into three faculties: vegetable, animal and rational. The first two 'souls' perish with the destruction of the body, while the rational soul, that is the acquired intellect, survives.

Maimonides defines his conception of the soul in the opening chapters of the *Mishneh Torah*.[9] The soul of all flesh is its form, given by God. The acquired knowledge found in humanity constitutes the individual's complete form. Of this form it is said in the Torah: 'Let us make humanity in our image, according to our likeness' (Genesis 1:26). In other words, the form is the consummation of knowledge and there is nothing compared to it. When the body perishes, the form is not destroyed, but endures for ever. 'And the dust returns to the earth as it was, but the spirit returns to God who gave it' (Ecclesiastes 12:7). It is no accident that this definition of the soul is found at the beginning of Maimonides' Code. It follows from his statements about God's existence, God's uniqueness and unity and the command to love, fear and sanctify God's name. Knowledge of God ultimately resides in God and thus humanity's way to God is through reason. It is the rational soul that links the individual with God and that enables us to understand something of God's essence.

In his commentary on the Mishnaic tractate *Avot* known as *Shemonah Perakim*, Maimonides emphasises that the individual has only one soul, although that soul has different functions. It is wrong to believe that these functions constitute different souls in themselves; they are merely activities of the soul and are called 'physical', 'vital' and 'psychical'. Each of these three activities in turn governs various functions of the soul. The physical or nutritive faculty governs nourishment and pro-creation; the vital or sensory faculty controls movement, sense-perception and imagination; while the psychical or rational faculty governs the power of reasoning, which is exclusive to humankind alone. Just as the doctor is required to know the whole of the body before a part of it can be treated, so therapy of the soul requires knowledge of the whole, although these 'divisions' of the soul are not component parts in the same sense that limbs are a component part of the body.

The highest possible reward for the individual is immortality of the soul.

> Each soul that is being spoken of in relation to this matter, does not require a body for its spirit, only the form of a soul, that is the knowledge with which it grasps the Creator according to its strength, and with which it grasps the separate intelligences and the rest of these things. And this is the form which we explained in chapter four of *Hilkhot Yesodey Ha-Torah*. In this context, it is called a 'soul' (*nefesh*). This life, in which there is no death – hence its name, life, because the only kind of death is the death that happens to the body, and in the world to come there is no body – is called 'eternal life' as it is said 'the life of my lord shall be bound up in the bundle of the living' (I Samuel 25:29). And this is the highest possible reward, and the highest possible good, and this is what all the prophets desired.[10]

In *Moreh Nevukhim* (I, 41), Maimonides defines the word *nefesh*, which can among other things, he says, denote reason. 'That is the distinguishing characteristic of humanity, as in 'As the Eternal One lives that made us this soul' (Jeremiah 38:16). It denotes also the part of the human being that remains after death ...' While the welfare of the body is prior in time and nature, the ultimate perfection is the welfare of the soul, which is greater in nobility. The commandments found in the Torah promising reward or threatening punishment are a means, not towards a material end, but towards a far greater, nobler end. Most of the commandments serve for the attainment of moral virtues, not as ends in themselves, but in preparation for something higher. The acquisition of rational virtues which teach true opinions concerning divine things is the ultimate end, and this is what gives the individual true perfection.[11]

Therein, however, lies an ambiguity. Is Maimonides discussing the immortality of the soul or of the intellect? In *Moreh Nevukhim* (III, 70), he does suggest that the 'soul' that is to live on after death is not the same soul that entered a human being at their birth:

> For the soul that remains after the death of a human being is not the soul that lives in that person when they are born; the latter is a mere faculty, while that which has a separate existence after death, is a reality; again, the soul and spirit of a human being during their life are two different things; therefore the souls and spirits are both named as existing in human beings; but separate from the body only one of them exists.

In *Perek Chelek*, however, that distinction between the 'soul' and the 'intellect' does not appear to be quite so explicit. In this section of Maimonides' Commentary on the Mishnah, we are given an introduction to the Principles of the Faith in which Maimonides delineates different classes of thinkers who are characterized by their interpretations of statements made by the Sages and their beliefs about the world to come and resurrection. It is quite clear from the language he uses that Maimonides deprecates those who luxuriate in visions of a physical paradise, or who accept a corporeal form of resurrection. They are utterly mistaken in their interpretation of the Sages, he argues. Their literalism is absurd because they cannot distinguish the way language is used metaphorically in order to teach a moral lesson.[12]

Maimonides' exposition of reward in the afterlife begins with this introduction in *Perek Chelek*: 'Know that just as a blind person can form no idea of colours, nor the deaf comprehend sounds, nor a eunuch feel the desire of sexual intercourse, so the bodies cannot comprehend the delights of the soul.' Whatever is outside us is non-existent to us. Because we experience the world through our bodily senses, we imagine that the material world universe must constitute total reality. But we are wrong, because human beings have little conception of the pleasures awaiting the soul, only because they cannot penetrate the mysteries of the spiritual world and cannot conceive, except in lengthy contemplation, of non-physical, non-material pleasure. Maimonides allegorizes the famous passage from *Berakhot* 17a, understanding the phrase 'crowns on their heads' to mean the preservation of the soul in the intellectual sphere: 'In the world to come, there will be no eating and no drinking, no washing and no anointing, and no marriage; but only the righteous sitting with crowns on their heads enjoying the splendour of the *Shekhinah*.'

Maimonides' interpretation of the phrase 'enjoying the splendour of the *Shekhinah*' removes any possible misconstruing of this image. Souls will reap bliss in what they comprehend of the Creator, 'just as the Holy *Chayyot* and the other ranks of angels enjoy felicity in what they understand of God's existence'. Maimonides' understanding of immortality is specific, referring to the third faculty of the soul, the active intellect which is promised this reward as a result of exemplary intellectual and moral standing. The intellect of the soul (he still calls it the 'soul') continues for ever, like the continuation of the Creator, and this is the highest and greatest bliss to which humanity can aspire.

Hermann Cohen points out that Maimonides' interpretation of *Berakhot* 17a is defined in terms of the Aristotelian *theoria*, the enjoyment of thinking that is transformed here into the enjoyment of God's splendour. 'Thus theoretical intellectualism has become religiously purified.'[13] In the world to come, the self draws near to God in a world whose superiority and nobility pales everything else into worthless insignificance:

> The highest form of goodness will be the soul in the world to come, yet there is no way in this world in which to attain and to know this for the only kind of good that we

know in this world is the perfection of the body, and this is what we desire, but this same goodness, however strong it is, has absolutely no value in the world to come and cannot be compared to the goodness of material things in this world ... It is what David spoke of when he said: 'How great is Your goodness which You have stored up for those who fear You' (Psalm 31:20).[14]

Maimonides' thirteenth principle of faith affirms the resurrection of the dead. It is clear from the introduction to the principles that this affirmation is unequivocal:

The resurrection of the dead is one of the cardinal doctrines of the Law of Moses. He who does not believe in this has no religion and no bond with the Jewish faith. But it is the reward of the righteous only, as is shown by the statement in *Bereshit Rabbah*, 'The great benefits of the rain are for both the righteous and the wicked, but the resurrection of the dead applies to the righteous only.'

This is developed further in the *Treatise on the Resurrection of the Dead*, in which Maimonides makes it clear that this doctrine is a miracle connected with belief in God and God's existence: 'It is faith and not reason that can persuade us that it will occur, just as we have learned with certainty that other miracles have been performed on our behalf. But as it does not appertain to the natural, no proof can be advanced in support of it.'

Added to the transcendent and miraculous nature of this doctrine is the problem of the lack of Biblical verses that might substantiate belief in resurrection. Maimonides acknowledges the controversy that arises between those who doubt the truth of the doctrine of resurrection and those who are compelled to strain the sense of the verses in the Bible. Material substances will decompose slowly, he argues and belief in resurrection must rest on belief in the possibility that the impossible can become possible even when it appears to contravene Scripture. If God has created the world out of nothing, then surely we must concede the possibility of miracles, including the resurrection of the dead.

The controversy which broke during Maimonides' lifetime and continued into the early fourteenth century, centring on

Christian Spain and Provence, was not straightforward. Samuel ben Ali was outraged by Maimonides' statements in *Hilkhot Teshuvah* which, he said, appeared to deny the physical resurrection of the dead. Furthermore, a statement to the effect that the Messiah would not have to perform miracles or wonders or revive the dead appeared to compound the misunderstanding. If that were the case, then resurrection would be unnecessary and consequently would not occur. Maimonides dismissed the Ga'on's comments as women's tales, arguing that many of the 'resurrection' passages in the Bible are figurative or rhetorical, such as Ezekiel's vision of the dry bones. Only the passage from Daniel (12:2, 13) should be taken literally to teach the fact of re-existence. Resurrection will occur soon after the Messiah has appeared and will constitute the first great act of redemption.

Some scholars perceive a basic ambiguity around the theme of resurrection in Maimonides' writings. 'Why did Maimonides on the one hand establish physical resurrection as a pivotal principle of faith and on the other, limit resurrection to a minor and temporary function of the penultimate promise?'[15] Was it that Maimonides was unable to depart completely from affirming the doctrine of resurrection because it was already embedded in Talmudic tradition, and in attempting a synthesis between his Greek concepts and the most un-Greek one of bodily resurrection, he failed? Did part of him wish to 'explain away' the doctrine as part of the framework of promises that was to keep the Jewish people within the fold as moral and ethical people so that they would earn the higher good of the spiritual world to come? Perhaps he gives away his attitude to such doctrines as bodily resurrection in the introduction to *Perek Chelek*, in which he makes an analogy of the small child who has to be bribed with food and clothes as rewards for studying Torah. Humanity is frail and needs those kinds of 'props' to keep it on the straight and narrow – for not all individuals are so inclined to contemplation of God's existence for its own sake.

One of Maimonides' main detractors was the twelfth century Talmudic authority, Rabbi Abraham ben David (1125–98), who may have attempted to diminish Maimonides' overall popularity by his sometimes moderate, but occasionally intemperate, outbursts of invective. The statements of the Sages, argues the

'Rabad', all prove that the dead will be resurrected in their bodies.[16]

It was Meir ben Todros Abulafia of Toledo, author of *Sefer Kena'ot*, however, who sparked off the resurrection debate during Maimonides' lifetime. Meir considered Maimonides' doctrine on resurrection heretical and he penned his accusation in the form of letters to rabbis of southern France, known as the 'sages of Lunel'. They largely defended Maimonides against the accusations of Meir, who was out of his depth in the argument. Meir was a literalist, and his motivation in attacking the Rambam was to protect the traditional beliefs of Israel. He objected to Maimonides' apparent denial of bodily resurrection in *Hilkhot Teshuvah*. For Meir, the promise of resurrection was part of God's covenant with Israel. Nor could he accept Maimonides' interpretation of *Berakhot* 17a because it destroyed that promise: 'If God does not resurrect, where is the hope for those who at great personal sacrifice obey this law?'[17] In other words, Meir wanted to see some kind of material reward for practising the commandments. It was part of the covenant. If Israel kept the commandments, God would reward her. If you removed a belief in bodily resurrection, what remained? A response was sent to Maimonides from Aaron ben Meshullam, the son of the founder of the Lunel school. Aaron defended Maimonides' views, noting that Maimonides labelled anyone who did not believe in resurrection a *kofer* (unbeliever) or an *apikoros* (heretic). Aaron actually probably misinterpreted Maimonides by labelling him a disciple of Sa'adiah, who posited two resurrections – one during the Messianic Age followed by a second death, and a second period of resurrection in the world to come. Certainly, Maimonides speaks only of one resurrection, but when that resurrection takes place is not clear in his temporal scheme of things. Was it to precede the Messianic Age or come after it? It would make more sense to see resurrection taking place before the Messianic Era, so that the dead could arise to enjoy the life of that time. Yet it would be wrong to speculate too closely and to spell out the details. The doctrine of resurrection belonged to the realm of the miraculous and of faith. Perhaps the absence of details laid him open to criticism and controversy.

Although Meir might bring numerous proofs from Scripture to support his argument and would back his vigorous defence of resurrection with Talmudic and midrashic texts, it was clear that the argument was shifting imperceptibly to the issue of the limits of allegorical interpretation of Scripture. For some mediaeval thinkers, Biblical stories were to have no reality whatsoever, but were merely allusions to philosophical doctrines. Meir's belief in resurrection and the world to come were very firmly tied up with the position of Israel in this world. Resurrection was a hope for the oppressed and for a people in exile.

Maimonides also had admiring supporters. Abraham ben Nathan ha-Yarhi (*c.* 1155–1215) was troubled by a seeming contradiction between Psalm 72:16 and *Berakhot* 17a, the former promising gastronomic rewards, the latter non-physical rewards. If the Messianic Age was a political framework, marking the end of Israel's captivity and dispersion, the *olam ha-ba* was an exclusively spiritual age that would mark the salvation of the righteous. Similarly, Sheshet ha-Nasi ben Isaac of Saragossa (1131–1210) attacked Meir and couched his defence of Maimonides within philosophical frames of reference. To Sheshet, resurrection was 'the pleasure of the intellect which cleaves to its Creator'. In this respect, resurrection was seen as a philosophic immortality of the activated intellect when freed from its prison, the body, and rejoicing in the light of God. Resurrection would not take place at any one time in the future, but occurs daily. It does not rupture the material order of things, but is the happy result of that potential which God placed within certain individuals at their birth. The intellect once activated can live for ever.

This is certainly some distance from the expressions of Maimonides on the *olam ha-ba*, immortality of the soul and resurrection. Nowhere does Maimonides state that resurrection occurs daily. At his most vigorous, he exhorts Israel to sustain its belief in resurrection, in the same way that it sustains belief in the existence of God. That is certainly not to deny resurrection, but to declare belief in the *chatimah* of the second benediction of the *Tefillah*, placed in the mouth of Isaac following the return of the soul to his body. That Maimonides was misinterpreted and indeed reinterpreted by thinkers such as Sheshet was due not only to the sensitivity of such issues as resurrection and immortality, but to the climate of opinion which grew more frightened and more wary of the power of philosophy. For some, Maimonides had crossed a boundary and overturned the image of the world and God. For others, he had transformed the crude and literal statements of the Sages into a transcendent and spiritual expression of Jewish faith.

NOTES

1. G. Friedlander (ed.), *Pirke de Rabbi Eliezer* (New York, 1971), Chapter 31.
2. For a full discussion of this *midrash* and earlier sources, see S. Spiegel, *The Last Trial* (New York: Jewish Lights, 1993) pp. 28–37.
3. *Encyclopedia Judaica*, 'Maimonidean Controversy', Vol. 11, pp. 745 ff.
4. *Sifre, Va'etchanan*, para. 34, f. 74a.
5. *Genesis Rabbah, Lech L'cha.* 44.17.
6. D. J. Silver, *Maimonidean Criticism and the Maimonidean Controversy* (Leiden, 1965), p. 27.
7. For a full description of Avicenna's five arguments proving that the rational soul is a self-subsisting substance, see H. Blumberg, 'The Problem of Immortality in Avicenna, Maimonides and St Thomas Aquinas' in *Eschatology in Maimonidean Thought*, J. I. Dienstag (ed.) (Ktav, 1983), pp. 77–9.
8. Ibid., p. 80.
9. *Yesodey Ha-Torah* 4:8.
10. *Mishneh Torah, Hilkhot Teshuvah* 8.3.
11. *Moreh Nevukhim.* III, 54.
12. *Moreh Nevukhim.* III, 43; II, 29.
13. H. Cohen, 'Immortality and Resurrection', in *Eschatology in Maimonidean Thought*, J. I. Dienstag (ed.) (Ktav, 1983), p. 39.
14. *Mishreh Torah, Hilkhot Teshuvah* 8.6.
15. *Maimonidean Criticism*, Silver, p. 38.
16. E.g., gloss to *Mishneh Torah. Hilkhot Teshuvah* 8.4: 'The words of this man appear to me to be close to the position of one who says there is no resurrection for the body, only for the soul, and by my life, this was not the prevailing opinion of the sages.' Rabad refers to *Ketubbot* 11b: 'In the future, the righteous will stand up in their garments'; *Sanhedrin* 92a: 'The righteous will not revert to dust ... but remain in their accustomed form'; and *Sanhedrin* 90b–91a: 'They will rise in their deformities and be healed.' See I. Twersky, *Rabad of Posquieres* (Cambridge, MA: Harvard University Press, 1962).
17. Meir Abulafia, *Kitab al Rasail*, Y. Brill (ed.) (Paris 1871), cited in Silver *Maimonidean Criticism*, p. 116.

15

On the Impossibility of Prophecy: A Study of Isaiah 6

JONATHAN MAGONET

I consider it a privilege and a great personal pleasure to be able to contribute to this *Festschrift* honouring the achievements of John Rayner.[1] In addition to his major role in shaping the history of Liberal Judaism in the UK and his significance as a congregational rabbi, he has made important contributions as a scholar to the study of *Halakhah*. As a liturgist he has been responsible for major innovations and the restoration of traditional materials to our prayer life. His courage in raising moral challenges to the actions of successive Israeli governments places him firmly in line with the prophetic teachings about which he has preached throughout his rabbinic career. His influence on the history of the Leo Baeck College-Centre for Jewish Education has been considerable and through his role as teacher, mentor and guide he has helped generations of rabbis during the formative years of their vocation. As a student and colleague I offer this chapter on the challenge presented to the prophet himself by the prophetic word.

The authority of the Hebrew Bible is based on its contention that it records the word of God as conveyed to human beings through the history and experience of a particular people. Much of the drama of the Bible inevitably concerns itself with the reception of the divine word, the authenticity of the record of that reception and the way it should be understood and/or interpreted. In Genesis the narrator and the biblical figures, the patriarchal families, share a first-hand knowledge of the will of God. But in the subsequent books of the Bible, with the transition to tribes and the emergence of the nation, direct access to the word of God becomes increasingly restricted. Instead the word is to be mediated through a particular cadre of people, the prophets. We commonly think of them as God-intoxicated individuals who receive a call to prophesy. But the Biblical record suggests that most of them have been formally schooled to fulfil that task. Through some process of accreditation an individual could be designated as a 'prophet' and might be employed by the royal court or the Temple. Nevertheless the exceptional individual may receive a direct word from God, as Amos attests and asserts – he is neither a prophet nor the son of a prophet, the latter phrase understood to mean an apprentice, a product of such training, a 'professional' (Amos 7:14).

Though Abraham is called a prophet (Genesis 20:7), the figure *par excellence* to be so designated is Moses. A brief narrative in the Book of Numbers suggests that subsequent prophets are successors of Moses, having received a part of the divine spirit that has rested on him (Numbers 11:23–9). When Moses complains to God that he cannot lead this people alone, he is told to summon seventy elders and a transfer of prophetic spirit is effected. Already here anxiety is expressed about this apparent threat to Moses' unique authority as God's only spokesperson. When two of the elders continue to prophesy, Joshua suggests that Moses should stop them. Moses' response is not to suppress, but instead to empower. 'Are you jealous on my behalf? Would that all the people of the Eternal were prophets and that the Eternal would put the divine spirit upon them!' (Numbers 11:29).

Nevertheless scripture will distinguish the uniqueness of Moses. In the following chapter his special status is emphasized: 'If there is amongst you a prophet of the Eternal, I make Myself known to him through a vision, I speak to him through a dream. Not so to My servant Moses, the one who is trusted in all My house. Mouth to mouth I speak to him, clearly and not in riddles' (Numbers 12:6–7). At the end of his life this distinction is again emphasized: 'There arose not again a prophet in Israel like Moses whom the Eternal knew face to face' (Deuteronomy 34:10). The rabbinic tradition will spell out the nature of this distinction: 'All other prophets beheld visions through a blurred lens, but Moses beheld visions through a polished lens, or clear glass' (Succah 45b; Gen Rabbah 91; Lev Rabbah 1:14, Yebamot 49b). Another rabbinic statement adds a further dimension to the problem of prophetic utterances. 'A single *signon*, message, was given to many prophets, but no two prophets prophesied in the same *signon*, or "style".' The implication is clear. Unlike the case of Moses, the divine message that was conveyed to the people was affected by the individual personality and experience and even literary or rhetorical abilities of the particular prophet. That is to say, a significant degree of subjectivity entered into their prophetic activity. At the very least this coloured, if not distorted, the divine word they were charged with transmitting.

The Hebrew Bible itself acknowledges the problem of the power given to the prophets and the need to guard against its misuse. How do you know whether someone who is a legitimate, that is to say officially qualified, prophet has truly been the recipient of divine instructions or at least has conveyed them accurately? Two passages in Deuteronomy seek to address this but only serve to indicate the depth of the problem. One passage allows the judgment to be based on whether or not a particular prophecy about a future event comes true. But at the time of the prophecy itself, how does one distinguish the 'true' prophet from the 'false' (Deuteronomy 18:18–22)? A second passage presents the difficult situation of a prophet who makes a prediction that comes true, which would seem to authenticate his abilities, yet who calls upon the people to go after 'other gods' – here he is to be judged as a false prophet who deserves the death penalty (Deuteronomy 3:2–6). The prophet Jeremiah will wrestle with both these problems in two narrative chapters (Jeremiah 26, 28) where he too makes a prophecy about the future, warning of destruction to come. This seemingly contradicts previous prophetic promises about the inviolability of Jerusalem. Moreover, his words are contradicted by an equally qualified prophet, Hananiah, who holds a more encouraging view of the future. In another chapter, Jeremiah condemns the way his contemporaries distort the very language of prophetic discourse and feed off each other's words (Jeremiah 23). Jeremiah's tragedy was to live at a time when he could see the destruction of his nation coming yet his warnings went against government policy and popular belief. For his pains he was tried for heresy, imprisoned and almost put to death. Indeed, the rabbinic tradition has him killed by those who forcibly took him into exile in Egypt after the Babylonian invasion.

The Bible has no record of similar problems faced by Isaiah, though he too warned of future destruction. He seems to have been a man of rank within his society, with access to the king and with an intimate knowledge of the leading groups and of their corruption. Nevertheless a rabbinic tradition has him executed by King Manasseh. In the chapter we are going to study, Isaiah draws our attention to a paradoxical role that he has to play out as a prophet. His very words of warning are to have the effect of making the people even less receptive to God's threats and even more stubborn, so that God's purpose will actually be fulfilled and destruction will come. Indeed his very calling to be a prophet is to enact this task. In chapter six of the Book of Isaiah there is an extraordinary account of his personal call and the impossible task for which he volunteers. This is a brilliantly constructed chapter and deserves a detailed analysis which will take up the bulk of the rest of this chapter.

First the text itself:

1. In the year that King Uzziah died I saw the Lord
   (*Adonai*) seated upon a throne, exalted and lifted up,
   His robe filling the Temple.

2. Seraphs stood over Him, six pairs of wings to each
   one. With two they covered their face; with two they
   covered their feet, and with two they flew.

3. They called to each other and said,
   'Holy, holy, holy is the Lord (*YHWH*) of hosts,
   the whole earth is full of His glory.'

4. The pillars of the threshold shook at the voice of the
   one who called and the House was filled with
   smoke.

5. I said, 'Woe is me for I am lost,
   for I am a man of unclean lips
   and I live among a people of unclean lips;
   yet my eyes have seen the Sovereign, Lord (*YHWH*)
   of hosts.'

6. But one of the Seraphs flew to me,
   and in its hand a hot coal, plucked from the altar
   with tongs.

7. It touched it to my mouth, saying,
   'See, this has touched your lips,

your iniquity has departed and your sin is covered
over.'

8. Then I heard the voice of the Lord (*Adonai*) saying,
   'Whom shall I send and who will go for us?'
   And I said, 'Here I am, send me!'

9. He said, 'Go and say to this people:
   Hear and hear again, but do not comprehend!
   See, and see again, but do not understand!

10. Make fat the heart of this people,
    dull their hearing,
    seal their eyes,
    lest, seeing with their eyes,
    and hearing with their ears,
    and understanding with their heart
    they repent and heal themselves.'

11. I said, 'How long, O Lord (*Adonai*)?'
    He answered,
    'Till cities lie waste without inhabitants,
    houses without people,
    and the ground is waste and desolate.

12. For the Lord (*YHWH*) will send people away
    and great will be the desolation in the midst of the
    earth.

13. But a tenth will remain in the land which shall
    revert to grazing;
    like the terebinth and oak that leave a stump even
    when cut down.
    That stump shall be a holy seed.'

The rabbis noted the difference between Isaiah's vision of
God here in chapter six and that of Ezekiel in the first chapter
of his book. Isaiah sees God seated on the throne with the fiery
seraphim around him and is immediately engaged in conversation. By contrast, Ezekiel offers an elaborate and complicated
description of the chariot of God that will become the basis of
later mystical speculation. The rabbis compared the two prophets
to a man from the country and a man from the town who
visited the king. The town dweller was sufficiently familiar with
the royal court to get on with the business at hand. But the
man from the country was so overwhelmed by the visit that he
spent a lot of his time describing the furniture!

In working through the details of the chapter we will turn to the original Hebrew text. One self-evident reason is that many of the nuances, especially those dependent on the repetition of particular words, can usually be seen only in the original. The translation, being true to the usage of the host language, will often use different words for the same Hebrew term because of the context or literary convention. In this way many internal links within the original text may go unnoticed.

The first thing to observe is the justly celebrated passage, the words said by the seraphim: 'Holy, holy, holy is the Lord of hosts, the whole earth is full of His glory!' It is a phrase that has understandably taken a central place in both Jewish and Christian liturgy, enabling us mortals below to participate with heavenly beings in their praise of the Creator. Familiarity with the passage however, may blunt us to the extraordinary theological sophistication of its meaning.

The English word 'holy' carries a weight of theological implications, some of which may distort the meaning of the original Hebrew term. The word translated as 'holy' is *qadosh*, whose root meaning is 'separate', 'set apart', 'other'. It emphasizes the 'otherness', the 'apartness' of God. The call to Israel in Leviticus 19, 'You shall be holy for I the Lord your God am holy', is an invitation to be separated out from other nations, to be specially dedicated to God. In Isaiah this sense of otherness is fully extended. The simple repetition *qadosh qadosh* would suggest that this 'otherness' of God is even more 'other'. The threefold repetition extends this even further. Such is the otherness of God that the divine becomes immeasurably distant, unknowable, or, to use the more conventional language of theology, 'transcendent'. But the second part of the sentence offers an entirely different image: 'The whole world is filled with God's glory.' Again, the traditional translation 'glory' conceals a very particular Hebrew term. *Kavod* in its original sense means 'weight', 'heaviness'. It is the word familiar to us from the Ten Commandments as 'honour' your father and your mother, perhaps in the sense, 'give due weight to your father and your mother'. In this sense *kavod* comes to mean the 'weightiness' of an individual, their selfhood, their presence. On this understanding the second part of our verse suggests that the whole world is filled, 'weighted', with the 'presence', the immediacy, of God, or to use once again the technical language of theology, the immanence of God.

Thus our sentence establishes the paradox that God is at one and the same time 'other', 'unknowable', transcendent, yet also 'present' in the world, here to be encountered, indeed 'filling' the world with that presence, immanent.

Before exploring the implications of this twofold perception of God, we need to see how Isaiah has reinforced this image in the verses that surround it. The key Hebrew term is *malei* which means 'full'. Thus verse one has God seated upon a throne, 'exalted and lifted up', while His robe *fills* the Temple. In verse three, God's 'glory' *fills* the earth. Finally, verse four has the pillars supporting the Temple shaking, the outer walls, while the House is *filled* with smoke. Both these surrounding verses reinforce the two dimensions: the image of transcendence (God on high, the outer walls) and of immanence (the robe and smoke filling the building).

This twofold imagery has a further effect, however, one that will be addressed in the rest of the Isaiah text. The imagery helps define two domains: the heavenly where the seraphim and the divine court are located, and the earthly. This distinction is a commonplace of biblical thought. The frequently used terms 'heaven and earth', either together or linked within adjacent passages, will make use of this distinction, though also play with the implications in different ways. The builders of the Tower of Babel try to reach up to heaven, only to be scattered over the face of the earth, which is their domain. A number of psalms play with the problem of where the two domains meet one another. According to Psalm 115, the making of idols is a human attempt to invade the divine domain but with earthbound forms. Our passage will now explore the problem of how communication is to be effected between the two domains.

Isaiah's immediate reaction to this vision is one of fear and horror. He is schooled in the language of the cult, so his first response is to view himself as ritually unclean (*tamei*), something that violates the sanctity of the Temple and could lead to destructive forces being unleashed on the people. (In order to appreciate the awe evoked by the Temple – the dwelling place of God – and the consequences of inappropriate behaviour within it, the nearest contemporary image is that of an atomic reactor. When properly harnessed it can provide power for society; if something goes wrong it can discharge enormous destructive energies. The strict hierarchy of the Temple personnel, priests and levites with their carefully distinguished roles, is to ensure that boundaries are not crossed that might lead to some such disaster.) Isaiah speaks specifically of his lips being unclean, an appropriate image for one whose task is to speak as the mouthpiece of God. But the imagery may also relate to the legal regulations about the leper (Leviticus 13:45). Though it is not clear what disease is intended by the biblical term translated as 'leprosy', those so afflicted have to be quarantined. Their mouths are to be covered with a cloth and as they walk they are to call out, presumably to warn those nearby of their presence: *'tamei, tamei'*, 'unclean, unclean'. Thus Isaiah evokes the state of being most distant from the holiness of the Temple and uses the term to describe himself. Not only that, but he himself dwells among a people of unclean lips. There are a number of possible ways of understanding this doubling of the image of uncleanness. It could be an excuse – it is not my fault, look where I come from! Or it could be a way of deepening the shock and danger of his state – not only am I unclean but I belong to an entire society that should be so designated. What it does do, however, is firmly link him to his people and the domain to which he belongs, as remote as possible from the holy domain he has encountered. We will see a further consequence of this linkage later.

How are the two worlds to be bridged? One of the seraphim is to be the agent, but acting with suitable caution, presumably for fear of contamination. Though itself a fiery being, the *seraph* uses the intermediary of tongs to take a burning coal from the altar and touch it against the lips of the prophet. The coal is a purifying agent, presumably because it comes from the altar, which plays a role in the removal of sins from the people. Yet this is a particularly unpleasant act against the prophet. The rabbis noted this and they found an explanation in a Hebrew word play. The term for 'coal' is ritzpah, which they divided into two words, *retzatz peh*, which would mean 'strike the mouth'. Isaiah, they thought, was too harsh in his criticism of Israel. However bad they might be in their behaviour, they were still the special people of God and should be treated with due respect and appropriate forms of rebuke. Isaiah, they thought, went beyond what was permissible, and so needed a form of purification that brought home this lesson to him.

Whatever the reason for this method of purification, the result is immediate. Isaiah hears the voice of God for the first time directly. He has become party to the internal dimensions of the divine realm. As often in the Hebrew Bible, God asks a question, one intended to evoke a response from the hearer. (We may think of the question to Adam hiding in the garden, 'Where are you?'; to Cain after the murder of his brother, 'Where is Abel your brother?') Who will go to deliver God's message to the people? Isaiah volunteers.

What follows is seemingly a negation of the whole purpose of prophecy. The more Isaiah is to convey the word – 'hear and hear again ... see and see again' – the less it is to be effective, indeed it is to be counterproductive. The full horror of this subversive activity is reinforced through a powerful literary device, a chiastic structure, where each of the three organs of understanding are listed, and then repeated in reverse order, underlining their ineffectiveness.

> Make fat the *heart* of this people,
> dull their *hearing*,
> seal their *eyes*,
> lest, seeing with their *eyes*,
> and *hearing* with their ears,
> and understanding with their *heart*
> they repent and heal themselves.

There is yet another dimension to the scandal of this action, because the prophet himself has *seen* God and has *heard* God, but will be unable to convey any of this reality to the people who so desperately need it.

If we now look again at the action of the seraph we can understand how this divine being requires some kind of barrier, the tongs, to prevent being contaminated by direct contact with this human creature. But Isaiah, having been purified by this action, has passed over into the divine realm. The effect is to cut him off from his own people who will no longer understand what he says. Thus his comment that he belongs to 'a people of unclean lips' is given an additional bitterly ironic dimension. It is no surprise that this message evokes a cry of anguish from the prophet, 'How long, O Lord?!' But the word Isaiah receives is relentless:

> Till cities lie waste without inhabitant,
> houses without people,
> and the ground is waste and desolate.
> For the Lord will send people away
> and great will be the desolation in the midst of the earth.

Only at the end comes the promise of some kind of future. A remnant will survive the destruction, like the stump of a felled tree from which some new growth may be possible, a holy seed.

I would like to draw attention to a few structural elements in this chapter before pulling together some of the implications. One of the ways of noting structural matters is through the repetition of key words. We have already focused upon the word *qadosh*, 'holy'. Its threefold repetition at the beginning of the chapter emphasizes the otherness of God, but it is important to note the return of the same root at the very end of the chapter in the phrase *zera qodesh*, 'a holy seed'. There is still a faint echo of the divine to be found in the devastated earth. The other word that similarly repeats is indeed the Hebrew word *eretz*, 'earth', which can mean 'the entire earth' or a single piece of land or territory. Just as in the opening the earth was filled with the presence of God, now the land/earth is desolate and empty of its inhabitants. The bleakness of the image is complete, even though a small ray of hope remains. It is understandable that when the rabbis chose this passage as the prophetic reading to accompany the chapters in Exodus telling of the revelation at Mount Sinai and the giving of the Ten Commandments, they felt the need to add a few verses to soften the negative impact. They chose a couple from chapter 9 of Isaiah with their promise of a messianic future of peace.

But an additional effect of these two repeated words 'holy' and 'earth' is further to define the two domains of which we spoke earlier: the divine domain of the royal court with God's throne and servants – the subject of the first four verses – and the emptied domain of the earth, which is the subject of the last three verses. In fact the full effect is to define three regions, heaven, earth and an intermediate zone, the one where the seraph and the prophet encounter one another. It is the place where the altar is located representing the Temple. The latter is, in one understanding, the place where heaven and earth meet, and where some kind of exchange is possible. Technically this divides the chapter into three distinct parts: verses 1–4, the divine domain; 11–13, the human domain; and 5–10, the intermediate zone. (Though it is only putting a cherry on the icing of the structure, it is interesting that another verb in the identical grammatical form is found in each of the three sections. The verb *yoshev* means to 'sit' and hence to 'reside', 'dwell' or 'inhabit'. In the first section, God 'sits' upon the throne. In the second, Isaiah 'dwells' among a people of unclean lips. In the final section the earth will be without 'inhabitant'. The distinction between divine and earthly existence is further reinforced.)

There is one other feature that must be pointed out, something which is always of importance in Biblical texts, namely the choice of the names used for God. Throughout the chapter the same English word, 'Lord', is used conventionally in translations, but there is an important distinction in play here in the Hebrew original. The term used of God that describes Israel's intimate relationship with the divine is the four-letter name, the Tetragrammaton. It is made up of four letters, *yod, hey, vav* and *hey*. The form seems to be an unusual version of the verb 'to be', containing features of both a past and future form of the verb. It is a fittingly unknowable word for the God who was revealed to Moses as *ehyeh asher ehyeh*, 'I am what I am', to use one possible translation. Jewish tradition from the earliest times has refused to pronounce the name, the only exception being once a year on the Day of Atonement when the High Priest spoke it aloud in the Temple. Instead a substitute was used, namely the word *Adonai*, which is a variant of the form 'my Lord', hence the conventional translation of 'Lord'. The word *Adonai* itself, spelled with the appropriate Hebrew consonants *alef, dalet, nun, yod*, also occurs. But in our chapter something unusual is happening. Both the Tetragrammaton and the consonantal form of *Adonai* are to be found. Perhaps it will now not be a surprise to learn that both forms, one of each, are to be found in each of the three sections of the chapter. Moreover it is likely that this is deliberate and a distinction may well be intended. When Isaiah says that he 'sees' the Lord (verse 1), when he 'hears' the Lord speak (verse 8) and he asks 'How long, O Lord?' (verse 11), it is the consonantal form that is used.

The Tetragrammaton is reserved for the formal title 'Lord of hosts' (verses 3, 5) and the third-person description of God sending people away from the land. I would suggest that the use here of the two names echoes the same 'transcendent/immanent' distinction we discovered at the beginning. The God that Isaiah can 'see' and 'hear' and address is the God who is immanent in the world, accessible to human experience and encounter, so the consonantal form is used. Yet that self-same God remains at the same time unknowable in the divine fullness and otherness, determining human destiny according to God's own intentions, and for this aspect the Tetragrammaton is reserved.

A final word on the structure. The threefold framework coincides with the three parts of the Jerusalem Temple. The innermost part where only the High Priest may enter is the *qodash qodashim*, literally the 'holy of holies', the most holy place. Outside is the section restricted to the priests and levites, the *heichal*, the place of the altars, the intermediate zone in Isaiah's vision. Outside that is the outer court where the people could assemble, coinciding with the earth, the human world.

Isaiah's carefully crafted piece attempts to convey both the prophetic experience and the impossibility of conveying that experience. It calls to mind an analysis by George Steiner of Schoenberg's opera, *Moses und Aron*. In the Biblical account, Moses has a speech impediment. When sent to Pharaoh, Aaron his brother is to become his mouthpiece for he is one who 'speaks very readily' (Exodus 4:14). In the opera, Moses talks but does not sing. Aaron is the one who sings. Moses, who alone is party to the word of God, is unable to communicate it directly. Aaron, who can communicate, does so, but by the very power of his command of language distorts the message that is to be conveyed. Aaron is the one who builds the golden calf.

Though Isaiah speaks out of the specific context, vocation and training of an Israelite prophet, the visionary experience he draws upon may be common to other human realms, notably that of the artist. The struggle is likewise to convey the vision through the limited means of the particular craft of the artist, who is always aware of how far the result falls short of what has been experienced and what ought to be conveyed. However inadequate, the attempt has to be made. The artist alone knows what has not been achieved or conveyed.

Of course that is not quite the end of the story or of the power of Isaiah's writing. If such communication was impossible, why did the prophets even try, and why did their followers bother to preserve their words? On one level prophecy is not actually about predicting the future, or rather, that is only a limited aspect of the task. The prophet is the one who sees most clearly the present, attempting to see the world with the detachment and moral commitment of the divine perception. If the prophet reads the future it is in terms of what is currently happening, and the degree to which the Israelites are living up to their covenantal obligations to one another and to God. The future is conditional upon how people react to the divine word in the present. So we must take a step back from Isaiah's actual words and ask about his strategy, and how his words might have been received, at least in the form that we have them in the book that bears his name. For whatever else, Isaiah is a master of rhetoric. By proclaiming that he will not be understood, that his words will indeed dull the minds of his listeners, perhaps he is seeking to have the opposite effect. This would be a desperate ploy to express what Viktor Frankl has termed 'paradoxical intention'. The message of their incomprehension may force his hearers to do precisely the opposite. And indeed, enough people heard the message to ensure that the passage was preserved.

There is an ironic sequel to this success of Isaiah. In the following chapter he predicts that despite the immediate danger it faced from invading armies, Jerusalem would not fall. In the event he proved to be right. Thus grew the myth that Jerusalem and the Temple as God's special places were inviolable. It was against this tradition that Jeremiah was to struggle a century later when a different prophetic word was needed, one equally unpopular and unheard in its time.

Is that the ultimate fate of prophecy? That by its very nature it cannot be accepted in its time? Moreover that it may be valued in retrospect and indeed become the religious truth of a later generation that must in turn be challenged by a new prophetic voice. Isaiah offers no answer to this conundrum. But if Jeremiah best expresses the pain of living with the divine word, Isaiah is the biblical prophet who comes nearest to expressing the paradox and the impossibility of the prophetic word.

NOTE

1. This chapter is a revised version of the Aquinas Lecture delivered in Glasgow on 30 January 2003.

16

Christ Through Jewish Eyes

MARK L. SOLOMON

It is rare, in most inter-faith dialogue, to venture to offer a frank and constructive view of the central doctrines of one religion from the perspective of another.[1] Perhaps it is not attempted because it is a foolhardy and presumptuous thing to do, or because of the fear of causing offence, where the aim is to build up understanding and trust. So we talk to one another about our own religions, or about issues of mutual concern, or about interesting historical items, rarely venturing a comment about how we *see* the other.

Between Jews and Christians a special dynamic exists, driven by the idea that Christianity grew out of Judaism, and the memory of centuries of persecution, so that the dialogue is all too often one-way: Jews explaining Judaism to respectful Christians, who are often timid about explaining Christianity back. A number of Jewish scholars are beginning to advance the view that, within some circles, we have built up sufficient trust and confidence to take our dialogue to a more profound level, where we can share our deepest convictions without fear of being misunderstood, explain what the beliefs of the other might signify for us, and reflect on our meaning for each other.

For many years, and particularly in the post-war period, Christian theologians have formulated personal theologies of Judaism, attempting to replace the old anti-Jewish doctrines and stereotypes with something more positive, which can take account of the guilt and horror of Auschwitz. On the institutional level, several churches have issued collective statements embodying a new theology of the Christian–Jewish relationship. Until very recently, this endeavour had found little echo on the Jewish side.[2] A major step forward was taken with the publication in 2000 of *Dabru Emet*, the first modern collective Jewish statement about Christianity, written by a group of American Jewish academics and subsequently endorsed by numerous rabbis and scholars around the world.[3] The beginnings of a Jewish theology of Christianity have appeared, but in the dialogue encounter the need continues to be felt for Jewish voices that can make positive spiritual sense of Christianity for other Jews from within the Jewish Rabbinic tradition.

The following ideas are offered as a partial and preliminary attempt to formulate a Jewish theological understanding of the significance of Jesus Christ for Christians. It is the fruit of many years' reflection on my own profound encounter with Christianity, while trying to remain true to my understanding of Judaism. Some may feel that, in trying to find positive theological space for the Christ of Christian faith, I have strayed too far from the Jewish historical consensus. No doubt I still have much to learn, and this essay is offered as a contribution to an ongoing discussion, through which we might continue and deepen our shared learning process.

THE JEWISH JESUS

Perhaps the most moving and important level of Jewish–Christian dialogue has centred on the person of Jesus, and in particular on getting 'behind' the theological picture of Jesus built up over centuries of Christian dogmatics, to rediscover the man Jesus, and above all the Jew Jesus. One of the pioneers of this great work, in this country, was Claude Montefiore. This extraordinary scholar, who died in 1938, exhibits in his many writings, including his great two-volume commentary on the Synoptic Gospels, a love and respect for Jesus that can still take the breath away. To him, Jesus was above all a prophet, 'in the genuine succession to Amos and Isaiah'. Montefiore calls him 'the prophet of inwardness', and he certainly saw in Jesus a prototype for the Liberal Judaism he was labouring to create. He writes, 'As Liberal Judaism derives so greatly from the prophets, is it not wonderful that it should rightly find much to admire and use in the prophet of Nazareth.'[4] Many other scholars, both Jewish and Christian, have delved into the Jewish context and identity of Jesus, including more recently Geza Vermes. Some emphasize Jesus as a quasi-Pharisaic teacher, some as an Essene-type dissident, some as a wandering healer and *chasid* (holy man), some as a messianic aspirant. Thanks to their work, it is becoming less and less common, in intellectually respectable circles, to hear Jesus spoken of as though he were quite separate from the Judaism and Jewish people of his time. Vital as this insight is, however, and spiritually nourishing as I believe it has become for many Christians, it is, in a way, a dead end in dialogue. However Jewish Jesus may have been, and however inspiring we find the idea of the deep unity of Judaism and Christianity in his person, the fact remains that, for the vast majority of Christians in the world, the significance of Jesus does not lie in the fact that he *was* a Jew, or a prophet, or even a teacher and healer. The significance of Jesus is that he *is* the Christ, the Son of the living God, the saviour of the world and the second person of the Holy Trinity. It seems to me that real progress in dialogue can come only when Jews acknowledge the importance, the *meaningfulness* of these ideas for Christians, and find a way to respond to them from within Judaism.[5] That is why I have entitled my contribution '*Christ* Through Jewish Eyes', not 'Jesus Through Jewish Eyes', to indicate that I want to grapple, not with Jesus the man, but with Christ the Lord.[6]

MESSIAH

Even the word Christ, though, is problematic, for as we all know Christ means 'the anointed', the Greek equivalent of the Hebrew *mashiach* – messiah, and Jesus's status as Messiah is another dead end in our dialogue. That is not to say that Jesus' messianic role is not of central importance to Christians. It is just that Jews and Christians mean such utterly different things by the word 'messiah' that the question, 'Was Jesus the Messiah?' leads, and has always led, to hopeless muddle and misunderstanding. My own answer, which will not clear up the muddle right away, would be – *of course* Jesus was not, and is not, the Messiah for the Jews, but *of course* he was, and is, the Messiah for Christians.

I am quite sure that, in the first century, there were many and varied beliefs circulating, some of them quite esoteric, about the nature and function of the Messiah; and it may be that, for Jesus's earliest Jewish followers, the role Jesus played in their lives and their faith was one to which the name Messiah naturally attached itself. As Judaism and Christianity continued to develop, however, the meanings of Messiah diverged dramatically. For Christians it came to mean the one who delivers the individual from sin and death, while for Jews, especially after the destruction of the Second Temple, it meant the one who would deliver the people from Roman oppression, gather in the exiles, restore Jewish sovereignty under the Davidic dynasty, rebuild the Temple, and, having vanquished Israel's foes, reign over a just and peaceful world. Messiahship is not where Jews and Christians should look for shared, or at least increased, understanding of the significance of Jesus. The Messiah of Rabbinic Judaism, above all, was a mortal human being, albeit a great and holy one, whereas the risen Christ of Christianity came increasingly to be regarded as a divine being, indeed, in the words of the Nicene Creed, as 'Light from Light, true God from true God'. It is to this very divinity that we must look now for light.

INTERMEDIARIES

Jews and Christians have both built up, throughout their centuries of co-existence yet estrangement, many comfortable myths about one another's faiths in relation to their own. One of the favourite Jewish myths about Christianity is that Christians approach God only through intermediaries, from the priest in the confessional, to the saints and the Blessed Virgin, to Christ himself, while we Jews, God's elect children, approach the Father directly, face to face, without any need for intermediaries whatsoever. There is, of course, a kernel of truth in this picture, but even more falsehood, and that on both sides of the picture. I won't comment here on the extent to which many Christians may encounter God the Father directly in prayer. It is the other side of the coin that concerns us more: the assertion that Jews don't need intermediaries to approach God. This is a deep misconception. Jews indeed address their prayers and confessions directly to God, but their image of God, their conception of themselves in relation to God, and the very words of the prayers they say, do not spring ready made from the mind of the individual Jew. We learn about God, and our relationship with God, through our sacred texts and our people's religious tradition, to which we give the name *Torah* – God's teaching.

I would argue that this is a universal law of spiritual life: no finite being has direct, unmediated access to the absolute, the infinite and unknowable God. Every spiritual tradition provides a sacred bridge to link us to the One, the source and ground of all being. I shall not take time here to attempt to substantiate this assertion for all religions, but it is clear enough, I think, that for Christians the vital bridge between humanity and the divine is found in Jesus Christ. I will argue that for Jews the bridge is the Torah, and that many of the functions (if I may so put it) served by Jesus in Christianity, are performed by the Torah in Rabbinic Judaism.[7] Jews, therefore, can best understand and appreciate the theological role of Jesus for Christians, by delving into the significance of the Torah in their own religion.

LOGOS

The similarity in the roles of Christ and the Torah in Christianity and Judaism respectively goes beyond the fact that they are, in the two religions, the sacred bridge between the finite and the infinite. The two are actually linked together profoundly in the way the beliefs about them developed in the early Church and early Rabbinic Judaism. The clearest articulation of these beliefs is found, for Christianity, in the Gospel of St John, and for Judaism, in the teachings attributed to the circle of Rabbi Akiva, the central figure in the Rabbinic movement that created Judaism as we know it after the destruction of the Second Temple. Rabbi Akiva flourished as a teacher between about 90 and 135 CE, precisely the period during which most New Testament scholars place the authorship of the fourth Gospel. Both these authorities seem to have based their teaching on ideas that began in the wisdom books of the Bible, such as Proverbs and Job, were further developed in Hellenistic Judaism in such books as *Ben Sirach* and the *Wisdom of Solomon*, and were given philosophical expression by the Jewish philosopher Philo of Alexandria, a contemporary of Jesus. These ideas centred on

Wisdom or Reason as the first creation of God, before the universe began, which became God's companion, instrument or plan in the creation of the world, and also the way for human beings to encounter the transcendent God. In Philo's Greek, the reason or order of God is called the *logos*, which is most commonly translated 'word'.[8] For Christians, the word and wisdom of God became incarnate in Jesus; for Jews, the word and wisdom of God were, and remained, embodied in the Torah. I shall now look at each of these, to try to discern their similarities, which are profound, and their equally profound differences. I shall do so with the help of the threefold rubric commonly used in modern Jewish theology to describe the main ways in which God relates to the world and the individual: creation, revelation and redemption.

TORAH AND CHRIST IN CREATION

The seminal text regarding wisdom in the creation of the world is in Proverbs, where wisdom speaks:

> The Eternal One created me as the beginning of his way, the first of his works of old. I was set up from everlasting, from the beginning, before ever the world came to be ... then I was with him as a skilled workman, and I was daily all delight, playing always before him ... Happy is the one who hearkens to me ... for whoever finds me finds life, and obtains favour from the Eternal One. (Proverbs 8:22–3, 30–1, 34–5)

By the time of the writing of the apocryphal books, in the second and first centuries BCE, wisdom is already identified with the Torah,[9] but the first explicit statement in Rabbinic literature is the saying of Rabbi Akiva in the Mishnah: 'Beloved are Israel, for to them was given the precious instrument; even greater is the love, for it was made known to them that they were given the precious instrument with which the world was created, as it says: For I give you good doctrine; forsake not my Torah.'[10] The Rabbis taught that the Torah pre-existed the creation of the universe[11] and that 'God looked into the Torah and created the world.'[12]

The fourth Gospel famously opens, 'In the beginning was the Word, and the Word was with God, and the Word was God ... all things were made through Him ... and the Word became flesh and dwelt amongst us' (John 1:1, 3, 14). This belief was included in the Nicene Creed: 'I believe in one Lord, Jesus Christ ... through whom all things were made.'

So both the Torah and Jesus were seen, in strikingly similar terms, as God's creative Word. The difference between these conceptions – and it is a big difference, at least at first sight – is that, already in John, the Word is not just *with* God, it *is* God. Nowhere does Rabbi Akiva, or any Rabbi, state that the Torah is God, although that step is indeed taken in mediaeval Jewish mysticism, which sees the Torah as an aspect of the Godhead itself.[13] Nevertheless, as we shall see soon, the difference even in formative Rabbinic Judaism may not be as great as it seems at first.

TORAH AND CHRIST AS REVELATION

For Jews and Christians alike, the nature of God is not to remain forever hidden from humanity. God reveals, not just divine laws, but as much as human beings can bear to receive of the divine being. For Jews, God's self-revelation is contained in the Torah, the expression of divine will and wisdom, but also of divine love and mercy. In the daily evening service, Jews bless God for giving the Torah, in the words: 'With everlasting love have you loved your people the House of Israel. Torah and commandments ... have you taught us.' The corresponding morning blessing reads: 'With abounding love have you loved us, Eternal One our God; great and exceeding grace have you bestowed upon us.'[14]

Jesus too, for Christians, is the supreme revelation of God's loving nature: 'For God so loved the world that He gave His only begotten Son' (John 3:16). In the life and character and redemptive sacrifice of Jesus, Christians find the ultimate revelation of God's love.

It is intriguing that, as Rabbis and Church Fathers alike reflected on God's revelation between the first and fifth centuries, they both came to the conclusion that it is of a dual nature. Christ, as defined by the councils of the fifth century, is one person in two natures, both fully human and fully divine.[15] The Torah, for the Rabbis, is one Torah in a twofold revelation: the Written Torah, which came, as it were, straight from heaven and consisted of God's words alone; and the Oral Torah, which was the unfolding human interpretation of the written text.[16] The intuition of both sets of sages was that revelation is never a one-way process, imposed by God. It calls forth, and depends upon, human co-operation for its completeness and success.

TORAH AND CHRIST AS THE WAY TO REDEMPTION

While most Jews would think of the Torah primarily as revelation, it can probably be said that most Christians would see Jesus primarily as their redeemer. Theologians have differed, over the centuries, about the precise manner of the redemption wrought by Jesus. Some, especially in the Western churches, have emphasized the expiatory sacrifice of Jesus's death on the cross, atoning for the sins of the world and particularly for the original sin of Adam and Eve – that is, the inherently sinful disposition of all human beings.[17] Jesus's supreme sacrifice liberates those who accept it from guilt and death. Other Christian theologies, especially in the East, have laid more stress on the transfigured Christ as the type of glorified, perfected, divinized humanity, showing the rest of us the way to divine life.[18] In Teilhard de Chardin's phrase, Jesus is 'Omega Man', the goal and destiny of all humanity.[19]

Original sin is one Christian doctrine which Jews commonly reject absolutely. We are not born with any inherited taint, destined for damnation if left to our own devices. One Jewish scholar went so far as to describe Judaism's belief as 'original virtue'.[20] There is some truth in this, and we certainly say in our morning prayers, 'My God, the soul you have given me is pure' – but that does not exhaust Judaism's teaching on the subject. The Rabbis maintain that we are born with a *yetser ha-ra*, or evil inclination, and even say that it holds undisputed sway over us in our earliest years, until, with the birth of the *yetser ha-tov* (good inclination) around puberty, we develop a sense of altruism and learn to control our selfish instincts.[21]

The evil inclination, for the most part, has little to do with the sin in the garden, but is part and parcel of God's creation, and, as such, is fundamentally a good thing. When, after creating humanity on the sixth day, 'God saw all that He had made, and behold, it was very good' (Genesis 1:31), a remarkable *midrash* comments: 'good' means the good inclination, but 'very good' includes the evil inclination as well; for without it, no one would build a house, marry and beget children, or work for a livelihood.[22] The *yetser ha-ra*, then, is our life force with its basic drive for self-preservation. It is positive and vital, but being self-centred it habitually, and inevitably, leads us to put ourselves first, to seek our own gratification, even at the expense of others, and hence to do evil. There is little to distinguish this doctrine from some versions of the idea of original sin. The question is, how can we overcome our selfish, sinful tendencies? Here the two religions seem to differ radically. Jews will say, we have it in ourselves to act rightly, follow God's laws, and work out our own salvation, while a Christian might say that we are unable to free ourselves from the grip of our selfish nature, and only God, through Jesus's pure, voluntary atoning sacrifice, can free us and bring us to eternal life.

Once again, the difference is not as great as it seems, for the Rabbis do not teach utter self-reliance in our struggle with evil. For them, it is only God's gift of the Torah that offers us the chance of self-mastery and salvation. As one famous Rabbinic saying puts it, 'The Holy One, blessed be He, says to Israel: My children, I have created the evil impulse, and I have created the Torah as the antidote to it; if you occupy yourselves with Torah, you will not be delivered into its power.'[23] Another saying runs: 'If that base fellow' – meaning the evil inclination – 'should waylay you, drag him to the House of Study: if he is stone, he will melt; if he is iron, he will shatter.'[24] An even more radical expression of the idea – and one which most Jews nowadays, if they ever heard it, would probably reject with outrage as 'too Christian' – is the oft-repeated Rabbinic legend that the serpent in the Garden of Eden injected Eve with filth, which is passed on to all her descendants, and only when Israel stood at Sinai and accepted the Torah was their filth removed.[25] Sinai, then, is our Calvary, and only the Israelites' collective surrender to the will of God, when they declared, 'We will obey and we will learn' (Exodus 24:7), liberates us from our baser nature. As Hillel put it, 'One who has acquired words of Torah, has acquired for himself the life of the World to Come.'[26]

The most profound Rabbinic statement on atonement is attributed, once again, to Rabbi Akiva, and comes at the very end of the Mishnaic tractate *Yoma*, on the laws of the Day of Atonement. It reads:

> Happy are you, O Israel! Before whom do you purify yourselves, and who is it that purifies you? Your Father in heaven, as it is said [Ezekiel 36: 25] 'I will cast on you pure waters, and you shall be pure', and it says [Jeremiah 17:13], 'The Lord is the hope [*mikveh*; read: ritual bath] of Israel.' Just as the bath purifies the defiled, so the Holy One, blessed be He, purifies Israel.[27]

It is easy to miss the full force of this statement, and the trenchant polemic it contains against early Christianity. Let us consider the literary and historical context. The preceding seven chapters of tractate *Yoma* dealt in detail with the Temple ritual of Yom Kippur, which was seen as vital to the annual reconciliation between God and Israel. But the Temple had been destroyed; the High Priest, the Holy of Holies, the sacrifices and the scapegoat were no more. Israel was bereft of its divinely appointed means of atonement. There were those in the Church, by the early second century, who declared to the Jews that God had rejected them because they had rejected their Messiah. The only hope for sinful Israel was to embrace the salvation offered through baptism in the faith of Christ, the Son of God. Into this misery steps Rabbi Akiva, and proclaims, 'Happy are you, O Israel!' – not rejected or abandoned – 'Before whom do you purify yourselves, and who is it that purifies you?' Atonement, indeed, is not wholly in our own hands, nor yet wholly in God's, but is a joint endeavour.[28] Akiva answers, not as one might expect 'The Holy One, blessed be He', or the like, but 'Your *Father* in heaven', that is, not the Son whom others preach, but the Father alone.[29] We do not need baptism in a pool for salvation, but immersion in the purifying waters of God alone, the waters only God can sprinkle on us to free us from the defilement of death.[30] God, our pool of water, is our all-sufficient hope – a play on the word *mikveh*, which has both meanings. But *how* is God our pool of water? Rabbi Akiva no doubt expected his students to be familiar with his other teaching, which became a watchword of Rabbinic life: 'There is no water but Torah.' Torah is the well-spring of life-giving, purifying

water, which all who are thirsty can come and drink by studying its teachings.[31] Immersion in God, then, means immersion
in God's Torah.

Rabbi Akiva did not only preach this message, he lived it.
The story is told that, when the public teaching of Torah was
banned on pain of death during the Hadrianic persecution,
Rabbi Akiva defied the ban and continued to teach. A friend
rebuked him for his folly, asking why he could not yield for the
time being, rather than risk his life. Rabbi Akiva answered with
a parable. Once, he said, some fish were swimming in a river,
when a fox came to them and said, 'Why are you swimming
in the river, O fish? Do you not know that fishermen are there
waiting to catch you in their nets? Come out, and I will carry
you away to safety on my back.' To which the fish answered,
'O wily Mr Fox, do you not realize that, if we are in danger
here in the water, which is our element, how much more will
we be in danger if we leave our element altogether?' Even so,
said Rabbi Akiva, with the Jews: if we are in danger when we
learn Torah, the source of our life, how much more will we be
in danger if we cease to learn.[32] In due course, Rabbi Akiva was
indeed arrested and died a martyr's death.[33]

So much, then, for the Jews – what about the rest of
humanity? Part of the answer, it seems to me, is clear: God gave
God's self, in the Torah, to the Jewish people for their salvation;
and then God gave God's self, in Christ, for the salvation of the
Gentiles. I see no reason why a Jew should not affirm joyfully,
in the words of St Paul, that 'God was in Christ, reconciling the
world to Himself' (II Corinthians 5:19).[34] Christ is the Torah
incarnate, the living word of God spoken to the nations,
enabling them to participate equally in the same covenant God
made with Abraham and Israel.[35]

COMMUNION

Why God acted in just this way, I will venture to speculate in
a moment. First, I would like to reflect on the way our beliefs
are reflected in our liturgy, and in the idea of communion. I
have to admit that the Christian liturgy I am most familiar with
is the Eucharist, and Protestants for whom the Eucharist is not
central to their faith may not identify with some of what I will
say here.

Jews and Christians alike may commune with God in their hearts, in prayer. Each community, however, has a pre-eminent act of communion, which, for many, is central to its life and identity. For Christians, it is the sharing of Christ in the Eucharist. For Jews, it is Torah study, represented in the liturgy by the ceremonial reading of the Torah. The two rituals display some remarkable similarities, which reinforce the idea that the Torah fulfils, for Jews, the role that Jesus performs for Christians. In the Eucharist, prayers and scriptural readings – the 'Liturgy of the Word' – form the introduction and lead-up to the culminating and most sacred part of the service, when the real presence of God becomes, for Roman Catholics, manifest in the bread and wine, and is shared by the worshippers.[36] In the main service of the Jewish week, on Shabbat morning, as well as on Monday and Thursday mornings, the climax of the *shacharit* service is reached with the reading of the Torah. It is taken from the Ark, clothed in splendour; carried in procession and venerated (although not in many Liberal synagogues), and, like the host in the Catholic mass, elevated on high to be seen and honoured by the congregation. The tabernacle, in which the consecrated host is kept in Catholic churches, is strikingly like a miniature Ark. Of course, there are differences: nobody would say that the Torah scroll can be worshipped as God, and each of these ceremonies has its own separate history and development. On a phenomenological level, though, the similarities reveal a great deal about the inner meaning of these rituals for the communities that perform them.[37]

On a deeper level, the Rabbis insist that, wherever the Torah is studied, the *Shekhinah* (divine presence) is there[38] – which reminds one strongly of Jesus's assurance in Matthew: 'Where two or three are gathered together in my name, there am I in the midst of them' (Matthew 18:20).[39] In later Jewish mystical literature, the study of Torah is spoken of as spiritual food in language reminiscent of that applied to the Eucharist.[40]

GOD'S REASONS

A question that naturally occurs is, why did God, in the divine wisdom, choose to reveal the Word in one way to the Jews, and in quite a different way to Christians? I would add, as well, that

I believe God reveals God's word and light to every people in a way appropriate to them: the Qur'an for Muslims, the Vedas and other scriptures to Hindus, and so on. But our focus here is on Jews and Christians. I certainly cannot claim to have fathomed the divine mind, for as we know, 'My thoughts are not your thoughts, nor are my ways your ways, says the Eternal One' (Isaiah 55:8). Nevertheless, the following speculation has occurred to me, which I would like to share. For me, as a Jew, there is something supremely beautiful, precious and inspiring about the Torah, and the centuries of devoted scholarship that have created the Talmud and *Midrash* which we call the Oral Torah. The process of studying, questioning, debating and discussing, the restless curiosity, marvellous creativity and intellectual adventurousness of Judaism: without these the universe would be a poorer and duller place, and something of divine – and human – wisdom and splendour would remain forever unknown. So God gave us the Torah, as our sacred bridge to the infinite, and our means of helping to perfect the world. But to participate in the life of Torah one needs to be able to speak the language, to belong, as it were, to the elite scholarly society, and have around one a community that, even if it can't share fully in that process, has the tradition and dedication to foster it. It is no accident, therefore, that the Jews are 'the fewest of all the peoples' (Deuteronomy 7:7), a kind of godly experiment in creating, out of a band of slaves, a 'kingdom of priests and a holy nation' (Exodus 19:6). Since we are only human, the experiment has never definitively succeeded, but at least we, and God, have kept it going for nearly three and a half thousand years, and it is still going, yielding new and interesting results all the time. But the word could not remain in this esoteric, if beautiful, form, if it were to be communicated to the masses of humanity who don't speak Hebrew or Aramaic and haven't cultivated a taste for Rabbinic dialectics. God, therefore, chose one Jew to become the vehicle for a renewed revelation that would bring the light of Torah, in a modified form, to the peoples of the world. Since a book can be read only by those who can read, know the language and are used to intellectual thought, God chose a medium of revelation that every human being can understand, that is, a human life – and a human death.

The Rabbis, at least from the time of Rabbi Akiva onwards, knew that God was with them in their human suffering, for thus they interpreted the verse in Isaiah: 'In all their afflictions, he was afflicted' (Isaiah 63:9),[41] and they taught, 'Wherever the people of Israel go into exile, the *Shekhinah* goes into exile with them.'[42] Rabbi Meir, the pre-eminent disciple of Rabbi Akiva, even went so far as to state that whenever any human being feels pain, the *Shekhinah* also cries out in pain.[43]

This faith in God's presence and participation in our human condition, however, was given perhaps its most moving and powerful expression in the idea of the Incarnation. For, once the word ceased to be a body of teaching, and entered into a body of flesh, it had to come to be regarded as God. The alternative was to worship a being other than God, which is idolatry, so however hard it is to understand, it was natural that Christians came to regard Jesus, by the third or fourth century, not just as a divine being, but actually as God, and thus was born that stumbling block to Jewish–Christian (and Muslim) understanding, the doctrine of the Trinity, which is too much for me to deal with in this essay.[44]

MODERN CONCEPTIONS OF TORAH AND JESUS

To conclude, it is important to acknowledge that the beliefs here described as constituting Judaism and Christianity may not be ones with which all Jews and Christians identify, or with which they are comfortable. The fact is that neither Jewish nor Christian beliefs are static and unchanging. Both have evolved over the centuries and are still evolving. From a modern point of view, shared by the present writer, all religious beliefs arise mainly – some would say solely – in the human mind. That does not mean that they are not divine, or do not partake of ultimate truth. It simply concerns the way in which God works, which I believe is primarily from within us. As a Liberal Jew, I do not believe that the five books of Moses came down from heaven, or that every word in them is God's own truth; and the same certainly applies to the teachings of the Rabbis. Nevertheless, these are our sacred traditions in which we have found, and are still finding, new truths and inspiration, even as we discard what we see as outmoded or unhelpful beliefs and practices. I know that many Christians see their own tradition in a similar way, and that, just as Jews debate the nature, purpose and divinity of the Torah, so Christians are debating the nature of Jesus and his divinity.

If we can come to recognize that the same God who gave light to us, in a way appropriate for our character and culture, has given light to others also, fitting to their culture and character, the result can only be an ever deeper appreciation of the boundless greatness, generosity and loving-kindness of God, and increased understanding, harmony and peace between human beings.

NOTES

1. This essay is a revised version of a talk originally given to the Central London Branch of the Council Christians and Jews, at the Liberal Jewish Synagogue, on 3 May 2001.
2. A relatively early and fascinating essay in this direction is E. Borowitz, *Contemporary Christologies: A Jewish Response* (New York/Ramsey: Paulist Press, 1980).
3. The text of *Dabru Emet*, and a superb series of theological essays on the issues it raises, can be found in T. Frymer-Kensky, D. Novak, P. Ochs, D. Fox Sandmel and M. Signer (eds), *Christianity in Jewish Terms* (Boulder, CO: Westview, 2000).
4. Quotations from *The Old Testament and After* (London, 1923), pp. 229–32.
5. J. D. Rayner, in a letter to the present writer of 16 May 2001, commented, 'I have often thought that the theological Christ *should* be discussed from a Jewish perspective, since otherwise one is not really talking about Christianity at all.'
6. By coincidence, in the year this talk was first delivered, a book appeared entitled *Jesus Through Jewish Eyes: Rabbis and Scholars Engage an Ancient Brother in a New Conversation*, B. Bruteau (ed.) (Maryknoll, NY: Orbis, 2001). The focus is firmly on the Jewish Jesus, and the designation of Jesus as 'brother' is probably an echo of the memorable statement of Martin Buber, 'From my youth onwards I have found in Jesus my great brother. That Christianity has regarded and does regard him as God and Saviour has always appeared to me a fact of the highest importance which … I must endeavour to understand.' M. Buber, *Two Types of Faith*, trans. N. P. Goldhawk (London: Routledge and Kegan Paul, 1951).
7. For the presence of angelic intermediary figures, sometimes functioning as God's vice-regent, in ancient and mediaeval forms of Judaism, see G. Scholem, *Jewish Gnosticism, Merkabah Mysticism, and Talmudic Tradition* (New York, 1960), ch. 7. Many Rabbinic texts stress the vital role of the ministering angels in carrying the prayers of an individual up to God. For a *halakhic* application of this idea, see Babylonian Talmud (BT) *Shabbat* 12b.
8. See, e.g., Philo, *De Opificio Mundi*, iv–vi (16–20).
9. See Ben Sirach 24; Baruch 3:9–4:4.
10. *Avot* 3:18.
11. See *Bereshit Rabbah* 7:2; *Avot de-Rabbi Nathan* 31.
12. *Bereshit Rabbah* 1:1.

13. See *Zohar* II, 60a: 'The Holy One, blessed be He, is called Torah ... and Torah is nothing but the Holy One, blessed be He.' See G. Scholem, 'The Meaning of the Torah in Jewish Mysticism', in *On the Kabbalah and Its Symbolism* (New York: Schocken, 1965), esp. p. 44; and see E. Wolfson, 'Female Imaging of the Torah: From Literary Metaphor to Religious Symbol', *Circle in the Square* (Albany NY: SUNY), 1995.

14. Texts according to the Ashkenazi rite. The formulation 'with everlasting love' alludes to Jeremiah 31:2, and begins the 'Blessing of the Torah' in both evening and morning services according to the Sephardi rite. See BT *Berakhot* 11b; I. Elbogen, *Jewish Liturgy: A Comprehensive History*, trans. Raymond P. Scheindlin (Philadelphia, PA: JPS, 1993), p. 19.

15. The dogma of the two natures was defined at the Council of Chalcedon in 451 CE.

16. The doctrine of the two Torahs has traditionally been ascribed to the Pharisees, but recent scholarship has shown that, although the concept of authoritative oral traditions can be traced at least to the Tannaitic period (before 220 CE), the term *Torah she-be'al Peh* 'Oral Torah' first appears in texts dating from around the fifth century.

17. This dominant view in Western Christianity was given its definitive statement by St Anselm (d. 1109) in his work *Cur Deus Homo?*.

18. In the Western Church this view was upheld by Duns Scotus (d. 1308) and St Francis de Sales (d. 1622), among others.

19. Pierre Teilhard de Chardin (d. 1955) in his works *The Divine Milieu* (New York, 1960) and *The Future of Man* (New York, 1964).

20. S. Levy, *Original Virtue and other Short Studies*, (London: Longmans Green, 1907), p. 1.

21. See BT *Sanhedrin* 91b; *Avot de-Rabbi Nathan* A, 16; *Kohelet Rabbah* to Ecclesiastes 4:13. On the concept of original sin in Judaism, see S. S. Cohon, 'Original Sin', *Essays in Jewish Theology* (Cincinnati, OH: Hebrew Union College Press, 1987), pp. 219–72 (originally published in 1948).

22. *Bereshit Rabbah* 9:7, to Genesis 1:31.

23. BT *Kiddushin* 30b.

24. Ibid.

25. See BT *Yevamot* 103b; *Avodah Zarah* 22b; *Shabbat* 145b–146a; it is attributed to Rabbi Yochanan, the leading Palestinian sage of the mid-third century.

26. Mishnah, Avot 2: 8.

27. Mishnah, *Yoma* 8:9, conclusion. The opening phrase alludes to Deuteronomy 33:29, which speaks of Israel's salvation by God. In *Pesikta de-R. Kahana* (ed. Buber 157b) the saying about the bath is attributed to R. Eliezer, R. Akiva's teacher, while in *Midrash Tehillim* 4:9 and *Yalkut Psalms* 627 it is attributed to R. Eliezer b. Jacob, probably R. Akiva's disciple of that name. For a discussion of this *mishnah* (with different conclusions from those offered here) see J. Goldin, 'Reflections on a Mishnah', *Studies in Midrash and Related Literature*, B. L. Eichler and J. H. Tigay, (eds), (Philadelphia: JPS, 1988), pp. 141–9.

28. I am grateful to J. D. Rayner for his suggestion, in the letter cited in n. 5 above, that one could adduce here, for example, the words of Malachi 3:7, 'Return to Me, and I will return to you.' For the Rabbinic parable elaborating on this mutuality of *teshuvah*, see *Pesikta Rabbati* (ed. Friedmann, Vienna, 1880) 184b–185a.

29. See R. Akiva's saying in *Avot* 3:18, quoted above, which in an earlier clause states, 'Beloved are Israel, for they are called children (or: 'sons') of God ... as it is said: You are children of the Eternal One your God'

(Deuteronomy 14:1). I think this is a polemic against the Christian claim that Jesus is, in a special sense, the Son of God.

30. Sprinkling of water, containing the ashes of the red heifer, was the rite of purification for those who had been defiled by contact with death. Ezekiel 36:25 is playing on this image, as noted by Rashi ad loc. R. Akiva is pointing out that God alone acts the priest's part in the purification of Israel; see Hebrews 9:11–14.

31. See, e.g., *Sifrey Devarim* 48, *Shir ha-Shirim Rabbah* 1, 2b, 3, *Midrash Tehillim* 1:18. Note the formulation in *Sifrey Devarim*: 'Just as water elevates the impure from their impurity, so words of Torah elevate the impure from their impurity' (see *Tanchuma, Ki Tavo* 3). See also the striking statement in *Shir ha-Shirim Rabbah* and *Mid. Tehillim*, 'Just as the waters cover the nakedness of the sea, as it is said: As the waters cover the sea (Isaiah 11:9), so the Torah covers the nakedness of Israel, as it is said: Love covers all transgressions (Proverbs 10:12)' – where it is clear that 'love' is taken as a synonym for Torah!

32. BT, *Berakhot* 61b.

33. On Jewish and Christian martyrology, and the early interaction between Christianity and Rabbinic Judaism, see D. Boyarin, *Dying for God: Martyrdom and the Making of Christianity and Judaism*, (Stanford, CA: Stanford University Press, 1999). On texts concerning the martyrdom of R. Akiva, see especially pp. 102–13.

34. For many Christians, the saying of John 14:6, 'I am the way, the truth and the life; no one comes to the Father, but by me', is a major obstacle to religious pluralism. Perhaps, however, it could be understood as meaning, not 'I, Jesus of Nazareth, am the sole embodiment of the way, and without me no one can come to the Father', but instead, 'I, Jesus, am one manifestation of that way, the true and living Word, which, in its many forms, is the route by which all people come to the Father'.

35. I am trespassing here on the ground of a vigorous debate among contemporary Christian theologians, whether Christ's coming ushered in a 'new covenant', even though the covenant with Israel may still be valid, or whether Christians were 'grafted on' to the same covenant God had made with Israel; see Romans 11:17ff.

36. Even the structure of the Liturgy of the Word reflects the centrality of Christ, with the Gospel reading in the final and most honoured place, and the congregation standing. In the Jewish liturgy, the order is reversed, with the more sacred reading from the Pentateuch preceding that from the prophets. I am aware that, especially in post-conciliar Catholic teaching, the Liturgy of the Word has been presented as equal in importance to the Eucharist.

37. The fact that, even in the most liberal Jewish communities, there is great stress on the Torah being read from an unvocalized, hand-written parchment scroll, strongly suggests the supra-rational, 'sacramental' quality of the act of reading, which would not apply if the portion were read from a printed text.

38. See *Avot* 3:3, 7.

39. A further dimension, which there is not room to explore here, is the sense in which the Jewish people and the Church, respectively, come to embody the Torah and Christ, and thus manifest the divine presence and action in the world.

40. See S. Zalman of Liadi, *Likkutey Amarim (Tanya)*, ch. 5, and the references cited there.

41. Following the *kere* version of the Masoretic text. This is the final verse of the *haftarah*, or prophetic reading, on the Sabbath preceding the Jewish New Year; in other words, the final prophetic word of each Jewish year.

42. BT *Megillah* 29a; *Mekhilta de-Rabbi Ishmael, Bo* 14; *Sifrey Bemidbar* 84.

43. Mishnah, *Sanhedrin* 6:5. While no normative form of Judaism has ever held that God can appear in a human *body*, the assertion that God cannot be manifest in human *form* is a product of mediaeval, especially Maimonidean, rationalism. It is contradicted by the pervasive anthropomorphism of the Bible, with its assumption that the prophets' visionary experience of God takes human shape (see Exodus 24:10, Isaiah 6:1, Ezekiel 1:26, Amos 9:1, etc.). For visionary anthropomorphism in Rabbinic Judaism, see BT *Berakhot* 7a, the saying attributed to Rabbi Akiva in *Mekhilta, Shirta* 3, the *Shiur Komah* and the profound anthropomorphism of mediaeval Kabbalah. See E. Wolfson, 'Judaism and Incarnation: The Imaginal Body of God', *Christianity in Jewish Terms*, pp. 239–54.

44. Jewish difficulties with the Trinitarian idea seem to me to arise from two main causes: on the one hand, the prominence the doctrine attained in Christian liturgy, which in turn arose from the centrality of the incarnate Christ in the Christian experience of God; and on the other hand, the Maimonidean philosophical interpretation of divine unity, which became normative from the Middle Ages onwards. Classical Rabbinic Judaism presents significant analogues to Trinitarian thinking, for example in the frequent collocation of God and God's twin attributes of Justice and Mercy, forming a dynamic and dialectic entity; and epithets like *Shekhinah* and *Ruach ha-Kodesh* (Holy Spirit) as manifestations of God's presence and inspiration. The mediaeval Kabbalistic doctrine of the *sefirot*, which include divine hypostases entitled Father, Mother, Son and Daughter, is (as some of its mediaeval Jewish critics noted) difficult to distinguish conceptually from some versions of Trinitarian theology.

17

Moses Montefiore and Jews, Christians and Muslims

ANDREW GOLDSTEIN

Claude Montefiore was at home across the spectrum of Anglo-Jewry. He was a founder of the Liberal Jewish Synagogue and a council member at West London Synagogue, and collaborated with the Orthodox scholar Herbert Loewe, on the *Rabbinic Anthology*. Claude Montefiore was also one of the first Anglo-Jewish scholars to delve deeply into Christianity and he had very close relationships with Christian clerics and academics. His first wife was the granddaughter of a Polish rabbi, his second a convert to Judaism.

Chaim Bermant describes Claude Montefiore's last hours as follows:

> As he lay dying he called for his friend, the Rev. W. R. Matthews, Dean of St Paul's, to minister to him. 'This was a privilege which embarrassed me,' the Dean later confessed, 'because he was deaf and one had to shout to make him hear, and it was difficult for me to pray in a manner which would imply no Christian belief.'
>
> And so a compromise was reached. They intoned the Lord's Prayer together – to which not even the most Orthodox Jew can object – the Dean at the top of his voice, the dying man in a whisper, the former addressing one Father in Heaven, the latter another.'[1]

Claude Montefiore died in 1938 and was the great-nephew of Sir Moses Montefiore, the most famous Anglo-Jew of the nineteenth century. At Sir Moses' death in 1885 he was surrounded by Jews. In fact a *minyan* had gathered round his bedside, including the minister of his private synagogue in Ramsgate, Rev. Herman Shandel, and his faithful secretary and confidante, Dr Louis Loewe, the grandfather of the Loewe with whom Claude Montefiore collaborated. It was with Dr Loewe that Moses Montefiore repeated his last words on earth; this time the traditional Jewish last words, and I use the translation Loewe has in his account of the incident, 'Hear O Israel, the Eternal is Our God, the Eternal is One!'[2] So, in a way, either Sir Moses or Louis Loewe preferred the translation of our *Siddur Lev Chadash!*

From the deathbeds let us go back to Moses Montefiore's earlier life and consider the relationships he and his wife, Judith, had with Christians and Christianity; with Jews and Judaism – and add a few comments about Muslims and Islam.

Moses' family were Sephardim from Italy and he was to become a grandee of the Spanish and Portuguese Congregation in London. Judith Cohen's family had originated in Holland – and they were Ashkenazi. It has often been said that the marriage of Moses and Judith in 1812 was the first mixed marriage to take place in Anglo-Jewry; that is between an Ashkenazi and a Sephardi.

This has been shown to be an exaggeration[3] but what is true is that the marriage was most successful and the religious life and concerns of the couple took in both communities. Although Judith joined her husband's congregation, Moses always gave full consideration to Ashkenazi practice. He would consult the Ashkenazi rabbinate as well as the Sephardi *Haham*, he supported Ashkenazi and Sephardi charities in England and the Holy Land on an equal footing. This point can be seen in concrete form in the design of his *Mishkenot Sha-ananim* in Jerusalem. Planned as alms houses, they were to accommodate Ashkenazi and Sephardi residents on an equal basis and at one end of the block that still stands by Montefiore's windmill was an Ashkenazi synagogue and at the other a Sephardi synagogue. On his first visit to the Holy Land in 1827 he took with him a letter from the Ashkenazi Chief Rabbi, Hirschel, to the two Chief Rabbis in Jerusalem, Ashkenazi and Sephardi, urging them to co-operate and not fight with each other.

Over the following years his many missions of mercy took him to his native Sephardi Italy, and to Ashkenazi Poland and

Russia, to Romania and Morocco, to Egypt and Constantinople, Damascus and Jerusalem. He was in touch with distressed Jews in Persia and Yemen and India and corresponded with and raised money from Jewish communities in America and Australia. It mattered not if they were Ashkenazi or Sephardi, oriental or occidental. Before the advent of e-mail he must have been in touch with more Jewish individuals than any other person, and by the time he died, aged 100, he had probably travelled to more Jewish communities around the northern hemisphere than any named person since Benjamin of Tudela.

What sort of a Jew was he? He was a religiously observant Jew and usually depicted as a pillar of Orthodoxy. The future Chief Rabbi, Herman Adler, said of him in 1883, 'His firmness and constancy had been further shown … He had never touched forbidden food, no matter where he might have been … '[4] In fact, in the early years of their marriage there are a number of references to Judith and Moses eating non-kosher meat while travelling and they were frequent travellers at home and abroad.

In 1823, for example, they were on a holiday tour of the Low Countries, Germany and Italy. Judith wrote a letter to her sister, Hannah, 'We are well pleased with the cooking when a slice of bacon does not cover the roasted poulay [*sic*], in that case Mr Mazzara [their Catholic travel companion] continues to finish the dish.'[5] A reference in Judith's unpublished diary of that tour indicates that the offending bacon was removed and given to Mr Mazzara while the Montefiores tucked into the chicken.

They never knowingly ate forbidden foods, however, and I suspect their guidelines in the early days were the Biblical rules of *kashrut*. They liked all sorts of wine with no query of its provenance. But this is clear – their first tour to the Holy Land in 1827–28 changed their religious life. Although they spent only eight days in Palestine, and three nights in Jerusalem, the object of their ten-month tour, they were so moved by the experience that, as well as returning six times, Moses wrote, on leaving Jaffa, 'This day I begin a new era. I fully intend to dedicate much more time to the welfare of the poor and to attend Synagogue as regularly as possible on Monday, Thursday and Saturday.'[6] Once home, he carried out his promise and he adopted a more fully Orthodox lifestyle, although he continued to eat fish in non-kosher restaurants. But such was an accepted level of *kashrut* until relatively recently.

Even in the early days he never travelled on shabbat and went to great personal inconvenience, for instance, in never boarding or disembarking from a ship on shabbat (and strangely the many ships he took on his travels invariably made shore on a shabbat). He did not write or smoke on shabbat although in the early years these rules were occasionally broken. Later on he would bend other rules a little, for example asking a servant to open a letter for him on shabbat.

Above all, he was a proud Jew. Many of his contemporary upper-middle-class Jews were only too eager to hide or deny their Judaism if it seemed an embarrassment or to hinder their social progress. Many went to the extreme of converting which, as we shall see, was for Moses Montefiore an anathema.

The story is well known of him standing on principle and, when appointed Sheriff of London in 1838 and finding the installation ceremonies were on *Rosh Hashanah*, getting the date changed and riding to the ceremony in a state coach with his own cooked kosher chicken in his bag for the banquet. How many subsequent Jewish notables have been less resolute when attaining civic honours? But there are many other examples of Montefiore's consistency. Early on at the Goldsmids he embarrassed his hosts by doing the full Hebrew Grace after Meals in the presence of their honoured guest, Lord Nelson.[7] And Judith was of a similar disposition: when Sir Sidney Smith visited her home on *Tisha B'Av*, she, unlike her sisters, was not ashamed to be seen sitting on a low stool – and she did not break her fast, patiently explaining to Sir Sidney the reason for it.

So much for the Montefiores and their personal Judaism. What about the Montefiores and the Jewish community? Again, the first trip to the Holy Land was the turning point that changed their lives. In their early holiday travels they had little interest in visiting synagogues or making contact with local communities. They knew from experience that once contact had been made it often cost them dear in time and money. When stuck in Alexandria in 1827, over the High Holydays, it was obvious they would go to *shul*. But on their continental tour of 1823 the first synagogue they visited was Mantua, six weeks after leaving home, even though they had spent *shabbatot* in towns with synagogues. Instead they prayed at their hotel. In

Prague in 1851 they went to the Altneu *shul* for Shavuot and on the second day visited seven synagogues and the old cemetery. (Nothing changes for tourists to Prague!) After his first visit to the Holy Land, Moses Montefiore got more and more involved with the care and charities of Jewish communities around the world – it filled a large part of the last sixty years of his life and regular synagogue attendance was *de rigueur*.

CHRISTIANITY AND THE NON-JEWISH WORLD

When Moses was born in 1784 the Jewish community in Britain was very small and mostly lower-middle-class with its top echelon soon rising in rank financially and in the class system. Yet Jews were far from politically emancipated, though there seems to have been reasonable acceptance within English society. One of Montefiore's early civic involvements was as a volunteer in the Surrey Local Militia. The militia had been set up at the height of fears of invasion by Napoleon, but by the time Moses joined in 1809 the danger was over and so one suspects there was about his joining something of the thrill of adventure.

Later Moses Montefiore was to play a prominent part in a number of organizations and bodies that would mean spending a considerable amount of time and energy on non-Jewish causes from royalty down. In 1831 he purchased a large estate in Ramsgate and the story is well known of his making a door in his boundary wall to allow the soon-to-be Queen Victoria, who stayed on the adjoining estate, to use his cliff-top garden. Subsequently, he had several meetings with the Queen and many with visiting royal families. In 1835 he became a member of the Merchant Taylors' Company, in 1838 he became one of the two Sheriffs of London and, it being the year of Victoria's accession, he was knighted. In 1843 he became a Justice of the Peace and 1844 saw him High Sheriff of Kent. In 1830 he had become a member of the Atheneum Club and in 1836 a Fellow of the Royal Society. Once could go on listing his contacts with English society and in all these bodies Moses Montefiore played as full a role as in the Jewish organizations.

And then there were his business interests; each of them involving close contact with non-Jews. His early partners were his brother, Abraham, and brother-in-law, Nathan Meyer Roths-child. By 1824 he and they had joined with non-Jewish bankers, mostly Dissenters, for instance Francis Baring and Samuel Gurney, in promoting the Alliance British and Foreign Life and Fire Assurance Company. It came about largely because the established assurance companies were prejudiced against Jews and Dissenters. At the same time, Moses and Rothschild were working with another circle of non-Jews in a project they would launch in 1825, the Provincial Bank of Ireland. This venture included leading Catholics who were excluded by the previously monopolistic Bank of Ireland – a prominent name being Daniel O'Connell. At the same time Montefiore was also involved in the setting-up of the Imperial Continental Gas Association, which invested in and developed gas-lighting systems across Western Europe. In all these ventures (and there were several others) Moses Montefiore involved himself actively as a director and they all brought him into very close contact with Christians of all sorts, but especially Catholics and Dissenters.

The Montefiores grew up in Protestant England and Judith sent her sister a letter from France in 1814 when the Montefiores had ventured to Paris on Rothschild business. At the end of Moses' business letter, Judith penned some lines to her sister:

> Yesterday morning we were at Notre Dame saw the Catholic ceremony of devotion. they have a variety of forms in their Adoration of graven Images to which they bow & kneel with great sanctity, then strew the frankincense, first to the Image, then to the Priests of which latter there were a great number viz.10 who appeared to be the chief, having most superb gold embroidered robes on them, several others seated on each side of the church; there is a fine organ. A Violin cello and two violins which compose the band; we did not stay to the Conclusion having seen Sufficient of their ceremonies very soon. On our journey from Dunkirk here we observed on the outside of the churches large Images with a cross, some of gilt, others of marble; every now & then M said, here we are coming to another Jesus.[8]

How different was Catholic France from Protestant England.

The Montefiores had shown an early interest in Christianity. On their honeymoon in 1812 they visited Canterbury Cathedral,

'Admired the statues and architecture and stayed for the service'.[9] In Bruges on 9 October 1823, 'Went to see the Church of St. Salvadore which contains many paintings by Vandyke, Rubens ... the Chapel Jerusalem contains a statue of the Virgin and Son by Michael Angelo.' In Aix la Chapelle, 20th October, 'Went to the Cathedral ... saw many valuable reliques ... such as the cord of the virgin Mary ... the priest however said the Church did not oblige the belief of their truth.' In Cologne they were amazed at the cathedral, and in Bonn (22 October) Judith noted, 'Under the Chapel is a vault where are interred about 40 of the deceased Monks open to the inspection of strangers. Montefiore and Mr. Mazzara went to see them, and were astonished at the perfect state in which they appear. Mr M. took a piece of skin of one'![10]

In 1827 in Rome they got tickets to visit the 'Sistern Chapel' [*sic*] to hear the Pope bless the Palms on Palm Sunday and returned with a consecrated *lulav,* and in 1839 they went to watch the Pope's Easter blessing at St Peter's.

In 1827, having landed in Messina, they went to the cathedral to hear Sicilian Vespers ... and so on. During the three days spent in Jerusalem in 1827 Judith took one day to visit the various Christian sites in Bethlehem.

The visits to churches seem to have become less frequent as time went by. Maybe they had visited the important ones; maybe as they got more deeply Jewish they had less interest in Christian places and experiences.

MUSLIMS AND ISLAM

By the time of Moses' first visit to the Near East (1827–28) several explorers and travellers had already been and described their experiences. Some (for example Joliffe and Chateaubriand) were very chauvinistic and describe Arabs and their towns and culture in very disparaging terms.

Several (for example, Clarke, Buckingham, Madden) showed great respect for Islam and the Arabs, and Moses and Judith belong to the latter trend. In 1839 they visited Hebron and tried to get into the Cave of Machpelah, but fanatical Muslims prevented their entry. Yet still Judith makes no condemnation of all Muslims, only the fanatics. In 1855 they visited the Mosque of Omer and the Temple Mount, despite the rabbis putting them in *cherem* for doing so. The rabbis were soon persuaded to remove the ban of excommunication when they were reminded that the Montefiores brought great financial benefit to the Jews of the Holy Land. In 1827 Moses had his first interview with the Pasha of Egypt, Mehemet Ali, and they seemed to have got on well. In later visits the friendship was renewed and Mehemet Ali wished to make Sir Moses a sort of financial representative in England. In 1857 the grandson of Mehemet Ali, Tousson Pasha, was sent to England to stay with the Montefiores for several weeks. They acted as guardians as well as hosts and had quite a difficult time of it, yet the young prince returned the next summer and on other occasions in the future. Dr Loewe makes clear in his *Diaries* that the Montefiores knew how to entertain the prince 'in the Eastern Style'. Such experiences and contacts must surely have aided Moses when he visited Muslim rulers in Egypt, Constantinople and Morocco.

TOLERANCE AND INTOLERANCE

His tolerance towards peoples of other religions is shown by the way he coped with Christian travelling companions. They travelled to Ireland in 1825 to open branches of the Provincial Bank of Ireland and the Montefiores went with Mr Medley, a fellow director, and his wife, both Protestants. The Medleys would not travel on a Sunday and the Montefiores on a Saturday. So, come the Jewish shabbat, the Montefiores rested and the Medleys moved on. On Sunday, the Medleys stayed put and the Montefiores caught up with them; both travelling on together on Monday. As we have seen, the Catholic Mr Mazzara took the Montefiores to church with him and in Alexandria in 1827 Mr Mazzara accompanied Judith to synagogue on Yom Kippur as Moses had walked to the main synagogue a distance away. In 1857 the Montefiores were again on their way to the Holy Land, this time with Dr Hodgkin, of Hodgkin's disease fame. The Montefiores went to the synagogue in Lyon on shabbat where Sir Moses found out there was a meeting of Friends in Nimes and arranged for Hodgkin to attend this Quaker meeting the next day.

As time went by the Montefiores became close friends with

many leading churchmen, especially Archbishop Tait of Canterbury. Moses would write letters of protest about the persecution
of Christians, just as he would for the Jews, and raise funds,
for example, for the Christians of Syria in 1856. He had always
given generously to Christian charities and in his will he left
£100 to each of eight churches in the Ramsgate area, six of
them Church of England, one Congregationalist and one Roman
Catholic. Again his ecumenism is illustrated. A significant amount
of money was sent to him for his extensive fundraising appeals
for the Holy Land by Christian clergy and lay people from
Britain and abroad.

But there was also his religious intolerance. The rate of out-
marriage in nineteenth-century England among the Jewish
upper middle class was high. Prominent Jewish families like
the Goldsmids all but disappeared by the end of the century
due to conversion and intermarriage. At first, Moses Montefiore
appeared to tolerate those who married out of the faith. A boy-
hood hero was Uncle Joshua, who had an exciting life leading
expeditions to West Africa and ended up in America. His first
wife was the daughter of a leading member of Bevis Marks
synagogue, but his second, whom he married at seventy-three,
was his first wife's maid and a Catholic. In the last eight years
of his life he sired eight children and sank into increasing
poverty. His nephew, Moses Montefiore, is said to have helped
him out with a pension. A little closer to home, Moses' own
brother, Abraham, married a non-Jew, Mary Hall. This led him
to be ostracized by his family and fellow Jewish stockbrokers.
Moses, however, supported him financially and took him on as
a business partner.

Perhaps his views hardened a little in old age. He asked his
secretary, Louis Loewe, to draft a letter in 1878 to Mrs Cohen,
a relative, to respond to her letter of distress about her daughter
marrying a Gentile: 'I wish you would be so kind as to sketch
for me an answer to Mrs Cohen's letter and express my concern
with some sympathy expressed on my part ... say all you can
to comfort Mrs C. but you cannot avoid the expressions of my
feelings on the intended marriage.'[11]

If Moses could live with the problems of marrying out, he
was certainly more forthright in his condemnation of Jews
converting to Christianity. He fought hard against those
missionaries who went to Palestine to convert the Jews and

against similar activities in Russia. In 1848 Moses and Judith went on their third visit to Palestine and on their return stopped at Marseilles and visited a spinster aunt, Lydia Montefiore. As Loewe puts it, 'Miss Montefiore assured Sir Moses that she had always endeavoured to follow the example of her parents and would live and die as a Jew.' [12] Moses was deeply taken with the old lady and sent her an annual pension. What the *Diaries* don't reveal is that some years later the lonely old lady, seeking friendship, converted to Christianity. When Sir Moses heard the news he cut her off and never sent her another penny.[13]

By the time the Montefiores began their continental travelling, Reform Judaism was beginning to spread in Germany and France. At first, Moses seemed to approve. He and Judith had often noted the lack of decorum in synagogues they visited. Moses could not tolerate this and in 1838 on the way again to Palestine, they visited Brussels and noted that the sermon was in German. In Strasbourg Judith remarked, 'We were impressed with the beauty of their chanting, but it seems the prayers were abridged.'[14] And then in Rome the sermon was given in Italian and the decorum had improved and Moses duly approved. Though Moses could tolerate these reforms on the continent, when they appeared in Britain he became an implacable opponent.

Thus it was that Sir Moses Montefiore vehemently opposed the founding and establishment of West London Synagogue in 1840, even though several close relatives were among the founders. He supported Ashkenazi and Sephardi Chief Rabbis who instituted a *cherem* against those who entered the synagogue or used its prayerbooks. And a decade later, as President of the Board of Deputies, he was most obstructive in getting permission for the West London Synagogue to conduct marriages and later on for the Reform Synagogues of West London, Bradford and Manchester appointing Deputies to the Board. There is some evidence that Sir Moses later on wanted a rapprochement with West London.

In 1879 Simon Waley invited him to the consecration of the new building; Montefiore replied he felt 'a sincere and deep anxiety for the unity of the Jews' but he wished to see the unity before the consecration.[15] It is sanguine to reflect that Sir Moses Montefiore, the champion of Jewish rights in so many foreign countries, could be so obstructive against the very modest reforms made by the founders of West London Synagogue.[16]

The former Bishop of Birmingham, Hugh Montefiore, would, I suppose, have been an anathema to Sir Moses. Bishop Hugh wrote a monograph on his great-great-uncle where he comments that 'Moses had a genius for religion like his great-nephew Claude Montefiore.' He later goes on to say that though Moses was on friendly terms with many Christians, he never mentioned Jesus. There is an early reference in 1814 but from all later material now in existence no mention can be found. Yet Sir Moses had a natural and deep religious faith and his wife even more so. Shortly after the death of his wife in 1862 he wrote: 'I hope that by divine blessing, I have been of some use to my fellow creatures, both Jew and Christian and I believe I may add Moors. To God above, who helped and sustained me be honour and glory. My angel guide of so many years being no longer with me in mortal form I pray the God of Israel to be my guide.'[17]

When Sir Moses died in 1885, among the large collection of letters of consolation there are many from Christians and Muslims, as well as Jews, all full of admiration for his achievements. As well as the *minyan* around his deathbed, vast crowds of non-Jews and Jews mourned the passing of this great Jew.

NOTES

1. C. Bermant, *The Cousinhood* (London: Eyre and Spottiswoode, 1972).
2. L. Loewe, *The Diaries of Sir Moses and Lady Montefiore*, facsimile edition (London, 1983).
3. S. Lipman, 'The Making of a Victorian Gentleman' in S. and V. D. Lipman (eds), *The Century of Moses Montefiore* (Oxford: Littman Library of Jewish Civilization in association with the Jewish Historical Society of England, Oxford University Press, 1985).
4. Ibid.
5. Ibid.
6. L. Loewe, *Diaries*, I.87.
7. L. Wolf, *Sir Moses Montefiore*, 1884.
8. Rothschild Archives R.Fam.C/30/1, Paris, 1814.
9. Honeymoon Diary, 1812.
10. Judith's Manuscript Diary, 1823.
11. R. Loewe, 'Louis Loewe, Aide and Confidante', in *Century of Moses Montefiore*.
12. L. Loewe, *Diaries*, II.7.
13. *The Conversion of Lydia Montefiore*, London (n.d.).

14. *Notes from a Journal*, 1835.
15. See A. Kershen and J. Romain, *Tradition and Change* (London: Vallentine Mitchell, 1995).
16. I. Feinstein, 'The Uneasy Victorian: Montefiore as Communal Leader', in S. and V. Lipman (eds), *The Century of Moses Montefiore*.
17. H. Montefiore, *Sir Moses and his Great Nephew: A Study in Contrasts*, University of Southampton, Eleventh Montefiore Memorial Lecture, 1979.

18

Religion, Civil Society and Inter-faith Endeavour

ANTHONY HARVEY

What is the place of religion, or rather of a diversity of religions, in a modern liberal society? In the past the question has been posed mainly as one of the relations of church and state, or of the rights of a religious minority. But today the freedom to practise one's faith is recognized, at least in theory, as a human right that can be claimed by all. The question then becomes: what is there about religion which makes believers into an association different from other informal groupings in society? Do they deserve special treatment? Are their customs in any way offensive to others? Is there any positive contribution they can make? And in an age when all religious and metaphysical propositions are thought to be relative anyway, is there any point in the kind of inter-faith friendship and dialogue which has been such a conspicuous and distinguished part of the ministry of John Rayner?

Until recently, political thought seemed to make little room for a creative answer to these questions. The model in most people's minds was more or less Hobbesian. Religions represent a stubbornly persistent and potentially conflictual element in human society. It is for the state to devise ways of protecting its citizens' right to practise their religion, on condition that they do not cause civil unrest or harm one another by blatant proselytizing. This model, though it implies a thoroughly negative view of the value of religion in society, nevertheless seems to have lost none of its relevance in a world where religious groups continue to inspire fear. Islamic fundamentalists associated with terrorism, extreme Orthodox Jews in Israel claiming absolute territorial rights on the ground of their religion, the 'Christian Right' in the USA prepared to contemplate Armageddon as a stage in the achievement of their political aspirations, religiously inspired attacks on mosques, temples and churches in the Indian subcontinent – all these seem to justify a secular policy of which the main concern is to protect society from sectarian conflict while guaranteeing the 'right' to freedom of religious belief and practice.

But there are also serious limitations to this approach. If religions are thought of as necessary but potentially subversive elements of society which have to be protected from one another and from which the public also may have to be protected, all the emphasis is laid on their differences from one another; what they have in common is overlooked. Moreover the question is seldom asked whether they may not have some positive contribution to make to the common good rather than being merely potential causes of disorder. It is this second question which comes into sharper focus today in the light of a somewhat different political philosophy which has emerged with the concept of 'Civil Society'.

Since it is one of the basic assumptions of a modern liberal society that all have a right to hold their own beliefs and live according to their own moral standards (so long as these do not cause harm to others), it might seem that the role of the state is necessarily limited to ensuring law and order and to providing the basic necessities for civilized social life. But the experience of nations which have gone down this path (which are most of the nations of the Western world) is that these basic provisions become more and more difficult to guarantee. All these countries have witnessed an unprecedented rise in the crime rate; the evidence of corruption and 'sleaze' in public institutions has become commonplace; and the relentless pressure of consumerism tends to erode the spirit of service and mutual obligation which used to undergird professional life and is driving the indigent into crime. Legislation is constantly brought forward, and as constantly revised, to work as carrot or stick to strengthen family life and communal institutions; but given the assumption (much more widely held than cynical references to Margaret Thatcher's dictum would suggest) that there is nothing in 'society' beyond families and individuals on the one hand and government on the other, it is not obvious what resources are available to government to reverse an apparent breakdown of public morality and social values.

What is missing from this analysis is the recognition than an important element in any civilized society is the network of voluntary associations and institutions which enrich the lives of most of its citizens and which have a significant influence on their behaviour. From trade unions to golf clubs, naturist clubs to choral societies, freemasonry to the British Legion, these associations exist in all strata of society and fill a significant part of people's lives.

They are, of course, extremely diverse, and their objectives are not necessarily benign. But one thing they all have in common (even those, such as racist groups and criminal gangs, which make no claim to be 'moral') is that they have *rules*. And these rules have a distinct moral character. They demand that members should be loyal to one another, should keep their promises, should be honest in their financial dealings within the society and should accept certain norms of sexual behaviour. The officers and members of a society are expected to be correct in their relations with members of the other sex; they must not cheat each other or mismanage the society's affairs; they may even be required to 'set a good example'. Failure to meet these requirements may result in expulsion: the moral code, whether implicit or expressed in a rule-book, is likely to be enforced by social disapproval if not by the infliction of actual penalties.

It is arguable therefore (and it is an argument now popular with some right-wing thinkers, who look back nostalgically to the astonishing burgeoning of voluntary associations and private civic initiatives in the nineteenth century) that these smaller social groups, standing between government on the one hand and individuals or families on the other, form an essential element in society, the cement in the fabric of the nation, the moral stiffening required to make any liberal society work. Hence the concept of 'Civil Society'. The term itself goes back at least to David Hume (though he used it in a rather different sense, that of 'civility' as opposed to 'barbarism') but it entered the discourse of political philosophy only about two decades ago and has already become accepted in popular speech. The concept relies on an analysis of society which takes seriously the contribution of these smaller social units (sometimes identified, not quite correctly, with Burke's 'Little Platoons') and finds the health of any society directly related to that of the voluntary associations which provide the standards and the motivation for responsible civic behaviour. At the same time, as we have observed, they have an important role in promoting a set of moral standards which, strictly speaking, may apply only within the group, but which inevitably exercise some influence on people's character and general behaviour.

This is not to suggest, of course, that society would necessarily be immoral without them. People may lament an alleged decline in moral standards; but the popular clamour that is regularly aroused by flagrant injustice or discrimination, the general approval of human rights as a high priority for legislation and social endeavour, the readiness of the great majority to respond to calls for humanitarian aid in times of natural disaster or political oppression, the general acceptance of the undesirability of a growing gap between the rich and the poor – these represent a degree of moral consensus which forbids us to decry our society as 'immoral'. Yet this consensus (as some philosophers have suggested) amounts only to a somewhat 'thin' morality. It is effectively 'thickened' by the existence of social groupings which actively promote their own code of conduct and give effect to their own moral aspirations. Their members are also citizens, and the moral standards learnt and practised in their informal associations are likely to have some influence on their general behaviour and to 'thicken' the moral texture of society.

Among these unofficial agents of moral education, the churches and other faith communities have an important place. Not only are their members more numerous than those of any comparable association, but the rules of behaviour they inculcate cover every aspect of life and are intended to be followed outside as well as inside their communities of faith. Moreover, their religious beliefs provide not only standards of conduct but a powerful motive for altruistic behaviour and service to others. Potentially, therefore, they represent a significant resource for strengthening the moral character of a nation and for 'thickening' its moral standards beyond the basic consensus surrounding human rights, justice, the obligation to provide for the disadvantaged and so forth.

To this it may be immediately objected, first, that these faith communities are often not in tune with the moral consensus now generally obtaining in a liberal society, and second, that in any case they do not agree with each other or even, in some cases, among themselves. How can we talk of a 'religious' contribution to public morality if the religions themselves display moral confusion? What contribution can be made to the public discussion of gay rights if Christians themselves are at loggerheads over the issue? How are equal opportunities for men and women furthered by religious ordinances which deny women an equal place in their own structures or impose on them a sartorial regime that does not apply to men?

To the first of these objections it has to be conceded that the major religions have been slow to endorse principles such as democratic government and human rights which are taken for granted in liberal societies. Christianity is not alone among the major religions in structuring its communities with a system of hierarchical authority which it believes to be derived from scripture and to be an article of faith (though Judaism has often been considerably more 'democratic'). But Christians, like Jews and many Muslims, now live in a world where they find themselves inescapably committed to the principles of democratic government, and even if they have been slow to modify their traditional organization they have been able to find, in their doctrine of the dignity and equality of all human beings before God, support for democratic institutions and in some cases even democratic political parties. Similarly with human rights. The reserve caused by the fact that obligations, rather than rights, are emphasized both in the Hebrew scriptures and in the New Testament, combined with the fact that Christian clergy were persecuted both by the French revolutionaries and by the Republicans in the Spanish Civil War, caused the churches to be slow in recognizing that the general principle of universal human rights follows from the doctrine (shared with Judaism) that all human beings are made in the image of God.

But these instances should not be read simply as examples of the churches and other faith communities slowly catching up with the norms of secular society and hitching themselves to current moral fashions. On the contrary, they illustrate the complexity of the relationship between these faiths and society. The influence of the one upon the other is never a one-way process, but rather a constant interaction. The general acceptance of these 'liberal' principles causes religious people to look again at some of their own doctrines and to understand them in a new light, while their own critical stance may itself influence the way in which these principles are applied and may feed into a wider debate.

This last point bears also on the other objection. The more that members of the historic faiths find themselves challenged by the generally accepted norms of society, the more they are forced to re-examine their own traditions and see how far they need to be reformulated in the light of modern knowledge and of the social and psychological pressures to which their fellow citizens are now exposed. If this is done ecumenically, and in the context of inter-faith dialogue and understanding, it will soon be found that all but the extreme conservative (or extreme radical) groups within their faith communities have a very large area of common ground when addressing the ethical problems with which we are all confronted today. Though differences of detail and of emphasis may still appear from time to time, what is impressive is the degree of moral consensus, which exists among people of faith and the support which this can give to a wider constituency of people of good will. Moreover these religions will share a heightened intensity of moral motivation in view of their shared belief that in so doing they are conforming themselves with the will of God.

In the context of Jewish–Christian relations, the following areas of ethical concern illustrate the degree of shared conviction which characterizes all but the most illiberal and conservative adherents of the two faiths:

1. A respect for the dignity of each human being as created in the image of God. This implies not only (as in political philosophy) that they are equal before the law and equal in rights, but that they are all of value also in the rich diversity of their individual gifts, relationships and callings, including the spiritual dimension of their lives. This shared understanding of the human condition not only reinforces the current popular enthusiasm for human rights but also enriches it with a deeper understanding of its implications and where necessary refines and criticizes it in the light of the social obligations which necessarily follow from the pursuit of rights and which tend to be neglected in secular discourse about rights.

2. The fundamental conviction of both faiths that the world was created by God and entrusted to human beings for their long-term flourishing entails a reverence and concern for the natural environment which adds a profound dimension to the prudential arguments usually advanced for environmental action, and is readily responded to by all (and they are the majority) who are moved by the beauty of the natural world and by an acute sense of loss when that world is exploited and its mineral and biological resources depleted.

3. The concern for social justice and the rule of law, which Christians have inherited principally from the Hebrew scriptures and which is a common heritage of the two faiths, inspires practical and prophetic action over a wide field of social concern.

4. The Hebrew scriptures, strongly endorsed by the New Testament, place great emphasis on the need to protect the interests of the vulnerable, the marginalized and the stranger. At a time when refugees and asylum seekers are politically exploited and represented as a threat to the security and welfare of others, this shared tradition of concern for the stranger in our midst is a significant witness to a basic humanitarian instinct now in danger of being suppressed, and has already borne fruit in many instances of shared social action.

But apart from these specific issues, there is a word to be said about inter-faith dialogue itself. This is a form of conversation which has to be slowly and often painfully learnt by those who take part in it. It involves patient listening, sensitive speaking, and a readiness to subject one's own deepest convictions to reappraisal in the light of the glimpses one obtains of the springs of another's faith. It is an experience which, if more widely shared, could have an incalculable influence on the climate in which disputed issues are discussed and handled within 'civil society', and it is an endeavour immeasurably furthered when those who undertake it display the courage, the tolerance and the wisdom which have characterized the man to whom this volume is gratefully dedicated.

19

Inter-faith Dialogue

CHARLES MIDDLEBURGH

Inter-faith dialogue is, like motherhood and apple pie, something that few people from mainstream religious communities are against. Across the world a profusion of organizations exist bringing the members of different faiths together to talk to and about each other, and new dialogue groups and permutations of faiths are being created all the time.

Why this profusion of faiths talking together? Perhaps it is the legacy of centuries of Christian triumphalism and persecution? Perhaps it is the legacy of the Nazis' attempt to destroy the Jewish people during the Second World War, which was seen by many to have been the logical end point of 2,000 years of institutionalized Christian anti-Semitism? Perhaps it is the widespread explosion of religious fundamentalism that threatens so many 'ordinary' Jews, Christians, Muslims and others? Or perhaps it is the surge of secularism in Western society that threatens all of us?

In the early years of the new century and a new millennium, Jews can look back at one of the worst centuries in their long history, full of hatred, persecution, mistrust and mass murder. We have endured the most extreme forms of hatred that any religious entity has ever had to suffer, we have had our beliefs and our standards travestied, we have endured imprisonment, ghettoization and expulsion. We have also witnessed the creation of a Jewish state for the first time in nearly 2,000 years, and the necessary accommodation between faiths and cultures that it has brought with it.

In the United Kingdom, Liberal Jews can look back with pride on their involvement in inter-faith work, be it in the London Society of Jews and Christians, the Council of Christians and

Jews, the International Council of Christians and Jews, the Three Faiths Forum or the Cambridge Centre for Jewish–Christian Relations. Inter-faith dialogue is a sine qua non of Liberal Judaism's commitment to pluralism and universalism, and probably accounts for the disproportionate role we have played in this area.

It is necessary for us to consider carefully, however, what the future direction of inter-faith debate should be, and what it should aim to achieve.

The legacy of a blood-stained relationship between Jews and Christians over many centuries made it imperative for the dialogue between these two faith groups to take the lead, and this was given added impetus by the events of the Shoah. Jewish–Christian dialogue has led the way throughout the world, and created an excellent model for others to follow. Within its constructs, deep and abiding cross-community friendships have been built, areas of misunderstanding and ignorance have been diminished, and valuable joint initiatives have been undertaken.

Yet it is to the credit of the Jewish community, and particularly the Progressive Jewish community, that in the closing years of the twentieth century we realized that the scope of inter-faith dialogue would have to be broadened and others would have to be brought in. The obvious starting point was Islam, a faith with a huge following throughout the world, and also, because of world politics, significantly misunderstood and misrepresented in many Western countries. The 1999 David Goldstein Memorial Lecture, sponsored by the Union of Liberal and Progressive Synagogues, invited a leading Muslim academic to consider Islamophobia and anti-Semitism as two sides of the same coin, and both these Abrahamic faiths have much in common of a positive and negative kind.

In a multi-religious and multi-ethnic society such as that in Great Britain, it is likely that in years to come inter-faith dialogue will need to be broadened still further, to include Hindus, Jains, Buddhists and others, and this will involve a range of new challenges, as well as opportunities. At the very least it may offer society in general a way of easing misconceptions and correcting misrepresentations that are divisive and intolerable in a country as diverse as our own.

Dialogue, however, is not enough on its own, for though two

people may talk amicably together they may still leave each other's company unchanged. It could be argued that the last few decades of inter-faith dialogue have merely been the first stage of a much longer exercise; they have been an opportunity for the worst misconceptions to be righted and the largest gaps in knowledge to be filled. Jews and Christians now have a better- informed understanding of each other than has ever been the case before, and together with that understanding has come respect and trust.

The great challenge of the twenty-first century is in building on that environment of trust so the genuine differences between faiths can be considered, reflected upon and understood. We will discover the real success of our dialogue only when we can confront the things that have always divided the religions from each other and share with each other how we feel about these matters.

For example, Jews must confront the concept of Jesus the Jew as Son of God in a way we never have before; Christians must grapple with the inherent problem that the Trinitarian concept of the Godhead poses to Jews who cannot reconcile it with pure monotheism. Muslims must try to accept that there are significant areas where the concepts and teaching of Islam, indeed its very worldview, raise serious issues for other faiths. All must acknowledge that the way their religion perceives others may be very different from the way those faiths actually see themselves.

These issues, and others, will be the litmus test of the value of inter-faith dialogue as it builds on the achievements of the past and looks to the future: we will have to learn to live with the doctrinal divergence that cannot and will not be changed and not allow it to alter our mutual respect.

Finally, as we look forward, there is yet a further level towards which those who are committed to inter-faith dialogue must aim. Those of different faiths who believe in dialogue are nearly always moderate members of their own religions, men and women who have reached a satisfactory accommodation between modern life and religious tradition and who have eschewed extremism and fundamentalism. It is likely that they will feel estranged from those right-wing members of their own faiths and will seek comradeship and partnership with those of other religions whose fundamental attitude to life is very similar to their own.

Inter-faith dialogue must then also be seen as a potential bulwark against extremism and a strong supporter of democracy, building a coalition of believers committed to stability, moderation and tolerance.

One of the proudest claims of Liberal Judaism is that in its past commitment to inter-faith dialogue it has made concrete the universalistic principle that underpins its distillation of Jewish tradition. Today, we must renew our determination to build on the achievements of the past and take our dialogue with other faiths on to a new plane whose worth to society could be incalculable.

20

Perceptions of the Other: Lessons from Jewish–Christian Dialogue

EDWARD KESSLER

If we take the twentieth century as our starting point it is quite clear that two immense events have combined to provide a dual focus to Jewish–Christian dialogue today: the Holocaust (*Shoah*) and the creation of the State of Israel. Both spurred an intense desire amongst many Christians and Jews to learn about the history, theology and other aspects of Jewish–Christian relations. The *Shoah* resulted in a general awareness of the immensity of the burden which the Church carried not only for its general silence, with some noble exceptions during 1933–45, but also because of the 'teaching of contempt' towards Jews and Judaism which it carried on for so many centuries. As Jules Isaac showed immediately after the war, it was this that sowed the seeds of hatred and made it so easy for Hitler to use anti-Semitism as a political weapon.[1] Although no one would deny that Nazism was opposed to Christianity, it is well known that Hitler often justified his anti-Semitism with reference to the Church and Christian attitudes towards Judaism.[2]

As a result of the soul-searching that took place after 1945, many Christians began the painful process of re-examining the sources of the teaching of contempt and repudiating them. Christian institutions, most notably the Vatican, the World Council of Churches (WCC) and individual Protestant denominations have, since then, issued declarations against the perpetuation of this teaching.

This meant from a Christian perspective that before dialogue could take place the history of the Church and its attitude towards the Jews had to be publicly acknowledged. This involved a proper appraisal of anti-Semitism, anti-Judaism and the significance of the *Shoah*. If we take the Roman Catholic Church and the Second Vatican Council (1962–65) as an example, the publication *Nostra Aetate* ('In Our Time') marked the beginnings of a fresh approach. The Roman Catholic Church came in from out of the cold and rejected the millennial teaching of contempt of Jews and Judaism and unequivocally asserted the Church's debt to its Jewish heritage. Most importantly of all, it ushered in a new era, fresh attitudes, and a new language of discourse never previously heard in the Catholic Church concerning Jews. The concept of a dialogue now entered the Jewish–Christian relationship.[3]

More recent Christian institutional statements have consistently condemned anti-semitism and documents such as the Roman Catholic *We Remember* and the Leuenberg Church Fellowship (Reformation Churches in Europe) *The Church and Israel* illustrate a willingness to tackle this subject.[4] Most Christian theologians involved in Jewish–Christian dialogue acknowledge that the slaughter of 6,000,000 Jews would not have been possible were the roots of anti-Semitism not deep within the Christian tradition.

Another example of the changes can be seen in the repudiation of the teachings of Martin Luther by the Lutheran World Federation, which rejected 'Luther's violent invective against the Jews and expresses deep and abiding sorrow over its tragic effects on subsequent generations'. In particular, it deplored the appropriation of Luther's words by modern anti-Semites and called for increasing Lutheran–Jewish co-operation.[5]

Documents such as these are directed to a Christian public and are primarily a sincere call for the renunciation of anti-Semitism. They reach not only Christians in Western Europe and North America, where dialogue has progressed, but also Christians in regions such as Eastern Europe, Africa, Asia and Latin America where many have never encountered a Jew. Thus, as far as anti-Semitism is concerned, the Protestant churches and the Roman Catholic Church, instead of being part of the problem, have now become part of the solution.

Unfortunately, the same is not true of the Orthodox Church. The changes that have taken place in what may be described as the Western churches find few parallels in the East. Despite a few inter-faith meetings, and despite some bold statements by a few Orthodox leaders, there is simply no comparison with the current state of play in the Roman Catholic and Protestant churches. Much has to be done before Orthodox Christianity abandons its repository of anti-Jewish polemic.

The *Shoah* not only caused Christianity to reassess its relationship with Judaism but also stirred greater Jewish interest in Christianity. Jonathan Sacks spoke for many when he stated that, 'Today we meet and talk together because we must; because we have considered the alternative and seen where it ends and we are shocked to the core by what we have seen.'[6]

The need to tackle such issues as the *Shoah* in Jewish–Christian dialogue is self-evident but there are dangers if it is not conducted in perspective. Fackenheim's proclamation that the Shoah resulted in a new commandment, the 614th, which stressed that it was incumbent upon Jews to survive as Jews, is a case in point. According to Fackenheim one remained a Jew so as not to provide Hitler with a posthumous victory.[7] As a result, however, Jewish identity became *Shoah*-centred and, at the same time, Jewish–Christian dialogue became *Shoah*-centred too. The danger is that by focusing solely on the Holocaust, Jews and Christians will gain a distorted view. For example, a young Jew will construct a negative Jewish identity, which without the positive side of Judaism, will not be a value to be handed down over the generations. A young Christian will come away with an exclusive picture of the Jew as victim without an awareness of the positive aspects of Jewish culture.

It is a result of the emphasis on *Shoah* and anti-Semitism that Jewish–Christian dialogue has often appeared to consist of an attempt to educate Christians about Judaism in order to prevent, or at the very least, to reduce Christian anti-Semitism. Thus, Jews and Christians become involved in dialogue on account of defensive factors, in other words, to stop the possibility of anti-Semitism from breaking out in churches in the future. Although Jewish–Christian dialogue proceeds at many levels and reaction to the Shoah is an important driving force, dialogue cannot be built solely on responses to anti-Semitism and Christian feelings of guilt. Indeed, no healthy and enduring relationship between people is built on guilt. If recent Christian soul-searching in the aftermath of the destruction of European

Jewry leads to a new approach and a revision of traditional anti-Jewish teaching, so much the better. The future relationship, however, cannot be built on the foundations of guilt. The sense of guilt is transient and does not pass to the next generation; moreover, it is unstable and inherently prone to sudden and drastic reversal.

This is acknowledged in *Dabru Emet* ('Speak Truth'), a broad-based Jewish statement about the relationship with Christianity, signed by over 250 Jewish leaders and scholars, including John Rayner. *Dabru Emet* is the first detailed modern cross-denominational document examining the place of Christianity in Jewish thought. Issued in September 2000, *Dabru Emet* stressed that it was time for Jews to reflect on what Judaism may now say about Christianity. It comments on the *Shoah*, assessing Christian guilt while separating Christianity from Nazism:

> Nazism was not a Christian phenomenon. Without the long history of Christian anti-Judaism and Christian violence against Jews, Nazi ideology could not have taken hold nor could it have been carried out ... But Nazism itself was not an inevitable outcome of Christianity ... We encourage the continuation of recent efforts in Christian theology to repudiate unequivocally contempt of Judaism and the Jewish people. We applaud those Christians who reject this teaching of contempt, and we do not blame them for the sins committed by their ancestors.[8]

This passage has been criticized by some for having gone too far; others were troubled to learn that some Jews do view Nazism as the logical outcome of European Christian culture and some expressed concern that Christians might feel completely exonerated by the Jewish statement. Most importantly of all, perhaps, is the fact that the statement illustrates that dialogue needs to move on to a more positive basis.

The second key issue in Jewish–Christian dialogue is the establishment of the State of Israel. There is little doubt that while the Church has for many years been grappling with issues related to Christian anti-Semitism, attitudes towards the Land and State of Israel have, from the theological perspective, proved more difficult to tackle. Theological difficulties have made a Christian reorientation to Israel problematic. Simply put, it has been easier for Christians to condemn anti-Semitism as a misunderstanding of Christian teaching than to come to terms with the re-establishment of the Jewish State. As a result, the subject of Israel has probably caused as much disagreement and division within the Church as any other topic in Jewish–Christian dialogue.

The Christian reluctance to accept the implications of the new state in the Jewish–Christian relationship has only served to reinforce its centrality in discussion. In addition, its significance lies in the fact that Israel is the only state in which Jews form the majority and this has important consequences for the Jewish–Christian relationship. For example, Jews have more confidence in their dealings with Christians. Also, most of the Christian holy places are now in Israel or in Israeli-controlled territory, which means that the entire Christian world takes a close interest in developments. This has led to strong reactions – both of a favourable and unfavourable nature – but the very existence of this spotlight shining so strongly on Israel, and especially on Jerusalem, gives particular importance to any attempt at mutual understanding between Christian and Jew inside Israel.

There are, however, a number of dangers with basing a theology of Jewish–Christian dialogue primarily on Israel. One is the fact that dialogue becomes linked to certain stages of achievement, which give an impression of a direct line of progress. Valuable as the stages of achievement are, they are often far from the complexities of the reality itself. There is great danger in arguing that what was once an interpretation of the Biblical promise is now in the situation of Israel concretized in a contemporary event. The challenge to Jewish–Christian dialogue as a result of an emphasis on fulfilment of Biblical prophecy can be seen in the writings of some evangelical Christians as well as fundamentalist Jews.

For example, what happened a hundred years ago to the Jews outside of Israel is considered by some as historically remote compared to Biblical events, which are viewed as almost contemporary. The present becomes transformed into Biblical language and geography, which leads to the danger of giving metaphysical meaning to geographical places. The fundamentalist Jew in Israel interprets the ownership of the Land of

Israel in terms of a divine gift. This creates a great danger of bestowing divine importance on Israel and the vocation of the Jew becomes a dedication to the existence and the restoration of the cosmic state. Thus, the return to the Land is a fulfilment of the divine promise. The Biblical promises,however, do not define the same borders and by choosing the widest ones the fundamentalist abuses the idea of the promise, which is related to the Land.

The dangers of Israel-based dialogue are also illustrated by those who, in the name of dialogue, move from a position of commitment for the well-being of Israel to one almost of 'Israel can do no wrong'. This is not conducive to dialogue, for it is not an honest and sober conversation firmly related to present realities.

The 1994 Vatican recognition of the State of Israel marks a significant shift in Christian thinking. Its significance is explained by David Rosen, who was intimately involved in the negotiations with the Vatican:

> This is the end of the beginning. The implications of *Nostra Aetate* and the subsequent documents called out for full relations between the Holy See and the State of Israel. Their absence had suggested that the reconciliation between the church and the Jewish People was not a complete one. Accordingly, for the last three decades, Jewish representatives have called on the Vatican to take this step. The agreement that was signed last week, therefore, has historical and philosophical importance as well as diplomatic significance. Now we can address the meaning of our relationship and get on to many other matters of common interest.[9]

The question is, what are the 'other matters of common interest' and what is their relevance to dialogue?

UNDERSTANDING THE MEANING OF DIALOGUE

Having described key issues in Jewish–Christian dialogue we now move on to consider the basis for dialogue. Two questions arise: how does modern inter-faith dialogue differ from the inter-faith disputations of the Middle Ages, and how does inter-faith dialogue differ from the bargaining of the market in which the aim is to find a mutually acceptable compromise.

In fact modern inter-faith dialogue is neither disputation nor seeking for compromise.

First, the word 'dialogue' and dialogue activity have been both misconstrued and ill-defined. A casual conversation between Jews and Christians that may add up to no more than a loose restatement of entrenched theological positions is sometimes claimed as dialogue. Any communication between persons of two differing religious points of view that does not involve a genuine hearing of the other is all too easily claimed as dia-logue. Today, one can communicate with others either by phone, fax or e-mail but dialogue requires more effort, and most of all, a face-to-face contact. Dialogue is not simply a method of communication.

Second, the word is sloppily used as almost an umbrella term to cover a whole host of related activities that are good in themselves, some of them even providing an essential frame-work for dialogue, but are not equivalent to dialogue. For example, some adopt the term Jewish–Christian relations as synonymous with dialogue. After all, you can have good or bad relations (as often the case with relatives) but relations in themselves are not the equivalent of dialogue; nor is the com-parative study of religions, which is also taken by some as a synonym for dialogue. Of course, dialogue does involve the serious study of the religion of others, but the understanding required before dialogue can take place consists of more, for example, than the understanding of the major festivals and life-cycles of Judaism and Christianity.

In reality, dialogue consists of a direct meeting of two people and involves a reciprocal exposing of the full religious conscious-ness of the one with the 'Other'. Dialogue speaks to the Other with a full respect of what the Other is and has to say. This is never less than personal but can develop in such a way as to be extended to a group and even to communities. It begins with the individual, however, and not with the community.

This is not an original definition, for the Biblical prophets were experts in this full personal communication and encounter. Isaiah in a famous passage powerfully commends Israel to enter into a personal relationship with God stating, 'Come now let us reason together' (Isaiah 1:18). We should also refer to Leviticus 19:33–4: 'When a stranger lives with you in your land, do not ill-treat him. The stranger who lives with you shall be treated like a native-born. Love him as yourself for you were strangers in the land of Egypt. I am the Lord your God.' These verses provide the theological basis for dialogue – indeed, the command to love the stranger is found on thirty-six occasions in the Pentateuch. Dialogue consists of embracing the dignity of difference and is dependent on a willingness to understand the difference and to get to know the Other.

Such a quest is never easy because it is not merely about the Other, nor about where the Other differs from us. The thoughts and experience of dialogue are well expressed in the writings of Franz Rosenzweig. Rosenzweig's emphasis is not on the subject matter that connects the speaker with the listener but the I confronting the Thou. The word is not only an expression of reality but also a means by which to express it.[10]

Speech for Rosenzweig consisted of articulating an awareness and comprehension in living contact with another person, which he called *sprachdenken*. Thus the use of words in a live encounter was for him more than just talking: something is not only said but something happens. This means that dialogue is dependent upon the presence of another person. It is not difficult to see how Rosenzweig became one of the main sources from which Martin Buber developed his 'I and Thou' formula.

Buber, in his exposition of the I–Thou relationship maintained that a personal relationship with God is truly personal only when there is not only awe and respect on the human side but when we are not overcome and overwhelmed in our relationship with God. This is illustrated by a famous story found in the Talmud in which Rabbi Eliezer appeals to heaven and the voice of God declares that he is right. However, the *halachah* (Jewish law) still follows the majority opinion (in opposition to Rabbi Eliezer) because of the principle 'it is not in heaven' (Deuteronomy 30:12). Many years later, the story concludes, Elijah tells Rabbi Nathan that when the incident took place God laughed and declared, 'My children have conquered Me'. The significance of the story for our study lies in its presentation of the personal relationship between God and humankind.[11]

This has implications for human–human dialogue because it means that two people must meet as two valid centres of interest. Thus one should approach the Other with respect and restraint so that the validity of the other centre is in no sense belittled. Further, not only is the essential being of the Other respected but the world of faith is also treated as valid and genuine; not an 'it' to be carelessly set aside but a distinctive value of belief. An I–Thou relationship is a meeting not of religions but of religious people. The emphasis is placed on the individual.

This illustrates the foundational principle of dialogue today: understand the Other as the Other wishes to be understood. In terms of Jewish–Christian dialogue, this means that Judaism and Christianity must be understood on their own terms.

This has significant implications for the perception of the Other because dialogue involves a respect that takes the Other as seriously as one demands to be taken oneself. This is an immensely difficult and costly exercise. We find it all too easy to relate to others in a casual way with a lack of concentration on the reality and good of the Other.

Thus genuine dialogue between Christians and Jews started only when Christians showed a willingness not only to repudiate anti-Semitism but also to show a desire to understand Judaism as Jews understand Judaism. This process began with a reawakening to the Jewish origins of Christianity.

Christians renounced many of the triumphalist doctrines, most significantly the renunciation of the teaching of the divine rejection of the Jewish people since the time of Jesus – in other words, the divine covenant with the Jewish people is now no longer viewed as having been annulled. According to the 1980 Evangelical Church of the Rhineland statement, 'We believe the permanent election of the Jewish people as the people of God and realize that through Jesus Christ the church is taken into the covenant of God with his people.'[12]

For its part, the Roman Catholic Church teaches Christians that 'the Jews remain most dear to God ... [who] does not repent of the gifts He makes nor of the calls He issues'. John Paul II spelled it out in the early years of his pontificate as follows: God's covenant with the Jewish people had never been broken, retains eternal validity; God does not renege on his promises. If the Jews were not rejected, then Judaism was not a fossilized faith, as had been taught previously, but a living, authentic religion.[13]

The ramifications were manifold. Christians were now told that Jesus, his family and his followers were Jewish and the Jewish background to Christianity was now stressed. Stated first in recent times by the 1947 Seelisburg document, Christians are commended to: remember that Jesus was born of a Jewish mother of the seed of David and the people of Israel, and that his everlasting love and forgiveness embraces his own people and the whole world, and to remember that the first disciples, the apostles and the first martyrs were Jews.

The rediscovery of the Jewishness of the origins of Christianity led to Christians being taught about the richness of the Jewish context, but also the perils of relying on the literal text of the New Testament. New subjects for consideration were also broached which included the closeness of the relationship between Jesus and the Pharisees. Catholics now learn that Jesus had very close relations with the Pharisees.

In addition, Christian ordinands were being taught that the final text of the Gospels was edited long after the events described and, for example, that the authors were concerned with denigrating those Jews who did not follow Jesus. At the same time they were concerned with vindicating the Romans, whose goodwill they were seeking. This was courageously admitted by the Vatican's 1985 *Notes* on the teaching of Judaism, which stated forthrightly:

> It cannot be ruled out that some references hostile or less than favourable to the Jews have their historical context in conflicts between the nascent Church and the Jewish community. Certain controversies reflect Christian–Jewish relations long after the time of Jesus. To establish this is of capital importance if we wish to bring out the meaning of certain Gospel texts for the Christians of today.[14]

There was a realization that too often Christians have pictured Torah as a burden rather than as a delight. Christians were reminded that Jesus was a faithful Jew and 'that from the Jewish people sprang the apostles'. Christian reacquaintance with Judaism resulted primarily from an increased awareness of the Jewish origins of Christianity. That Jesus was born, lived and died a Jew; that the first Christians were Jews; that the New Testament is, for the most part, a Jewish work.[15] From the

Jewish side individuals such as Martin Buber and Claude Montefiore reminded Jews that Jesus was a fellow Jew (their 'great brother' as Martin Buber described him).[16]

A COMMON MISSION

On many major issues, therefore, Jews and Christians find themselves on the same side of the fence, faced with the same challenges. The 'perception of the Other' has changed dramatically and this shift can be illustrated with a brief consideration of mission. This tenet has been, and still is, central to the Christian faith as illustrated by the legacy of the command found in the Gospel of Matthew to 'go therefore and make disciples of all nations' (28:19).

A great change has begun to take place only in the last ten or twenty years. For instance, when the WCC was established in 1948 its first report unsurprisingly condemned anti-Semitism but also, perhaps incredibly when viewed in hindsight, called for a redoubling of effort at the conversion of Jews. It recommended that the churches should 'seek to recover the universality of our Lord's commission by including the Jewish people in their evangelistic work'. The conclusion of the WCC was that, in light of the *Shoah*, an even greater effort should be made to convert Jews. The report stated that 'because of the unique inheritance of the Jewish people, the churches should make provisions for the education of ministers specially fitted to this task. Provision should also be made for Christian literature to interpret the Gospel to Jewish people.'[17]

Yet here lies a dilemma for all Christians, which explains why the subject has, until recently, been avoided. Nearly all Christians agree that in their witness of Christianity they should always avoid proselytism (in the pejorative sense); they should shun all conversionary attitudes and practices which do *not* conform to the ways a free God draws free people to Himself in response to His calls to serve Him in spirit and in truth. Yet, there exists a tension. According to the Catholic theologian, Thomas Stransky: 'In the case of the Jewish people, what is Christian proselytism in practice? And what is 'evangelisation' – the Church's everlasting proclamation of Jesus Christ, 'the Way, the Truth and the Life'? Is open dialogue a betrayal of

Christian mission? Or is mission a betrayal of dialogue?'[18] Interestingly, he also asks the reverse question, i.e. what is the continuing mission of the synagogue to the church? What is the *common* mission of the synagogue and church?

On the one hand, Christians are taught that the Church must preach Jesus Christ to the world; on the other, they must spread their Christian faith while maintaining the strictest respect for religious liberty. Such a tension is disturbing to many Jews. For example, the belief that salvation can come only through Jesus (or through the Church) relegates not only Judaism but also all other faiths to a position of inferiority. Have the changes in doctrine starting with Vatican II robbed this belief of its former triumphalism? Some participants in the dialogue remain unconvinced.

We must, however, remember that traditional Jewish eschatology, while not foreseeing the conversion of all to Judaism does anticipate that all nations will acknowledge the superiority and sovereignty of the God of Israel. Jews and Christians remain adherents of very different faiths and we must recognize that there are beliefs in all religions that characterize that faith and are too fundamental to compromise. This is acknowledged by *Dabru Emet* as follows: 'The humanly irreconcilable difference between Jews and Christians will not be settled until God redeems the entire world as promised in Scripture ... Jews can respect Christians' faithfulness to their revelation just as we expect Christians to respect our faithfulness to our revelation. Neither Jew nor Christian should be pressed into affirming the teaching of the other community.[19]

In 1988, the Lambeth Conference (which is a meeting of the Anglican Communion that takes place every ten years), confronted the issue of Christian mission. Unlike other gatherings, Lambeth 1988 emphasized, rather than minimized, the importance of missionary activity for Christian–Jewish relations. It re-examined the understanding of the Christian mission, which was seen not in terms of the conversion of Jews, but rather of a common mission. In the light of Christian–Jewish and Christian–Muslim relations, proselytism was to be rejected and the conference called for 'mutual witness to God between equal partners'.

It stated that although there are a variety of attitudes towards Judaism within Christianity today, 'All these approaches, however, share a common concern to be sensitive to Judaism, to reject all proselytising, that is, aggressive and manipulative attempts to convert, and of course, any hint of anti-semitism. Further, Jews, Muslims and Christians have a common mission. They share a mission to the world that God's name may be honoured.[20]

This is not to imply that there are no missionary problems today. There has, however, been a dramatic downscaling of Christian mission to Jews. Instances of missionary problems come mainly from some evangelical churches (including those 'messianic' movements such as Jews for Jesus). Relations with the Evangelical Protestants are especially complex. First of all, they often do not dialogue – even with other Christians. Their fundamentalist views are not to be discussed with others (similar to fundamentalist Jews) and mission is ingrained – as was again exemplified by the recent decision of the Southern Baptist convention, one of the largest groupings in the United States, to intensify mission to the Jews in a resolution 'to direct our energies and resources toward the proclamation of the gospel to the Jewish people'.[21]

Nevertheless, recent developments in mainstream Christian denominations illustrate another enormous shift in the Christian understanding from a mission to Israel to mission with Israel. We now encounter an emphasis on partnership and a common mission rather than the mission of Christians to Jews.

A COMMON BIBLICAL HERITAGE

In addition to a re-evaluation of mission, another subject under review is how to approach the Bible. Both Jews and Christians claim the Scriptures – the former use the term Hebrew Bible and the latter, Old Testament. Competing claims have unsurprisingly resulted in bitter argument and negative perceptions of the other.

Today we are witnessing an increased willingness to see a multitude of different possible meanings in the interpretations of Biblical texts. This is in marked contrast to the single 'authentic' meaning, backed by clerical or scholarly authority.

A Jewish justification for such an approach is found in the following passage from the Babylonian Talmud: 'In the School of Rabbi Ishmael it is taught: 'See, My word is like fire, an oracle of the Eternal, and like a hammer that shatters a rock' (Jeremiah 23:29). Just as a hammer divides into several sparks so too every scriptural verse yields several meanings.'[22]

Support for such an approach to Biblical interpretation can also be found in classical Christian exegesis, such as this passage from St Ephrem of the Syriac tradition:

> Who is capable of comprehending the extent of what is to be discovered in a single utterance of Yours? For we leave behind in it far more than we take from it, like thirsty people drinking from a fountain. The facets of His word are more numerous than the facets of those who learn from it. God depicted His word with many beauties, so that each of those who learn from it can examine that aspect of it which he likes. And God had hidden within His word all sorts of treasures, so that each of us can be enriched by it from whatever aspect he meditates on ... Anyone who encounters Scripture should not suppose that the single one of its riches that he has found is the only one to exist; rather, he should realise that he himself is only capable of discovering that one out of the many riches which exist in it.[23]

The tendency to offer a variety of different meanings, each of which claims validity, might be described in terms of exegetical relativity – in other words, traditional interpretations of Scripture represent breadth and plurality of viewpoint. In this way, both the Jewish and Christian exegetical traditions provide a framework to allow for multi-various interpretations of Biblical texts, which they both share. As a result, Christians and Jews may come to realize that the traditional (and sometimes negative) interpretations do not provide the final and authoritative meaning of the text.[24]

The approach may also be adopted in the tackling of texts which run contrary to fundamental ethical values or which may be read as a licence for violence or bigotry. In other words, exegetical relativity can be applied to those texts, which have been used for much evil, as for example, the way in which the Bible has been used to maintain slavery or second-class citizenship, to hold women in subjugation to men, and so on.

The application of exegetical relativity is dependent upon one criterion: that Biblical interpretation should reject any interpretation which would promote hatred, discrimination or superiority of one group over another. The use of a Biblical text for the purpose of the subjugation of women to men, black to white, Jew to Christian should be considered invalid, requiring reinterpretation.

This approach is justified by a hermeneutical principle shared by both Christians and Jews: humanity should live by the commandments and not die by their observance. To give two examples from Rabbinic Biblical interpretation:

- Deuteronomy 21:18–21 deals with the stubborn and rebellious son who is to be stoned to death. This law was turned into a purely hypothetical exercise and the command was restricted by so many conditions that it could never be applied.
- Exodus 21:24 includes the notorious 'eye for an eye' and 'tooth for a tooth'. Perhaps as early as Biblical times, this was viewed as a common Near Eastern artificial construct for addressing the legal problem of damages. The 'eye for an eye' was simply applied to the discussion of compensation, as explained by Rashi: 'If one blinded the eye of his fellow, he pays him the equivalent of the decrease of his value if he were sold in the marketplace; and similarly all of them; but it does not mean the taking of an actual limb.'

Interestingly, these passages assume that because God's word could not conceivably run contrary to the highest contemporary values at any given period, the doors of interpretation are open and problematic texts can be reinterpreted so as to conform to those values. They show that whatever appeared to be a contemporary problem could be reinterpreted and effectively abolished.

The recognition that the Biblical text can have more than one meaning is significant for Jewish–Christian dialogue. It is no longer essential to search for the one and only correct meaning of a text, but a number of different interpretations, each within its own context, each worthy of consideration in its own right, is an acceptable hermeneutic. As recently as 2002, the Pontifical Biblical Commission accepted formally that Rabbinic readings of Scripture were 'in continuity' with the Hebrew Bible.[25]

The existence of exegetical relativity may leave the interpreter with an uncomfortable tension because of the presence of a number of interpretations arising out of a single Biblical passage. The multitude of possible interpretations may be disconcerting, but their existence illustrates a greater reality, which exists not only outside of Scripture and in society at large, but also within Scripture.

Consider the following opposing translations of Job 13:15, which highlight an inherent ambiguity within the Biblical text: 'Behold, he will slay me; I have no hope' (Revised Standard Version – *RSV*); *and* 'Though he slay me, yet will I trust in him' (King James Version – *KJV*). The reason for the difference between the *RSV* and *KJV* is the result of a variation in the reading and spoken versions. The Masoretic vocalization (spoken reading) indicates that Job has hope while the consonantal text (written text) offers the view that Job has no hope. The Mishnah acknowledges the ambiguous meaning of the Biblical text and has recognized that both translations are possible:' the matter is undecided – do I trust in Him or not trust?'[26] The contradiction is meaningful as it expresses the tension of one who is torn between hope and doubt: the very tension that inhabits our mind when we read the Bible today. According to Andre Neher, 'Job pronounces two words which signify *simultaneously* hope and hopelessness ... I hope in Him, he shouts, but also do not hope in Him.'[27]

IMPLEMENTING THE CHANGES

It is clear that many of the main divisive issues between Judaism and Christianity have been either eliminated or taken to the furthest point at which agreement is possible. The efforts of Catholics and Protestants towards respect for Judaism are reflected in documents which project attitudes that would have been unthinkable a few decades ago. Christian theology has been profoundly revised at the official level – all churches are committed to the fight against anti-Semitism and to teaching about the Jewishness of Christianity. We have seen how this has impacted upon key areas such as mission and Biblical interpretation.

There is of course an important agenda for top-level dialogue and consultations but the emphasis should now shift to filtering to regional and local levels. It is possible today to respond effectively to regional requirements in the new global reality. Consciousness of the changes has been confined largely to the elite (although in certain regions, such as the United States, it has been more widely disseminated). The object now is to get these changes into the everyday understanding of all the faithful. The fields to be addressed are churches and synagogues, seminaries and *yeshivot*, schools and universities as well as informal education, including the media.

We must ensure that the positive developments achieved are properly applied at the regional level. This means attention to education and information to ensure that the new teachings are disseminated at grass-roots levels. It involves dealing with the fight against anti-Semitism in regions such as Russia, certainly to combat any manifestations within a religious context.

Most importantly, educational guidelines are required – designed for each region. This requirement is equally true for Jews as well as Christians. History has understandably moulded negative Christian stereotypes among Jews and we must now teach the Jewish community about the contemporary changes of attitudes by the churches. The beginnings can be seen in *Dabru Emet*, but this is simply the first step. Claude Montefiore's call for a Jewish theology of Christianity over seventy-five years ago still waits to be answered.

The challenge of today is to harness the growing interconnectedness and interdependence of Jewish-Christian relations, supported by the revolution in information technology, which is bringing all of us closer together. We need to broaden the dialogue to include, for example, Christians from the developing world, many of whom have never encountered a Jew in their lives and know little of them except from the New Testament accounts – not always a source of positive images of Judaism.

There is no guarantee of progress. There are risks, for example, that instability in one part of the world, such as the Middle East, will effect Jewish–Christian relations in another. Giant strides have been made but we are talking of a dynamic and relentless process. We will never be able to sit back and say, 'The work is done. The agenda is completed.'

It is clear, however, that we have come a long way in fifty years and Jews and Christians are more likely to share positive perceptions of each other than ever before.

NOTES

1. J. Isaac, *The Teaching of Contempt* (New York, 1964).
2. See excellent summary in R. L. Rubenstein and J. K. Roth, *Approaches to Auschwitz* (London: SCM, 1992), pp. 199–228.
3. *Declaration on the Relation of the Church to Non-Christian Religions Nostra Aetate*. See *Vatican Council II: The Conciliar and Post Conciliar Documents*, A. Flannery (ed.) (Dublin: Dominican Publications, 1981). For a summary of the importance of this document, see, E. J. Fisher, 'The Evolution of a Tradition: From *Nostra Aetate* to the *Notes*, in International Catholic–Jewish Liaison Committee', *Fifteen Years of Catholic–Jewish Dialogue: 1970–1985* (Rome: Libreria Editrice Vaticana and Libreria Editrice Lateranense, 1988).
4. *We Remember: A Reflection on the Shoah* and The Leuenberg Church Fellowship, *The Church and Israel: A Contribution from the Reformation Churches in Europe to the Relationship Between Christians and Jews*.
5. Assembly of the Lutheran World Federation.
6. Foreword to H. Fry, *Christian-Jewish Dialogue: A Reader* (Exeter: Exeter University Press, 1996).
7. E. Fackenheim, 'Transcendence in Contemporary Culture: Philosophical Reflections and a Jewish Theology', in H. W. Richardson and D. R. Cutler (eds), *Transcendence* (Boston, MA: Beacon, 1969), p. 150.
8. *Dabru Emet* can be found (with commentaries by Jewish and Christian scholars) in T. Frymer-Kensky, D. Novak, P. Ochs, D. Fox Sandmel and M. A. Signer (eds), *Christianity in Jewish Terms* (Boulder, CO: Westview Press, 2000).
9. Quoted from D. O'Brien, *The Hidden Pope* (New York: Daybreak, 1998), p. 383.
10. See Foreword to *The Star of Redemption* (South Bird, IN: University of Notre Dame Press, 1985), p. xiv.
11. See D. K. Novak, *Jewish–Christian Dialogue: A Jewish Justification* (Oxford: Oxford University Press, 1989).
12. See 'Towards Renovation of the Relationship of Christians and Jews: A Statement of the Evangelical Church of the Rhineland', in A. Brockway, P. van Buren. R. Rendtorff, and S. Schoon (eds), *The Theology of the Churches and the Jewish People: Statements by the World Council of Churches and Its Member Churches* (Geneva: WCC Publications, 1988).
13. See *The Evolution of a Tradition*, Fisher, p. 239.
14. *Notes on the Correct Way to Present Jews and Judaism in Preaching and Catechesis in the Roman Catholic Church*.
15. See the 2002 statement issued by the Pontifical Biblical Commission entitled *The Jewish People and their Sacred Scriptures in the Christian Bible*.
16. See D. Berry, *Mutuality: The Vision of Martin Buber* (Albany, NY: State University Press, 1985), pp. 69–88; also, E. Kessler, *An English Jew: The Life and Writings of Claude Montefiore, 2nd edn* (London: Vallentine Mitchell, 2002), pp. 136–41.
17. *The Message and Reports of the First Assembly of the World Council of Churches* (London: SPCK, 1948), p. 77.
18. T. F. Stransky, 'Holy Diplomacy: Making the Impossible Possible', in R. Brooks (ed.), *Unanswered Questions: Theological Views of Jewish–Catholic Relations* (South Berd, IN: University of Notre Dame Press, 1988), p. 66.
19. See n. 8.
20. *The Truth Shall Set You Free: The Lambeth Conference 1988* (London: Church House Publishing, 1988).

21. In 1989, fifteen evangelical scholars met in Willowbank, Bermuda under the auspices of the World Evangelical Fellowship and drafted a two-page declaration on the need for Christians to evangelize Jews because Jews need Jesus to be saved. See J. T. Pawlikowski's chapter entitled 'Reflections on Covenant and Mission', in M. J. Wright and E. Kessler (eds), *Themes in Jewish–Christian Relations* (Cambridge: Orchard Academic, 2004).

22. BT Sanhedrin 34a.

23. Commentary on the Diatessaron I:18–19.

24. J Magonet initially pointed this out to me. See his 'Reading our Sacred Texts Today', in T. Bayfield, S. Brichto and E. Fisher (eds), *He Kissed him and they Wept* (London: SCM, 2001), pp. 110–19.

25. See n. 15.

26. M. Sotah 5.5.

27. A. Neher, *L'Exil de la parole: du silence biblique au silence d'Auschwitz* (Paris: Editions du Seuil, 1970).

Notes on the Editors
and Contributors

Dr Edward Kessler (editor) is founding director of the Centre for Jewish–Christian Relations in Cambridge. He received a PhD from Cambridge University in 1999. Among his publications are *Bound by the Bible: Jews, Christians and the Sacrifice of Isaac* (Cambridge: Cambridge University Press, 2004), *An English Jew: The life and Writings of Claude Montefiore* (London: Vallentine Mitchell, 1989, 2nd edn, 2002) and *A Reader of Early Liberal Judaism: Israel Abrahams, Claude Montefiore, Israel Mattuck and Lily Montagu* (London: Vallentine Mitchell, 2004). He was a member of the LJS confirmation class of 1980, taught by Rabbis John D. Rayner and David J. Goldberg.

Rabbi David J. Goldberg OBE (editor) is rabbi emeritus of the Liberal Jewish Synagogue. His numerous writings include *The Jewish People: Their History and Their Religion* (co-authored with John Rayner, London: Viking-Penguin, 1987), and *To the Promised Land: A History of Zionist Thought from its Origins to the Modern State of Israel* (London: Penguin 1996).

Rabbi Dr Albert H. Friedlander OBE was formerly dean of the Leo Baeck College and until his death in 2004 was emeritus rabbi of the Westminster Synagogue. He was the senior editor of the German edition of Leo Baeck's writings (six volumes) and served as guest professor at many universities (including Basle, Frankfurt and Kassel). His writings include *Out of the Whirlwind: The literature of the Holocaust* (New York: Schocken, 1976), *Leo Baeck: Teacher of Theresienstadt* (London: Vallentine Mitchell, 1973) and *Riders Towards the Dawn: From Ultimate Suffering to Tempered Hope* (New York, Continuum, 1993).

Rabbi Frank Dabba Smith was born in California and educated at U.C. Berkeley. He currently serves as rabbi at Harrow and Wembley Progressive Synagogue. His published writings about the topic of photography and the Holocaust include *My Secret Camera: Life in the Lodz Ghetto* (London: Frances Lincoln, 2000) and *Elsie's War: A Story of Courage in Nazi Germany* (London: Frances Lincoln, 2003).

Rabbi Mark Goldsmith is rabbi of Finchley Progressive Synagogue, current chairperson of the Liberal Judaism Rabbinic Conference and a member of the Interim Steering Group of the International Interfaith Investment Group. He was fortunate to be among John Rayner's students at Leo Baeck College.

Rabbi Harry M. Jacobi was born in Berlin 1925 and went to the same school as Rabbi John Rayner. He escaped to England in 1940 (having been on the *kindertransport* to Holland 1939) and served in Jewish Brigade. He has been rabbi of Southgate, Wembley and Zurich Congregations as well as Chairman of Liberal Judaism Rabbinic Board.

Rabbi Dr Louis Jacobs CBE is one of the world's leading Jewish thinkers and teachers. Trained in the Orthodox world, he adopted some of the less traditional views of biblical scholarship, including elements of source criticism. Rabbi Jacobs serves at the New London Synagogue and among his most important works are *We Have Reason to Believe: Some Aspects of Jewish Theology Examined in the Light of Modern Thought* (London: Vallentine Mitchell, 1995), *A Jewish Theology* (London: Darton, Longman and Todd, 1973), *A Tree of Life: Diversity, Flexibility, and Creativity in Jewish Law* (Oxford: Oxford University Press, 1984), *Hasidic Prayer* (London: Routledge and Kegan Paul, 1972), *Jewish Preaching: Homilies and Sermons* (London: Vallentine Mitchell, 2004) and *Their Heads in Heaven: Unfamiliar Aspects of Hasidism* (London: Vallentine Mitchell, 2004).

Dr Eric L. Friedland received his PhD from Brandeis University and is professor emeritus of the Sanders Judaic Studies Program at three universities and one United Methodist seminary in Dayton, Ohio. He is author of *Were Our Mouths Filled with Song: Studies in Liberal Jewish Liturgy* (Cincinnati: Hebrew Union College Press, 1997), and served as consultant for *Machzor Ruach Chadashah*.

Rabbi Dr Walter Homolka serves as executive director of the Abraham Geiger College at the University of Potsdam for the training of rabbis on the continent of Europe. He is a Governing Body member of the World Union for Progressive Judaism and a member of the LJS.

Rabbi Dr Margaret Jacobi has been rabbi of Birmingham Progressive Synagogue since 1994. She qualified in medicine at Birmingham University and obtained a PhD in physiology before studying for the rabbinate. She grew up in the Progressive movement, where her father is a rabbi, and Rabbi Rayner officiated at her Bat Mitzvah.

Rabbi Dame Julia Neuberger was rabbi at the South London Liberal Synagogue for twelve years and then pursued a career in health and healthcare ethics. She has just finished as chief executive of the King's Fund, and is a new Liberal Democrat working peer. She broadcasts and writes extensively.

Rabbi Danny Rich has been rabbi to the Kingston Liberal Synagogue since his ordination at Leo Baeck College in 1989. He was a member of the LJS confirmation class of 1978, taught by Rabbis John Rayner and David Goldberg. He has been a justice of the peace since 1997.

Rabbi Sybil Sheridan read theology and religious studies at Cambridge before studying for the rabbinate at Leo Baeck College. Ordained in 1981, she has served as rabbi to Ealing Liberal Synagogue and the Thames Valley Progressive Jewish Community and is currently rabbi to the Wimbledon and District Synagogue. A lecturer at Leo Baeck College Centre for Jewish Education, she has edited two books: *Hear our Voice: Women Rabbis Tell their Stories* (London: SCM Press, 1994) and, with Sylvia Rothschild, *Taking Up the Timbrel: The Challenge of Creating Ritual for Jewish Women Today* (London: SCM, 2000).

Rabbi Elizabeth Tikvah Sarah received *semichah* from Leo Baeck College in 1989. Chairperson of the Rabbinic In-Service Training Programme for seven years, she continues to teach at the college and serve as a rabbinic tutor. She has been rabbi of Brighton and Hove Progressive Synagogue since December 2000.

Rabbi Sidney Brichto, formerly the first executive director of Liberal Judaism, is presently engaged in the translation of a reader-friendly Bible (London: Sinclair-Stevenson, 2000–). His most recent publication in the series is *The Apocalypse: The Writings of St John.*

Rabbi Alexandra Wright was born in London and grew up at the Liberal Jewish Synagogue, where Rabbi Rayner was the senior minister. Following ordination from Leo Baeck College in 1986, she returned as associate minister to the LJS until 1989, when she became rabbi at Radlett and Bushey Reform Synagogue in Hertfordshire. In 2004, she was appointed as senior rabbi to the LJS and once again returned home.

Rabbi Professor Jonathan Magonet is principal of Leo Baeck College-Centre for Jewish Education, where he lectures in Hebrew Bible. He is the author of several books on the Bible and co-editor of the prayer books of the Reform Synagogues of Great Britain. For over thirty years he has co-organised an annual Jewish–Christian–Muslim Student Conference in Germany about which he has written in *Talking to the Other: Jewish Interfaith Dialogue with Christians and Muslims* (London: IB Tauris, 2003). He is a vice-president of the World Union for Progressive Judaism.

Rabbi Mark L. Solomon is rabbi at the Liberal Jewish Synagogue and a lecturer in rabbinics at Leo Baeck College-Centre for Jewish Education. He studied at *yeshivot* in Australia and Israel and at Jews' College, London. He holds a BA from the University of Sydney and an MA from Leo Baeck College, and is currently working towards a PhD. He is a governor of the Ammerdown Centre, co-chairman of the London Society of Jews and Christians and a member of the Board of the Council of Christians and Jews.

Rabbi Dr Andrew Goldstein has been rabbi of Northwood and Pinner Liberal Synagogue since being ordained by Leo Baeck College in 1970. He chaired the editorial committee for *Siddur Lev Chadash* and co-edited *Machzor Ruach Chadashah*. His doctorate investigated the first journey of Moses and Judith Montefiore to the Holy Land in 1827–28.

Reverend Dr Anthony E. Harvey was educated at Eton and Oxford. He became a lecturer in theology and fellow of Wolfson College, Oxford in 1976. He became canon of Westminster in 1982 and sub-dean in 1987. He retired in 1999. Among his numerous publications are *Jesus and the Constraint of History* (London: Duckworth, 1982), *Strenuous Commands: The Ethic of Jesus* (London: SCM, 1990), *Promise or Pretence? A Christian's Guide to Sexual Morals* (London: SCM, 1994).

Rabbi Dr Charles H. Middleburgh is rabbi of Dublin Jewish Progressive Congregation and Denmark's Progressive Jewish Forum. He is a lecturer in Aramaic and rabbinic literature at Leo Baeck College Centre for Jewish Education, and in Judaism at Trinity College Dublin's Irish School of Ecumenics.

Bibliography of the Writings of Rabbi John D. Rayner CBE

BOOKS

The Jewish Youth Group (co-edited with Henry F. Skirball)
London: WUPJ, 1956

The Practices of Liberal Judaism
London: ULPS, 1958 (revised edition, 1960)

Strengthen our Hands
London: ULPS, 195?

Towards Mutual Understanding between Jews and Christians
London: James Clarke & Co. Ltd, 1960

Guide to Jewish Marriage
London: ULPS, 1975

Judaism for Today (co-authored with Bernard Hooker)
London: ULPS, 1978

The Jewish People: Their History and their Religion
(co-authored with David J. Goldberg)
Harmondsworth, Middlesex: Viking, 1987; London: Penguin
Books, 1989

An Understanding of Judaism
Providence, RI, and Oxford: Berghahn Books, 1997

A Jewish Understanding of the World
Providence, RI, and Oxford: Berghahn Books, 1998

Jewish Religious Law: A Progressive Perspective
Providence, RI, and Oxford: Berghahn Books, 1998

PRAYERBOOKS

Haggadah shel Pesach, Passover Eve Service for the Home
(co-edited with John Rich)
London: ULPS, 1962; illustrated by Jacob Shacham, 1964

Service of the Heart (co-edited with Chaim Stern)
London: ULPS, 1967

Gate of Repentance (co-edited with Rabbi Chaim Stern)
London: ULPS, 1973

Haggadah shel Pesach, Passover Haggadah
(co-edited with Chaim Stern)
London: ULPS, 1981

Siddur Lev Chadash (co-edited with Chaim Stern)
London: ULPS, 1995

PAMPHLETS

The Present Contribution of Judaism to Civilisation
London: ULPS, 1951

The Liberal Jewish Attitude to the Bible and Rabbinic Literature
London: ULPS, 1959

Liberal Judaism
London: LJS, 1966

Liberal Judaism: An Introduction
London: LJS, 1968

Life as I See it
London: LJS, 1972

The Greatest Commandment
London Diocesan Council for Christian Jewish
Understanding, the 1982 St Paul's Lecture, 1982

The Jewish Liturgy
Jewish Information Service, n.d., circa 1973

Me'ah Shirim, A Hundred Songs
London: LJS, 1978

Progressive Judaism, Zionism and the State of Israel
London: LJS, 1983

To Merge or not to Merge (co-authored with David J. Goldberg)
London: LJS, 1984

Fundamentalism
London: ULPS, 1998

Principles of Jewish Ethics from a Progressive Point of View
London: New Jewish Initiative for Social Justice, 1998

Aspects of Liberal Jewish Thought
(co-authored with David J. Goldberg and
Dr Charles H. Middleburgh)
London: ULPS, 1998